Bananas in Snow Country

A Benchmark Building's Lessons for a Green Future

Rob Knapp

Foreword by Norman Foster

 SUSTASIS PRESS

Published by Sustasis Press, The Dalles, Oregon

Library of Congress Publisher's Cataloging-in-Publication Data
Names: Knapp, Robert H., 1944- author. | Foster, Norman, 1935- writer of foreword.
Title: Bananas in snow country : a benchmark building's lessons for a green future / Rob Knapp ; foreword by Norman Foster.
Description: The Dalles, Oregon : Sustasis Press, [2024] | Includes bibliographical references.
Identifiers: ISBN: 9789403734835 | LCCN: 2024905649
Subjects: LCSH: Lovins, Amory B., 1947- | Sustainable architecture--Design and construction. | Architecture and energy conservation. | Sustainable design. | Buildings--Environmental engineering. | Architecture and society. | Architecture--Human factors. | Solar energy-- Passive systems--Design and construction. | Solar air conditioning—Passive systems--Design and construction. | Solar heating--Passive systems--Design and construction. | Insulation (Heat)--Design and construction. | Heat recovery--Design and construction. | Passive components--Design and construction. | Construction industry--United States.
Classification: LCC: NA2542.36 .K63 2024 | DDC: 720.47--dc23

Table of Contents

Acknowledgments

This has been a tortoise of a project. Seeing it through owes as much to Helena Meyer-Knapp's patience, thoughtful engagement with substance, and untiring practical support as to anything else. Wife; productive thinker, writer, and teacher; companion; mother and grandmother—Helena has kept many things alive in these years, and this book would not exist without her.

It would also not exist without the generous, wholehearted support Amory Lovins has provided from the start. Detailed interviews, ready access to documents, hospitality, time to prowl the building solo, introductions to key actors, complete editorial freedom left to me—he has done it all. Judy Hill Lovins, whose professional skill as photographer is on show often in this book, has been equally welcoming and helpful.

The Foreword by Baron Foster of Thames Bank is a generous contribution to this small project by a distinguished presence on the world stage.

As the book demonstrates, the Lovins building was the work of many hands, heads, and hearts. Hunter Lovins was hospitable and forthright in describing her multi-faceted involvement over the first 20 years. Special thanks go to other participants who met with me for interviews—Bill Browning, Chris Cappy, Robert Clarke, Steve Conger, Larry Doble, Jock de Swart, Rick Heede, Robert Hutchinson, Alexis Karolides, Charlie Manlove, Jimmy Mateson, Glenn Rappaport, Rob Watson. Their accounts, anecdotes and impressions have been invaluable.

The concluding sketches of present-day projects owe everything to what Chris Benedict, Ryan Cassidy, and David Baker told me and showed me of their work. A talk with Heather McKinstry of Dattner Architects improved my understanding of the Passive House process in New York City.

Marty Pickett, Titiaan Palazzi and RMI staff generally were helpful in finding and handling documentary traces, and good at keeping straight the distinctions between RMI the organization and RMI the Lovins brainchild.

Thad Curtz, prized long-term colleague, read my nearly final draft very closely and made many, many good suggestions for tightening the prose and improving the organization.

At Sustasis, Michael Mehaffy and Jenny Quillien have been thoughtful readers, prompt responders to even the smallest questions, and consistent supporters. Architect and illustrator Yulia Kryazheva's advice and final tuning of the design and layout have been crucial.

Foreword

By Baron Foster of Thames Bank OM
  Founder + Executive Chairman, Foster + Partners

I can tell you the exact date and place that I met Amory Lovins, but I cannot tell you when I first became aware of him. For me he was one of the few early pioneers in what we would now call the environmental movement. Going back in time perhaps the first visual awareness of the fragility, beauty, and loneliness of the planet was triggered by the Apollo 8 photograph, in 1968, of the Earth rising above a lunar landscape. (That was the year Amory wrote his first professional paper on climate change and what we must do to keep the Earth durably different than the Moon.) Six years earlier, Rachel Carson in *Silent Spring* wrote about the dangers to the planet of excessive use of pesticides. In 1969, Buckminster Fuller's *Operating Manual for Spaceship Earth* related Earth to a long space journey provisioned with a finite store of resources that cannot be replaced. This planetary awareness overlapped with the rebellion and questioning of a younger generation and its counterculture of the sixties, with the *Whole Earth Catalog* of Stewart Brand as its sourcebook. This was soon followed by the oil crisis of 1973, then a bigger one in 1979. The climate-changing potential of fossil fuels, which Amory's 1976 reframing of energy in *Foreign Affairs* clearly set out, was yet to be fully evident but in 1982, the resulting dependence and risks inherent in oil and coal as energy sources, along with these other background factors, set the context for Amory and his then wife Hunter to form Rocky Mountain Institute. In that same year, the early embodiment of these beliefs found form in the literally ground-breaking work on a very unusual house, office, and indoor jungle in Old Snowmass, Colorado. Its story is the subject of this insightful and entertaining book.

So, in December 2016, when my wife and I stood in the snow at the front door of Amory and Judy Lovins's home, 7,100 feet up in the Rocky Mountains of western Colorado, I felt that I had known him for decades even though he was a complete stranger—such is the power of a reputation. In reverse order, the book, with its graphic plan, tells me the route that Amory first took us, which for him as the scientist started with the black boxes and dials monitoring the house's technical performance as an autonomous living machine. I might have expected to see elaborate controls, but there were only a few simple ones, recently added when the last one percent or so of space-heating was changed from firewood to renewable electricity. Previously the only controls had been the light-switches and operable windows, because there was no heating or cooling equipment to control. If it got too hot, you could open a window; if it got too cold, you could close the window; either way, the building would passively keep you comfortable in a climate that then dipped well below -40°, the freezing point of mercury. These simple but subtly sophisticated means to a comfortable lifestyle, melding 6,000-year-old north Chinese passive-solar architecture with cutting-edge technologies, are an essential part of the story. Physicist and buildings expert Rob Knapp does much justice to that dimension, as indeed he does to the tactile experience of the spaces themselves. At the risk of some duplication, I would like to add our own first impressions.

Warmth is a key word: not just stepping in from the cold, but warmth in the organic sense of materials, spaces, and the paraphernalia of objects and furniture that populate the house. Even before the Lovinses start to tell you, it is evident that each piece has a story that makes it belong. It follows that there is a spiritual warmth to this building and its contents. The music of the waterfall, the smell of the flowers, the play of soft light on wood and stone all create a calm glow, an inner harmony.

Starting our visit in the entrance lobby, we're welcomed by the curious gaze of dozens of orangutan dolls, soft orange-furred creatures of many sizes and demeanors. The symbolic meaning of these toys as a playful reference becomes apparent as we exit the lobby to discover the heart of the residence—a green oasis of banana trees and a hundred other kinds of higher plants, resplendent in a soaring conservatory-like space with koi ponds and fragrant blossoms, all beneath a cascade of glass. The orangutans, we are reassured, quietly meditate by day but can come alive and might get a bit rowdy after midnight if (as has happened) all six banana trees fruit simultaneously, creating a "banana emergency"—a quarter-ton of ripe bananas needing immediate attention. Now we understand the entrance experience and sense a layer of dry humor that permeates this dwelling through its owners.

I often talk of Frank Lloyd Wright's skill at contrasting the compression of his entrance lobbies before you are welcomed into the grander living spaces. The Lovinses' home, although far removed from Wright, engages in similar contrasts between cubby-like spaces in which to hide away and the more airy circulation routes. Amory's ability to harness the power of youth in the building of this structure is also akin to Wright and his students at Taliesin. And this home's architect Steven Conger pays homage to Wright in strong horizontal beams, low ceilings, echoes of Japanese details, and seamless integration with nature, inside and out. The building's curves flow sinuously, with no corners where the roving eye can get stuck.

We came away knowing that this is a laboratory—a test bed for so many intertwined energy and environmental concepts—but above all it struck us as one of the most simple, cozy, and engaging of homes. Enchanted with its easy fit, impressed by the numerous benefits flowing from each design choice, and bewitched by Amory's enthusiasm, I reportedly called it an extraordinarily important building in the history of architecture, thanks to its combination of technical integration with technical-humanistic integration. I therefore urged Amory and Judy Lovins never to sell it, but to seek a way to put it in trust so it remains accessible to future generations of designers, students, and researchers. Now, reflecting on our visit of four years ago, I am delighted to learn that the Lovinses are seriously exploring how to do just that. This home's lessons for a sustainable future are even more valid now than they were in the nineteen-eighties, and earlier in this century when it was renovated.

In the conversations that followed our visit we talked about many topics, including our mutual friendship with Buckminster Fuller. Amory received from Bucky an important set of blueprints that he generously donated to the Norman Foster Foundation. Like Bucky, he is at heart an integrative designer of buildings, vehicles, equipment—anything that uses energy and resources, anything that can be made simpler, more efficient, more beautiful. And as Rob Knapp's book title neatly captures*, the home emerged from that precious quality that Asian philosophies call "beginner's mind": casting away all assumptions and preconceptions to grapple with raw reality. Never having built a house before, Amory and his partners didn't realize, as any expert could have told them, that what they wanted to do was impossible. Their childlike innocence thus made it possible to create something of distinctive and lasting value.

The opportunity to perpetuate the visits that Amory says well over a hundred thousand people have taken since 1982 may be a while off, but meanwhile, this excellent book is the next best thing to a first-hand experience. Indeed, it tells so much about the home's background and life, and its role in the evolution of superefficient buildings, that it becomes more than a substitute. I also very much hope that these pages will connect Amory Lovins, Rocky Mountain Institute, and this exceptional dwelling to a wider and younger audience, so that many more people who create, inhabit, and enjoy great buildings can be astonished and inspired by this one.

Norman Foster
May 2020

* Author note: The book's title at the time this Foreword was written was *Assembling the Possible,* chosen very much as Lord Foster says, to characterize Amory's approach; the current title (*Bananas in Snow Country*) aims instead to characterize the results which this approach is able to achieve.

1: Preface/Introduction

You might as well know one of my deep convictions from the start: this is not only a time of ecological, social and political dislocation and disruption, but also a time when there are abundant clues to prosperous, salutary reconnection. Clues, not Christmas presents—let's be clear about that. There are no magic vehicles just waiting to be unwrapped so we can hop in and zoom away from our troubles. But I'm convinced there are plenty of glimpses available of tools, practices, insights, and partnerships from which a world can be made that is not only sustainable but desirable.

This book doesn't ask you to share this conviction, though. Keep your own counsel, by all means, about how abundant the encouraging clues are. The book does ask you to watch carefully as I bring forward one of them, an unusual building in Old Snowmass, Colorado, and explain why I find it meaningful, a real signal about the potential reconnection of American lives to sustainable realities.

The building is 40 years old, a structure of curving stone walls and an expanse of sloping glass. It embodies a deep insight: by the late 1970s America had already generated the makings of major progress in sustainable building. The ingredients were there; bringing them together properly would have dramatic results. Sure enough, this building, in the heart of the Colorado Rockies at 7100 feet, in a valley where snow is frequent and abundant, has no furnace. That's right, no furnace. And it produces crop after crop of bananas in its indoor green space. It has also housed its prime mover, energy guru and gadfly Amory Lovins and his globally significant think tank since its completion in 1983. The sun provides the heat; judicious choice of materials and meticulous construction retain it. That is all it takes for comfortable living and professional working conditions all year round.

The story behind the spectacular energy efficiency and low emissions of this place offers badly needed clues about how to get to a sustainable future. But there is more. There are subtle but momentous clues to a sustainability that is unexpectedly satisfying. Lovins and his then co-worker and wife, Hunter, consistently (though not always consciously) made design choices that make the lived experience of the building enlivening, nurturing, stimulating. The place could be called "Less and More." It is far lighter on the planet than most buildings, and it does this in ways that enrich the lives it supports.

You will see where the ideas came from, hear about the adventure of getting the place built, learn that "More" did not include "more expensive," tiptoe gently through the workings of the place, and consider what was there and what it meant when it was legally approved for occupancy in 1984.

The book then discusses the features of US building that have deterred or distracted many from pursuing this lead, and briefly sketches the zigzag path along which progress has actually been made. The emergence of voluntary standards to certify green building is an important part of this uneven history, which includes obstruction by established interests and habits, the recognition of new dimensions of quality like biophilia and architectural wholeness, and the startling success of one new standard, Passive House construction, in the unlikely setting of affordable housing in New York City. The US is still far from building in truly sustainable ways, but this account will show that the ideas and techniques for making major strides are genuinely available across the country, no longer confined to a few extraordinary buildings.

You will hear two voices in the writing, a professional one ("Lovins did this") and a more personal one ("Amory did that"). This reflects the two selves I bring to this book. I'm a physicist, a long-time teacher of physics and sustainable design at a feisty, unconventional college in the Pacific Northwest, and a student of green building, especially in the commercial and institutional realm. That field needs a professional stance providing arm's-length analysis and evaluation for sifting true progress out of the mixed methods, intentions, and competences that are always in play. This book brings that attention to the Lovins building.

At the same time, I'm a long-time friend of Amory's; we have known each other since the earliest stages of his career. This will affect my views and choices about what I write; I hope it will be plain enough when this is happening. (My using his first name rather than his surname is one sign of the difference.) I actually also hope this personal engagement will help build a full understanding of what the building has to teach. A successful house must work at the level of feelings and meanings, not just as a smoothly functioning machine. My human connection to the place and its people may help illuminate that aspect of the whole.

What follows in this book is interesting, important, and never esoteric, but it quite often calls for careful reading. There are details and nuances some readers may want to savor and others may prefer to skim past.

> I will use an inset format and smaller typeface (as right here) to flag things I think are more for the former than the latter.

And if the main exposition in places is more than you want, you have other options. They are delightfully and helpfully set out in a work by Pierre Bayard, *How to Talk About Books You Haven't Read*, a minor classic about coping with the sad fact that no one can possibly read all the books they "ought to". Bayard points out that almost everyone resorts to skimming, jumping from introduction to concluding pages, or simply overhearing others as ways of connecting with what books have to say. Western civilization actually counts on this, he says. There is too much important writing for anyone to read it all, word by word. So hop from heading to heading in this book, if you like, skim when it suits you, read slowly and carefully when you choose.

It's a rare American who thinks of his home as a fulcrum for transforming the world. Amory Lovins is just such a person. He has been a remarkable individual presence for over 40 years in a vital sphere of American life—energy policy and practice. This sphere is deeply institutional. It's a realm of long-term planning, enormous capital investments, and lots of lawyers: think oil companies, think electric utilities, think Federal agencies, think major universities, think Congress. Its general goals are stability and the protection of established stakes. Its individuals, when visible, tend to the sleekly corporate or blandly organizational. American society has been content with this, on the whole. If there has been gas at the pump and the lights have come on when one flipped the switch, the energy sphere has been welcome to slide forward its own way.

Lovins stands out against this background. Both analyst and showman, both collaborator and controversialist, he has aimed at transforming the thinking and redirecting the activity of the energy sector toward a "soft path" that can support sustainable general prosperity. His success has been significant. A good deal of this book concerns his ideas and their evolution as they bear on buildings. He not only calls for, but also outlines in detail a transition in energy affairs from centralized high technologies like nuclear fission and liquefied natural gas to systems that are "flexible, resilient, sustainable and benign", like solar or wind electricity or (most importantly) efficient end uses. These constitute the soft path.

Stiffened by detailed research, the soft path concept has been Amory's lever for shifting the world, and it has shifted it. The focus here, however, will be on the fulcrum—the stone and glass, concrete and wood building in Old Snowmass which Amory and Hunter built with many collaborators in 1982-84 as a home, an office, and a material embodiment of what the soft path might mean. It is a place where vision and practicalities have merged.

Centering this single building in the field of view will keep things at ground level. We will be talking about practice, not policy, that is, about specific individuals and their situations, not averages. You will have brief but real encounters with Doug and Sara Balcomb and their house, and the same for Paul Leger, Wolfgang Feist, David Baker and their houses, Chris Benedict and the housing she designs, as well as with Amory and Hunter Lovins. It is at this individual scale, in the choices people make about buildings, that residential sustainability will ultimately stand or fall. Wide-view policy analysis, with its "view from 30,000 feet", has an importance. One wants to know whether ground-level moves add up to significant general impact. But the moves have to work individually before they add up to anything. So with few exceptions (one of which is about to appear), this book stays away from statistics and their unavoidable blurring of individual differences.

Here are two key statistics, though, to argue that sustainable building deserves your book-length attention. The first is simple: Americans spend over 85% of every day indoors. The published average[1] is 86.9%; people engaged in promoting wellness often round this up to 90%. Whichever number you prefer, the message is the same. Almost everyone in the US spends almost all their time inside a building, at home or work, in a mall, a place of worship, a health facility, or some other place. Parks, playing fields, hiking trails, farmlands, lawns and gardens are all in the outdoor average. So is time in or near cars. Taking the US as a whole, those all add up to less than 15% of each day.

Leading the lives we do inside all these buildings requires heating, cooling, lighting, fresh air, and all sorts of equipment, which together account for close to 50% of US energy consumption and its climate-threatening consequence, carbon emissions. Jet travel and intense industrial processes may be more eye-catching, but the unremitting hour-by-hour consumption by buildings adds up to much more. It may seem humdrum; it is mostly taken for granted. But there is no path to sustainability if the US fails to tame the building sector.

-----

[1] Klepeis, Neil E., et al. "The National Human Activity Pattern Survey (NHAPS): a resource for assessing exposure to environmental pollutants." *Journal of Exposure Science & Environmental Epidemiology* 11.3 (2001): 231-252.

2: **First Encounter**

No one approaches a building empty-headed. Even the first time, with no real idea what may be inside, one can't help bringing other buildings and other visits along, in fragmentary memories, unvoiced expectations, traces of feeling. I come to 1739 Snowmass Creek Road with a typical collection of such things—a moment from a walk with Amory in London 45 years ago, relief just now at having found the surprisingly modest "Rocky Mountain Institute" sign signaling where to turn off the road, some adrenalin from uncertainty about how the first steps in this book project will go, an awareness of not really understanding who lives in this valley—an eclectic mix of plaid working shirts, Sotheby's "For Sale" signs, pickup trucks, and horse fencing.

Seeing the soft red-orange contours of the low wall and entry gate to the house, I realize I am also recalling a visit some years ago to a friend in Santa Fe, where the soft red-orange exteriors of new houses are required by code, and the moment when I was shown how it is done there. The structure underneath is not usually the adobe it appears to be. Wood framing is most likely, cinder block or steel are possible; the local code requires they all be dressed to look like adobe. So part of me wonders what lies beneath the skin of this building I have come to study, and whether the skin and the guts make a single organic whole.

I'm on the alert for clues, but I also come as a person making a visit, so I am doing the ordinary practical things—pushing open the entry gate, following the slight bends in the flagstone path that takes me to the front door, looking for a doorbell, not hearing it ring, trying the door. I find it's open, and let myself in. I'm aware that the door is thicker, more solid and better seated in its frame than usual, but most of my attention goes to the somewhat narrow entry space, with its long bench. There's a large heap of orangutan dolls beside the bench. The space opens to the right, and presents me with a flash of bright green and sunlight at the far end of a darker passage. The textures, colors and decoration there are Western—stone, wood, a coat rack with cowboy hats, a simple wooden table with a lamp, a long display rack of publications. And as I move toward all this from the entry, there's Amory's voice from the far end, welcoming me and wondering if I want some tea.

Walk-through

What did I encounter then as I walked through the place? Here are some views from that time, now several years ago.[2] Details have changed since then as life has continued in the building, but the general layout and situation remain the same. The house flows east and west from each side of the entry door. East, through the passage I mentioned, takes you toward a dramatic green space, filled with plants of tropical lushness, and roofed by a very large expanse of sloping glass supported by a massive cantilevered arch.

Attracted by the foliage, you pass along one side of an open dining and sitting space with a substantial adjoining kitchen area. The slope of the glass must be toward the south. The sun is out there. The right-hand wall of the sitting space is a serpentine shape made of rough stones set in concrete, ending at south-facing tall windows looking out to a small garden space and the valley beyond.

View from dining area toward sitting area
(2016); kitchen is out of view to the right

View from dining area toward green space
(2016); passage to workspace is on the left

View from dining area toward work area
(2016); green space is out of view to the right

To your left, along the north wall of the green space is a series of doorways to small round rooms; past those the floor level drops in several stages as it leaves the greenhouse to reach the work zone.

The work zone is defined by floor to ceiling bookshelves, a continuous ribbon of desk surface, another serpentine wall, and more tall windows. The building was conceived from the start as both home and office, and this east end of the building was designed for 12 workers. It has held as many as 21. There were times when a work island was needed in the space now occupied by the ping-pong table, and when people's absences on business helped the stay-at-homes find places to sit.

The north wall of the work zone is largely books and document boxes; that space is open to the greenhouse on the west, and its south and east sides have the same rough stone walls and ample windows as the sitting/dining/kitchen area.

Work area looking south (2016)

Work area looking north (2016)

The ceiling and floor are the same, as well—massive wooden beams supporting planks above and smoothed red concrete with occasional scattered rugs below.

View back from edge of workspace toward
dining area (2016)

So much for a walk-through. Some questions present themselves at once. What are these tropical plants doing in the Colorado mountains? And what explains the overabundance of books and documents? What's with the orangutans? Some others are likely to occur if you keep thinking about the building, or get interested in its details. There's no sound of heating system air, so what sort of arrangements keep these plants alive? What's the story on the very solid front door? And what about the small slot to the right of that door that shows a fragment of foam board? Why are there almost no windows along the north side?

If you're actually being shown around by Amory, these questions and many more get answered before they even come to mind. He's not only proud of this house, he points many things out, and gives you a reason for everything. Few houses in the affluent world have been as thoroughly intentional. From the beginning in 1982, everything in it resulted from choice, not accident. Many of these choices have worked well, some have not; some have lasted from the start, some have been replaced; some are quite personal, even idiosyncratic, some have been widely taken up already in the wider world, some have wide future impacts to make. The rest of this book aims to make sense of what has happened in this structure and to explore its significance for sustainability now. This will take us deep under the skin of the house, backward and forward through its history, out to the social and political environment and back in from it. It will intermingle analysis and impression, evidence and intuition.

What makes a building significant?

What can a building mean to those who own it, use it, or consider it? I think that buildings carry just a few kinds of meaning in common use, though each has infinite variations. Looking back, a building can be a history or a testimony; in the present, it can be a resource but is often an albatross; looking forward, as Amory and Hunter Lovins were doing in 1982, it appears to most people as an investment or a personal dream. Six basic notions about why buildings matter, then—as history, testimony, resource, albatross, investment, personal dream. Thinking about each of these can help us understand what sustainability is and what it asks of us.

The Lovins house carries more meanings than these, though most of them could apply to it as well. Its primary significance is not a common one. The place was described correctly enough in a 2003 appraisal as "a combination residence/office building/appropriate technology research and demonstration facility", but its creators' intentions went beyond that true but plodding description. Calling it a "frontier benchmark" would be more profound and more accurate.

The intention was to radically expand the American understanding of what is possible in making a sustainable national life. That word, sustainable, is much labored, but the Committee on the Environment (COTE) of the American Institute of Architects now has a fine, simple way of putting it: "Sustainability envisions the enduring prosperity of all living things." Although it wasn't written until 2017, this would have been a fitting caption for the making of the Lovins house, 35 years before.

Efficient use of energy and a transition to renewable resources—the Lovinses saw these as vital to achieving a prosperous and enduring life in the United States, a country whose well-being would wither if it continued to squander its capital on conventional approaches to energy. They also knew prosperity only matters when it's embodied in people's personal lives, in homes and communities. Good policy is not enough by itself; great policy is not enough. Enduring prosperity as a matter of national well-being has to be worked out down at the level of windows, doors, cookstoves and all the other components of personal life, not just at the level of the GDP. The Snowmass house would be a benchmark for a universe of possibilities for doing this. As their residence, it would address the knee-jerk objection to efficiency and renewables, "This sounds great, but how do you actually live?" It would escape the synthetic aura of the "House of Tomorrow" exhibits one could see at world's fairs. As a place with comfortable furniture, artwork, and personal mementoes, it would soothe the anxious impression that environmentally sound living called for austerity or for a hippie home-brew of cast-off chairs and tie-dyed T-shirts. As Kenneth Boulding said, "What exists is possible." By its simple, solid existence, the house would demonstrate that the vision of a soft energy path Lovins had laid out in policy articles was not only possible in impersonal, functional terms, but also in terms of desirable personal life.

Looking forward from 1982, the house was to be a benchmark. However, looking at the place now, in 2024, means looking back as well as forward, and that means connecting with the common meanings. We want to know what kind of a benchmark the place has been. But we should also ask about its significance as history and as testimony. What about living there? Inhabiting a benchmark doesn't sound easy, and it is not for everyone. And what does the Lovins house have to teach about investments and dreams?

There is a lot to sort out. Even a single-family house is a very complicated tangle of physical things, not to mention the histories and hopes attached to them. Walls, roofs, attics, windows, doors, basements, beds, chairs, locks, sinks, toilets, shelves, hooks, plates, glasses, knives, cushions, photos, holiday decorations—the list is enormous, disparate, and ungainly. Everyday life avoids considering it as a whole; fortunately, we encounter it piecemeal. Breakfast brings a few things into focus, bedtime others, weekend mornings still others, and so on. Never the whole at once. But times for trying to see the whole do come up. Purchase and sale are the most obvious occasions; major renovations often call for it; and so does the rare attempt, like this book's, to stand back and appreciate a building and its place in the world.[3]

The housing sector of US society does have a well-established approach to such an encompassing evaluation of buildings. It is popularly called "economics," but it should be called "econo-mysticism." It consists of fixating on a few good insights into the operation of markets and investments and hardening them into a seemingly objective and unsentimental tool for making choices. One enumerates costs, quantifies benefits, subtracts the first from the second and allows the bottom line to decide.

As one tool among others, this has genuine utility. The search for sustainability trips and stumbles when economic analysis is omitted. But over time, in US policy circles, it has become the One Ring that claims to bring all considerations under its sway. And in personal housing decisions, the seemingly sensible aura of investment thinking has a way of dominating dreams and histories. What gets built or rebuilt gets decided largely by its possible effects on sale or resale value. This is the mysticism in econo-mysticism. Unfortunately, it is a shallow mysticism, in which certain numbers are allowed to stand for the whole rich experience of living in a place. In later discussion, I'll take up both the genuine usefulness of economic analysis for advancing sustainability in buildings and its ultimate limitations in that sphere.

What other ways are there for seeing a building as a whole? The other readily available approach is to hand the work to an architect. After all, architects are supposedly trained to think in terms of wholes, making buildings in which functions are harmoniously integrated with appealing forms. This, too, has genuine utility. Architects have made distinctive contributions to several of the buildings we'll look at closely, especially to the buildings' capacity to delight. But there are costs. Out of pocket cost, to start with. You're using a professional service and have to pay for it at professional levels. This by itself disqualifies architected design for almost all Americans, who have been taught by the housing industry that more square feet and more "features" are things their money can get them for sure, while less tangible things like balance, harmony, or integration remain out of view.

There's also a much less visible and ultimately more profound cost. There's an inevitable loss of connection between householders' real lives and the life the architect imagines for them. While many architects work hard at maintaining this connection, all are pulled by their training toward designs that are more oriented to an observer's aesthetic than to the ongoing daily lives to be carried on in the building. The aesthetic varies over a great range, from minimalism to what could be called 'profusionism' (the *Architect's Digest* look, for example), and there are many satisfied clients, who find they can live their lives well in what their architects have done, perhaps indeed improved by insights that emerged in the design process. But the danger of divergence is always there. Stories of willfulness, inattention, and impracticality are always close to the surface when architecture is the topic.

Sustainable housing has to live with the paradox of expertise: the best house would be the one you built yourself, if you only had the essential skills, knowledge, experience, and self-awareness, which there is no way to acquire in your finite lifetime. The Lovins building worked directly and intimately inside this paradox, as the story of its construction will show. What came out an unusual blend of the technical and the experiential.

Interestingly, the divergence between life observed and life lived also appears in the context of economic analysis. This seemingly objective tool works by confining attention to a few measurable dimensions. Likely to be lost in the process are dimensions of experience that are meaningful but not measurable, like the color and liveliness of wood-fire flames or visual access to mountain scenery. Discourse at the policy level is particularly prone to this narrowing of attention, for an obvious reason; it deals with society-wide measures and therefore with average or typical situations. Wood fires, scenery, and their cousins tend to get set aside, to the benefit of easier discussion but the possible detriment of the individual lives subject to the eventual generic policies. Building codes, for example, insist on detailed specification in advance of things like window location, foreclosing sensitive adapting of designs to opportunities emerging during construction. Fortunately, there are ways we'll consider of bringing these individual lives into the picture during design and construction, thanks to architectural thinkers like Christopher Alexander and Charles Moore.

Amory Lovins has spent much of his life on policy discourse and devoted much of his talent to it. He has been a keen observer of economic and social life, and is a master of quantitative analysis and debate. However, as he was already asserting in the 1976 article about an alternative soft path in energy policy that made him famous, he cared about that alternative because it would be more "compatible with social diversity and personal freedom of choice," more "consistent with traditional values" and more "pleasant", not just because it made geopolitical and economic sense. The Lovins house has served him as one reliable anchor to those values, and to possibilities for the lived lives of Americans outside the conference rooms.

––––––––––––––––––

[2] The walk-through photos are my own, taken at the time. The house had not been dressed up for public show; it was just being lived and worked in. I am grateful to the Lovinses for permitting this informality.

[3] The number of studies centered on single buildings and sustainability is very small. The architectural literature often takes up single buildings and at other times devotes some attention to sustainability, but very rarely brings them together.

3: From the Ferment of the 70s

The Lovins house went into construction in 1982, nearly ten years after the oil crisis of 1973, when the Organization of Petroleum Exporting Countries (OPEC) imposed an embargo on shipments of oil to the United States and a number of other countries because of their support for Israel in the Yom Kippur War. Those ten years witnessed dramatic political and economic ferment in the US. The near-impeachment of a president in 1974; the Iran hostage crisis, which brought about the defeat of a second president in 1980; the end of the Vietnam War with the fall of Saigon in 1975; another oil crisis in 1979; the widening scope of environmentalism—these are only some highlights of a period that also saw the genocidal Pol Pot regime in Cambodia, the brutal rule of Idi Amin in Uganda, European domestic terrorism by the Red Brigade and the Bader-Meinhoff Gang, and a brief easing of Arab-Israeli conflict in the Camp David Accords between Israel and Egypt, ending with the assassination of Anwar Sadat in 1981.

All of this came under the shadow of nuclear concerns, both global and domestic. The menace of global nuclear war between the US and the USSR grew starker and starker. The numbers of nuclear explosives and delivery vehicles grew in surges, spurred on by a governing concept, shared by both sides, that the capacity for "mutually assured destruction" was the key to preventing that destruction from taking place. The political and military power structures of both superpowers were convinced that the only way to avoid repeating the horror inflicted by two first-generation nuclear weapons in 1945 was to produce tens of thousands of more advanced and powerful ones and deploy them ready to use. For the US population at large this doctrine, coupled with the two decades of global confrontation with the USSR and China that culminated in the Vietnam war of 1959-1975, fostered widespread though often repressed dread, as Joanna Macy and other insightful observers have noted.[4]

Domestically, the question about nuclear energy was whether or not is should be used in electric power production for US commerce and home life. The prosperity that followed World War II had greatly increased energy use of all kinds, and electricity's share had grown three times faster from 1949 to 1973 than that of all other sources, owing to its convenience and flexibility of use. The enormous expansion of generating capacity came primarily from building new coal-burning power plants, using familiar technology that the industry had been improving incrementally in scale and engineering detail for decades. Looking to the future, however, power planners expected ceaselessly expanding demand that would require the services of "atoms for peace," that is, of nuclear power plants.

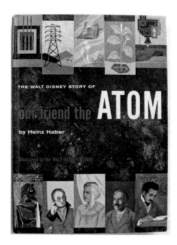

Nuclear power technology seemed to the electric industry and established policy makers at the time to be a magical combination of new and old. The actual generation of power in the new plants would come from steam-driven turbines, the same technology used in conventional coal plants. The new feature was generating the steam with heat from controlled nuclear fission, rather than from burning coal, oil, or natural gas.

The first nuclear generating plant in the US came on line at the end of 1957. The first applications of nuclear energy to produce controlled power rather than city-searing explosions had come several years earlier, and were military—nuclear steam generators for submarines. A given weight of nuclear fuel contains vastly more usable energy than any conventional source, and it offered the prospect of ships far more independent of resupply than in the past, so the Defense Department had funded adapting nuclear technology for controlled use. With the risks of technical development absorbed by the defense establishment, and a society that rejoiced in the transfer of technologies to profit-making use, the electric power industry of the late 1950s looked forward eagerly to a future of steady nuclear growth.

By 1973, however, the bloom was off the rose. Environmental concerns —air pollution, water quality—already had the wider public looking at electric power industry practices in unprecedented detail, with suspicions heightened by the society-wide struggles of the 1960s.

The nuclear arms race, and its evident links to civilian nuclear power, was equally disturbing. The more people looked, the more problems appeared. The health hazards of nuclear material came into sharper focus. So did the severe consequences of any serious loss of control over the nuclear reactions in a plant. No serious preparation had been done for dealing with used nuclear fuel, which was not only very dangerous due its intense radioactivity, but also could be processed into bombs. Even today, forty years later, we are only dealing with nuclear waste through stop-gap measures. Long-term handling remains an unresolved problem, politically, organizationally, and even technically.[5]

Critiques of nuclear power grew naturally and rapidly into an anti-nuclear movement that was a mainstay of environmental activism. Amory Lovins came into the energy scene through just this route. Born in 1947 and growing up in the Washington, DC area and points north, he showed early scientific promise, winning a number of national awards for high school science projects. By the time he entered Harvard in 1964, it was clear that he had prodigious intelligence and energy, coupled with multi-faceted interests, of the extraordinary kind that attracts the patronage of top scientists but fits uneasily in educational institutions, even the most elite.[6] He had also developed a deep interest in the environment, becoming an accomplished nature photographer who guided hikes in the White Mountains of New England.

Still centered in the physical sciences but not yet focused in a specific direction, Lovins transferred to Oxford in 1967, abandoning his Harvard degree. Two years later, still with no degree, neither graduate nor undergraduate, he won a Junior Research Fellowship, normally awarded to very promising new Ph.D.s, at Merton, one of the university's leading colleges. Simultaneously, his outdoor interests had led to his doing extensive hiking in the Snowdonia mountains of North Wales, where a major environmental controversy was under way over the extraction of minerals from ostensibly protected national park land. The issue became the focus of one of the first campaigns of Friends of the Earth UK, an outgrowth of David Brower's outspoken North American environmental advocacy.

Brower had been executive director of the Sierra Club, and had played a large part in its evolution from a mostly social and recreational group in California[7] to national prominence as an outspoken opponent of dam-building and industrial incursions into sensitive natural areas. Brower was charismatic, eloquent, imaginative, willing to be abrasive, and increasingly persuaded that environmental issues needed urgent attention and very sweeping measures. His initial opposition to a nuclear plant at Bodega Bay in northern California had been based on local impacts and proximity to the San Andreas Fault, for example, but within a few years he stood opposed to all nuclear power, anywhere.

Highly visible and uncompromising stances like this created significant tensions within the Sierra Club, and Brower was eventually ousted in 1969. He wasted no time; that same year he found support to start a new organization, Friends of the Earth, which coordinated and gave a national voice to local campaigns for environmental preservation and defense, including a widely shared commitment to anti-nuclear activism. By two years later, there were Friends of the Earth organizations in Sweden, France and the UK, as well as the US; they met to establish an umbrella group, Friends of the Earth International.

Lovins had already become engaged in the Snowdonia campaign and at Brower's invitation he wrote and co-photographed a book of images and essays about the region—*Eryri: The Mountains of Longing,* which appeared in 1972. From Snowdonia to energy affairs was a short step, given Friends of the Earth's deep opposition to nuclear power and Lovins' unusual array of talents, values, and personal qualities—including environmentalism and physics; a very quick mind and a passion for detail as well as a gift for phrasemaking. Energy extraction, production, and use were also at the heart of other major environmental issues of the time, from mining to acid rain to supertankers to the damming of wild rivers. Here at last was a suitably ambitious and significant direction for him. So in the spring of 1971 he proposed to Oxford that he do a Ph.D. in energy. When the university rejected the idea—energy was not an academic field they recognized—Lovins quit Oxford and his fellowship and went to London as the first employee of Friends of the Earth International.

Oxford was where I met Amory. In fact, I was a link in the chain that took him there. A lightweight link, rather like the light line fired from one ship to another to allow a heavy-duty hawser to be pulled across and make the working connection, but a key link all the same. At Harvard, Amory met my brother, who told him I was also doing physics, and had gone across to Oxford, where I was happily pursuing a doctorate in statistical mechanics. Amory wrote me to ask whom to contact about possibly transferring, and I gave him a name. Oxford's acceptances at the time were largely based on trust and the reputation of recommenders, especially for foreign students who had no British exam results to offer. Amory's gifts had likely impressed enough of the right people at Harvard for recommendations to be strong. Certainly his acceptance came through without drama.

Once Amory arrived in Oxford in September 1967, we got together occasionally to walk around town and talk physics and related things. Amory was a fount of intriguing ideas, and did a good deal of the talking. I remember one outing, near Notting Hill Gate in west London, when we got so absorbed in a notion about using strong atomic electric fields to make a particle accelerator that we lost track of where we were walking and only re-engaged reality when a policeman's voice from immediately in front of us announced that we were at the entry to Kensington Palace, a royal residence, and not welcome to go any further.

Notting Hill at that time was reasonably middle class, not the unreasonably upmarket district it later became. Through an introduction from American friends, I had got to know a family there, three daughters and their widowed mother, who were all memorable as well as hospitable. I later married the youngest daughter, Helena, a political studies scholar, student of peace-making, and mother; the other two went on to become a space planning architect and a world-class Chinese art historian, as well as raising families of their own. It was the mother, Paula Quirk, who matters most for Amory's history.

She was born Paula Weber, a daughter of August Weber, a German banker and anti-Nazi member of the Reichstag until Hitler's election as Chancellor in 1932. Wishing to continue his opposition to the Nazis without exposing his teen-age children to reprisals, August Weber sent all four out of the country to relatives in Switzerland in 1933. Paula, the eldest, and her brother found sponsors in England and shortly went there. (The other two children, twin girls, each had somewhat different trajectories in the US, and eventually settled near each other in Los Angeles.)

By the time we met, Paula had married Roger Quirk, a fast-track British civil servant, lost him to a heart attack, and raised the three daughters to university age. Civil service pensions were tiny, and Paula, at 50, had resolved to get a job, accepting that it meant starting at the bottom, surrounded by much younger people. She brought to her new working life a refugee's tough-mindedness, as well as intelligence, independence of mind, and a ready grasp of technical matters, and quite quickly created a niche for herself in market research for British engineering products. Her fluency in German and French, her appreciation of technical matters, and her considerable courage equipped her for cold calls and site visits with European businesses, and her knack for friendship with younger adults helped her do well in the home office.

She had also made a practice for a long time of sharing her house with others, beginning with various family connections who were also refugees. By 1971, she had sold the large family house in Notting Hill to provide starting capital for the two older daughters, and had moved to a much smaller place in the same area. It had a second bedroom; Helena, the youngest, had left for graduate study in the US; and Paula offered the place to Amory. He stayed for ten years, and remained a loyal friend until her death in 2005. I have no doubt that Paula's strong common sense, which was coupled unusually with an adventurous spirit, had a steadying and deepening effect on Amory in the years he boarded with her.

His room in Paula's house was the cockpit from which he planned, organized, and developed his commitment to energy affairs. It was so full of books that she once had a structural engineer check to see whether the floor might collapse. His first energy books and his seminal *Foreign Affairs* article of 1976 were written there; his lifelong whirlwind of speaking and consulting was launched from there; and when he married L. Hunter Sheldon in 1979, Paula's house was where they lived until moving back to the US in 1981.

In one of Amory's stock biographical statements, he writes,

> A Harvard and Oxford dropout, former Oxford don, honorary US architect, and Swedish engineering academician, he has taught at ten universities, most recently Stanford's Engineering School and the Naval Postgraduate School (but only on topics he's never studied, so as to retain beginner's mind).

The voice here is classic Lovins—confident, proud of his achievements, consciously boundary-pushing, and touched with purposeful whimsy. The closing phrase about topics not studied also contains an important truth about the way he has placed himself in the intellectual and political world of energy affairs. He did not train as an energy engineer, nor as an energy economist, nor as an energy policy analyst. He did not complete formal training in any field. The phrase "topics he's never studied" is somewhat disingenuous, of course. Lovins studies any topic of interest hard and in great detail. "Never studied formally" would be more accurate. He follows his own nose, rather than allowing himself to be channeled in conventional ways. His pride, then, rests on having achieved a sophisticated understanding of a series of specialized discourses, enough to participate successfully in their professional debates and to shape their development on occasion, without being captured by their conventional assumptions. "Beginner's mind," the openness to deep insights treasured in the Zen tradition, is a Lovins stock in trade.

Joining Friends of the Earth International in 1971 freed Lovins to concentrate on energy affairs on his own terms. Over the next few years, his networking talent and quick comprehension allowed him to turn the existing jumble of disparate, disconnected investigations at many different American and European locations into a rich compost in which to germinate and grow a major new rootstock for energy analysis. It blossomed in a 1976 article in *Foreign Affairs* that established him as a genuine trailblazer.

The soft path

The substance of the *Foreign Affairs* article (October 1976) is what matters most, but its presentation is worth a moment of attention. The face that looks out at the reader is more boyish than the others in the issue, which include career diplomats, senior academics, and Israel's defense minister of the time. And it is more bespectacled, more egghead or brainiac than those of the other younger contributors, who present themselves as vigorous future policy leaders. The poetic subtitle is unique among the other articles, which stick close to business—"policy," "control," "economy," "China," "Latin America," and the like. Leading off by quoting the original poem is equally unique. The author of this article is definitely not from the usual places: readers should prepare themselves for something other than the usual content.

ENERGY STRATEGY:
THE ROAD NOT TAKEN?

By Amory B. Lovins

Two roads diverged in a wood, and I—
I took the one less traveled by,
And that has made all the difference.
—Robert Frost

 WHERE are America's formal or de facto energy policies leading us? Where might we choose to go instead? How can we find out?

Addressing these questions can reveal deeper questions—and a few answers—that are easy to grasp, yet rich in insight and in international relevance. This paper will seek to explore such basic concepts in energy strategy by outlining and contrasting two energy paths that the United States might follow over the next 50 years—long enough for the full implications of change

The opening also shows him wasting no time getting down to business—"outlining and contrasting two energy paths that the United States might follow over the next 50 years."[8] The two paths are the hard (centralized high technologies) and the soft (efficiencies and flexible, resilient, sustainable technologies). The article finds the hard path not just ineffective (because it doesn't solve foreign oil dependence), but also infeasible (because it needs too much capital too fast) and undesirable (because it's too centralized and socially coercive). His opposition on the last point is forceful:

> The hard path, sometimes portrayed as the bastion of free enterprise and free markets, would instead be a world of subsidies, $100-billion bailouts, oligopolies, regulations, nationalization, eminent domain, corporate statism.
>
> . . .
>
> We are becoming more uneasily aware of the nascent risk of what a Stanford Research Institute group has called ". . . 'friendly fascism'— a managed society which rules by a faceless and widely dispersed complex of warfare-welfare-industrial-communications-police bureaucracies with a technocratic ideology.' "

The US, Lovins argued, should shift to the soft path—pursuing energy efficiency and building a diverse portfolio of energy flows from renewable sources such as sun, wind and biomass. This strategy would not only provide the energy for a thriving economy without loading the atmosphere with CO_2, but would also avoid the hard path's sociopolitical burdens. Soft technologies largely existed already, and did not depend on scarce resources. Installing and maintaining them required only modest skills.[9] And the fact, most unwelcome to conventional energy thinking, that sunlight and wind are dispersed, not concentrated, would have the actual advantage of reducing the impacts and expense of distributing energy from plant to user.

His reasoning rested on information and estimates by established mainstream sources, data and descriptions already available at that time to anyone who looked. Lovins had bothered to gather it together. His truly unusual thoroughness and his drive to develop a whole-system view had kept him at it; his outsider status, as an egghead with beginner's mind, gave him the mental space to connect it all in new ways.

The article caused a storm. Letters to the journal itself, reports and rebuttals in other professional publications, even Congressional hearings —opposition was quick and vocal, and though largely phrased as a technical discussion, did not hold back from ad hominem attacks. (He was called 'irresponsible', 'seductive', even a 'liar'). The article evoked apocalyptic visions, supposedly heralding the 'onset of a new Dark Age'. Though much of this opposition was regrettable, it was comprehensible. Opposition to the soft path proposition found little in the way of facts or methods to fasten onto Lovins had done his homework well and was rapid, detailed, and commanding in his rebuttals. He was able to show that conventional analysis of energy options ignored important kinds of costs (and benefits), and that careful assembly of the full range of needed information favored the soft options.

At this distance it seems clear that the virulence of the opposition reflected some deep unease and anxiety about threats to US values and practices in general, and about the energy establishment's position in particular.[10] The mid-1970s were years when the social upheavals of the

1960s—civil rights, Vietnam, the counterculture and the rest—were still playing out, with all their challenges to received wisdom, threats to established positions, and unresolved contradictions. On top of these widespread social stresses, the energy establishment was finding its own economic and political position shaky. The OPEC crisis of 1973, which caused oil prices to triple in three months, produced block long lines at gas stations, and upended all assumptions about global politics, showed that business-as-usual was a weak base for such an economically vital resource as energy. What seemed the obvious way forward to most insiders—a rapid expansion of nuclear power—was already being resisted. So the nerves Lovins touched in the energy establishment were already raw, and since his work was too well constructed to be successfully dismissed, virulence was one way to discharge feeling.

The storm played itself out without a clear resolution. The soft path survived as an approach with widespread appeal, but the hard path continued with widespread support of its own. In some ways, the contest between the two continues to this day.

The storm was also, of course, a good way to drive a calling forward into a career. From 1976 on, Lovins was in continuous demand as a speaker, consultant, visiting professor, and research participant. His nominal base was Friends of the Earth in London, but his life was itinerant in the extreme. In a later interview, he said, "I worked from my London base all around the world, chiefly Europe, and then I'd come back to the US to guide in the White Mountains each summer. The trips with Dave [Brower] were learning journeys, increasingly about energy. A lot of the work was on nuclear energy and nuclear proliferation issues. . . . Dave was paying me enough to more or less cover my phone bill [not small in those pre-Internet days for an intensive international networker]. I would live by my wits for the rest by writing, lecturing, broadcasting, and consulting."[11]

In 1978, he met Hunter, who brought legal training; a background in political science, sociology, and forestry; and her organizational talents to their joint professional work. They married the next year. The itinerant life continued. "It was a kind of nomadic hunter-gatherer existence.

Hunter hunted and I gathered."[12] Two years later, David Brower got fired from Friends of the Earth, ending the viability of their London existence. The Lovinses decided to move back to the US.

Snowmass

Two key questions now presented themselves. The questions were: where do we settle? and what are we? The answer to the first turned out to be out to be Old Snowmass, Colorado. The second led to the founding of Rocky Mountain Institute. There were plenty of invitations and offers, from all parts of the country. The couple's own inclination was to avoid big cities, partly from shared tastes for mountains and country settings, partly from a shared belief that big cities would be targets in any nuclear violence that erupted over the next 20 to 40 years. However, their itinerant professional life demanded certain services that were very rare in rural places at that time—multiple flights in or out each day, FedEx, international touchtone dialing, computer repair. Today, the Internet provides great help with getting this kind of work done, but in 1981, it was still experimental, very restricted, and a maddening patchwork of barely compatible hardware and software.

One of their professional stopping points was met both sets of needs. Aspen, Colorado was already well established, not only as a ski resort but as a significant year-round cultural center, through such initiatives as the Aspen Institute and Aspen Music Festival. Founded in 1950, the Institute had originally focused on the humanities, but by the late 1970s it had greatly broadened its range of seminars, public programs, and policy programs, and had become a mecca for business leaders, cultural figures and public intellectuals. Amory had been attending and speaking at sessions of the Institute for several years, and the summer of 1981 gave an extended stay in the area and opened up the possibility of setting up a new institute of some kind within Windstar, a foundation established by the singer John Denver. It was located up a small side valley in Old Snowmass, just northwest of Aspen, in an area Hunter already knew from her high school years at Colorado Rocky Mountain School further down the main valley of the Roaring Fork, in Carbondale.

A constituency like the Aspen Institute's expected and got just the kind of services that the Lovinses needed for their work. In addition, the Rocky Mountain setting was extraordinarily beautiful, and at a suitable distance from big cities. Ready access to the national and international leadership class as its members passed through the area would be an extra advantage for the high-level influence the Lovinses aimed for. As the summer of 1981 ended, they found and purchased a just-affordable building site next to Capitol Creek.

As the summer had progressed, however, affiliating with Windstar had seemed more and more problematic, and the idea faded from view. It was a few more months before the right idea for an organizational base emerged. Hunter turned to Amory sometime during their March 1982 drive east toward a teaching stay at Dartmouth College and suggested they set up their own, independent institute. Amory would focus on the quality of the research; Hunter would focus on administration. Rocky Mountain Institute was born.

Looking back from today to the *Foreign Affairs* article, it seems clear that if Amory the person needed a definite base location, his case for the soft path also needed more than analytic definiteness. It needed something like the Snowmass house. The article asserts that:

> Both paths, like any 50-year energy path, entail significant social change. But the kinds of social change needed for a hard path are apt to be much less pleasant, less plausible, less compatible with social diversity and personal freedom of choice, and less consistent with traditional values than are the social changes that could make a soft path work.

The decisive virtues of the soft path, and the deficiencies of the hard, were to appear at the level of individuals, households, and communities, where social diversity, freedom of choice and traditional values are experienced and matter personally. Analysis of relative system costs and national policy considerations don't reach down convincingly to that scale. But the soft path's support for these things virtues only materialize when embodied there. The question Amory and Hunter encountered often on the lecture circuit—"Do you yourselves live on the soft path?" or its equivalent—was not just a facile "Gotcha!" or a test of good faith.

It called for evidence that the political, social and human appeal of the soft path could actually be realized in people's lives. That call could only be answered by having a place and some life in it, some life on view.

Already in 1976, the building sector could provide important support for Lovins' claims about energy efficiency. In the article's words:

> To take one major area of potential saving, technical fixes in new buildings can save 50 percent or more in office buildings and 80 percent or more in some new houses.

The footnote backing this claim cites studies by a major US engineering firm, the National Bureau of Standards, the British Building Research Establishment, and the Owens-Corning-Fiberglas corporation. Hardly a group of wild-eyed idealists. Lovins' success in the soft path debates owed a good deal to showing that the ideas, techniques and materials in question were already in existence, and what sounded radical was actually just recognizing the potential of assembling them properly.

The impulse to look hard at energy efficiency in buildings, and the examples that established how great its potential was, had come as much from outside the establishment as inside. This history is worth a closer look. So do the reasons for opening it up at some length.

The 1973 oil crisis made the later 1970s a fertile and busy time in North America for exploring, testing and demonstrating bright ideas in energy-conscious houses. The three pictured below embody the significant themes of the time. The very visible differences in their appearance reflect a genuine lack of consensus about techniques and even about goals. They aren't obvious in the buildings, but there were also very important differences in these early projects' origins, owners, financing, audiences, supporters. and and constituencies. What they had very much in common was the goal of dramatically reducing energy use compared to what was needed in most American houses.

Three icons of alternative housebuilding in the 1970s (Saskatchewan House, Leger House, Balcomb House)

From left to right, the three exemplars are the Saskatchewan Conservation House (Regina, Saskatchewan), the Eugene Leger house (East Pepperell, Massachusetts), and the J. Douglas Balcomb house (Santa Fe, New Mexico).[13] Between them, they represent the two main low energy approaches of the time, the three main streams of building research, and several of the besetting tensions of the period—form vs. function, history vs. clean-slate, and lab vs. garage, at least. The two main approaches paralleled the two parts of the soft path vision—efficiency greatly reducing the need for energy, and soft technologies to supply the need that remained.

Solar heating

The energy problem for American houses in 1973 was about heating. and at that time heating came from furnaces—distinct single-purpose items of equipment. Since the usual fuel supply was now seen to be unreliable, a natural step was to search for some other single-purpose kind of

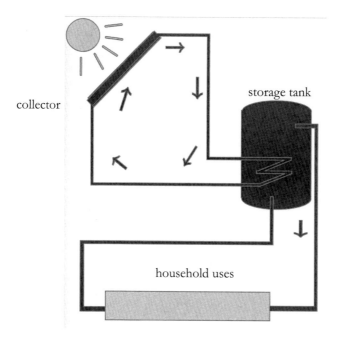

Basic elements of household water-based solar thermal collection. Fluid circulating to collector heats the fluid in the storage tank but does not mix with it. Heat for household use is sometimes in a similar closed loop.

equipment which could do the job.[14] Ideas for using solar heat were not far to seek, thanks to university research during the 1950s. Americans often have short time horizons, looking to neither the past or future in much detail, and the solar awareness of the mid-1970s did not reach far enough back to register the diversity of solar experimentation and even commercialization that had gone on in earlier decades in the US, in various waves of interest. In fact, almost all of the solar ideas of 2017 had precursors from before 1950, as far back as the third millennium BC in China. However, it was not until 1980 that awareness of this deeper history began to spread. At the outset, only the 1950s were in view, and that was a decade dominated by studies of just one of the many solar ideas that had emerged over time.

That idea was the flat plate thermal collector. Sunlight falling on a roof was to be absorbed by a black-painted metal sheet in contact with pipes or ducts holding flowing water or air. The plate would get hot, heating the water or air, and the pipes (for water) or ducts (for air) would carry the flow back inside to heat the house. The basic idea was simple, and the research of the 1950s had shown reasonably effective ways to develop it into workable systems. The systems were moderately complex, since the heated elements had to be insulated against losses to the outside air, ways of storing heat had to be provided to smooth out the day-to-night and weather-related variability of solar heating, and controls were needed to start, stop, or redirect the flows. Water systems had to prevent freezing; air systems had to find room in the house for the fairly sizable ducts.

This was a system concept well suited to engineering research. The basic science was in hand; there were enough variables to provide challenge; there was plenty of scope for incremental invention; and everything was measurable. There was uncertainty and healthy controversy about significant details, too, for example about which circulating fluid should be used. Most importantly, the systems could be studied without much regard for the households they were serving, just like familiar oil or coal furnaces.

The engineers active in solar research in the 1950s came to function as an insiders' club, a natural enough consequence of their small numbers. That this clubbiness narrowed its members' perspectives to the topics of greatest ease is not surprising; and that other actors such as architects, policymakers, or bankers let the definiteness of engineering narrow their thinking or allowed themselves to stop thinking is regrettable, but not the engineers' fault. Denzer's excellent account of all this in *The Solar House* shows how this conjunction of tendencies slowed and stopped official progress on solar energy from 1958 or so on.[15]

Research to that point clearly showed that flat plate collectors could do a fine job of heating houses. It also clearly showed that such systems would be expensive compared to other modes of heating such as conventional coal or oil furnaces or the up and coming option of electric heat. This had become a kiss of death for their commercial prospects by the end of the decade, and since they were the only solar game in town, it was a kiss of death for all solar energy at that point.

It's worth noticing that expense is not automatically fatal in many household decisions about equipment. In buying a car, expense matters, but so do capacity, styling, acceleration, and reputation. Bathroom fixtures and kitchen cabinets and appliances are notorious for their ability to get budgets set aside in favor of dreams, images, and feelings. Large screen televisions, home exercise equipment, curtains and upholstery—there are many things of this sort. Making household decisions purely on grounds of expense is the exception, not the rule.

Household heating, however, has been a prime exception. Expense has been in charge of decisions about heating systems. I think this was simply because the engineering approach of solar researchers at that time considered it as purely and totally utilitarian. They assumed householders only wanted reliable heat, and didn't care how it was provided. They left any delight or enthusiasm that might be part of the experience of studying or living with one system or another out of their analyses and reports. They didn't concern themselves with ethical issues that might be involved in choosing among them. They stuck to conclusions on the basis of relative convenience and relative reduction of nuisance. Like the general public at the time, they probably thought it was obvious that coal furnaces should be out of sight, out of mind, and that made it harder to see that one might think about solar heating differently. That assumption, and their engineering approach to the problem left expense as the only major variable.

Thus, solar energy in America was first widely introduced to the public and to policy makers through the framework of econo-mysticism, and our thinking about household energy use has often been limited by it ever since. One of Lovins' main goals in the Snowmass house, and one of its achievements as a project, was to broaden the view and to reinject the possibility of delight into the experience of sustainability.

Widespread interest in solar options reawakened after the OPEC shock of the 1970s. The ground had been well prepared by the memorable 1960s, whose turmoil included the appeal of countercultural phenomena in all their glory. Dropping out led people to multiple paths away from the world of the 1950s, which they saw as buttoned-up, sanitized, conformist, and corporatized. Though not many people may actually have started life anew, in literal communes or alternative households, living by bartering or starting ad hoc ephemeral businesses, the sudden sense of freedom to explore was very profound. Those explorations were sometimes naive, self-limiting, or short-sighted, but often enough they shed real light and opened real possibilities. The realization that one might profitably explore beyond conventional boundaries spread well past the tie-dyed and bearded or braided minority to all sorts of less rebellious people.

The sun symbolized much in the counterculture of the 1960s, and enabled much. It was outdoors, not in; health promoting, not draining; easily available, not confined or limited; free, not bought or sold. Its very lack of commercialization was appealing. Flat plate collector ideas found a new constituency, one which embraced the simplicity of the technology, wasn't flustered by the absence of a supplier network for parts and warranties, and took pleasure in the potential for home-grown versions made of cheap, locally available materials, such as used offset printing plates, expanded metal lath, and castoff electrical conduit.

This popular enthusiasm inspired a new wave (or wavelet) of university research, investigating more advanced collector configurations, such as evacuated tube designs which reduced losses by putting collector surfaces and piping in a glass vacuum bottle, like the insulating spaces that keep liquids hot in thermos bottles. The Saskatchewan House photo shows a horizontal row of such evacuated collectors on the steep south-facing roof just below the ridge-line. These mark it as one of the heirs to the solar work of the 1950s, the first of the three main streams of building research available to the Lovinses.

An icon of passive solar design

The most significant solar developments, however, were not conceived as furnace substitutes. They sprang from realizing that an even less corporate/industrial opportunity existed. Houses themselves collect solar energy through windows; proper attention to the placement and size of windows and to wall materials could make this the primary source of heat. This was called "passive solar" because it needed no pumps, valves, or mechanical controls. The idea sparked extensive experimentation through the 1970s, grew steadily in importance and largely supplanted the previous "active" approach. It is the second of the three main streams. The Balcomb house, dating from 1977, is an excellent example of where this led, and a side-by-side view makes the connection with the Lovins Snowmass house immediately apparent.

Left: Balcomb House (Santa Fe). Right: Lovins House (Old Snowmass)

Built in 1977 and occupied continuously since, the Balcomb house has been called the "quintessential solar adobe house".[16] It gained this status from a fortunate blend of entrepreneurial, regional and academic energies. The "Balcomb" in its conventional title refers to J. Douglas Balcomb, a scientist at the Los Alamos National Laboratory who became intrigued by and then deeply involved in measuring and modeling the thermal performance of passive solar houses. He was neither the designer or nor the builder. The architect of record was William Lumpkins, a New Mexico native and noted regional artist/architect, who contributed importantly to the layout and aesthetics. However, the drive and the insights for this well-integrated passive solar design came from Susan Nichols, a Stanford-trained mathematician who moved to Santa Fe in 1973 with her MBA husband, Wayne, and plunged with him into solar residential development.

The Balcomb house was officially Unit One in the Nichols' first subdivision, called First Village, which aimed to be a test bed for a variety of solar heating approaches. Like the Lovinses in Snowmass, their mood was experimental. The experiment at First Village was physical, of course

—would the houses achieve low energy?—but more importantly, it was a business experiment about creating commercial niches for sustainable building. This was not a priority for the Lovinses, but Susan and Wayne Nichols were trying to be developers, the people whose business is in bringing investment, construction and purchasers together. The biggest unknowns for them were the size and boundaries of the market for solar-heated houses in mid-1970s Santa Fe.

They went about defining their niche in stages. They described First Village as aimed at "a professional affluent market that can afford homes in the $100,000-$170,000 range. [This is equivalent to $690,000-$1.2 million in today's dollars.] The buyers of these homes often tend to be in their thirties and forties, some single, some with small families, all with individual lifestyles and strong environmental concerns."[17] Construction also went in stages. Units One and Two, one passive solar, the other active, were completed and sold before the design of later units was fixed. The Nicholses quickly concluded that the passive option performed as well as the active and was much easier to build and maintain; the remaining units were all variations on that theme. They built eight houses; three were commissioned by their owners and five were 'spec' built. to be sold on the market for better or worse. Each one was a different, 'custom' building, and all sold, at prices 15-20% higher than conventional homes of comparable size and style. [18]

The Nicholses were well aware that their success depended on building a reputation compatible with their desired niche. Their announced goal was to be seen as "quality, innovative builders who are environmentally responsible".[19] The Lovins house at Snowmass had related but quite distinct aims. Environmental responsibility, innovation, and quality were all to be part of it, but expressed so as to transmit a new, wide sense of possibility to a national audience rather than to embody the values of potential local purchasers. Their house was to be a benchmark demonstrating the existence of a path and offering a view along it, not an endpoint.

Unit One was also an experiment in the sense that it was closely monitored. Doug and Sara Balcomb bought the place because they had been actively studying passive solar buildings for several years, and this was a chance to experience one first hand. Their involvement was somewhat accidental. Doug had come to Los Alamos to work on nuclear-powered rocket engines, hardly a green initiative. But that funding ended, and in casting around for a new research area, Doug discovered the budding passive solar movement, was attracted to its possibilities, and saw that monitoring and modeling, familiar work for him, would be needed to validate good approaches and spread knowledge and trust.

New Mexico's passive experimentation grew out of the counterculture, partly from communes like Drop City, partly from feisty contrarians like Peter Van Dresser and Steve Baer.[20] The heritage of adobe construction and the examples of long inhabited pueblos close at hand, now recognized as passive solar buildings,[21] supported ideas about the potential of low-tech methods. The low budgets and modest technical training of counterculture people generally made those methods attractive or necessary. There were plenty of ideas and plenty of active building, but information about what to do and what worked was all anecdotal.

Balcomb and some Los Alamos colleagues began fitting thermocouples and data loggers to small, would-be passive solar buildings during their construction at places like the Sun Dwellings project at Ghost Ranch, NM—three different solar buildings and one conventional one as control. At the Los Alamos lab itself, they also set up a series of 10'x7'x5' test cells for comparing different window and insulation arrangements. Thus, it was not a big step for Balcomb to start measuring temperatures, humidities, and solar energy inputs in and around Unit One, his home.

The next page shows the kind of data he collected at Unit One—for two weeks bracketing New Year's, 1979. It also presents typical difficulties for the reader, so I'll give you a quick summary.

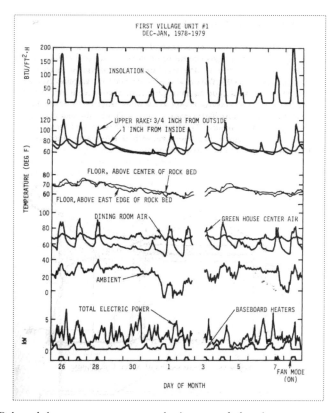

Balcomb house temperatures, solar input, and electric power use:
Dec. 26, 1978 to Jan.8, 1979.
See Supplement to this chapter for accessible explanations.

Twelve data streams are presented over two weeks of time using six different scales (one unlabelled) and four different units of measurement (one barely labelled). The chart appears in a paper by Sara Balcomb,[22] and in fairness, it is clearer and better adapted to its purpose than most engineering graphics of its period. It truly supports the high claims made for this building, and is thus worthy of some disentangling.

Most importantly, it shows the temperatures outside were never above 40° F in this period, and only got that high a few times. It was below zero for most of Jan. 1 and 2, with another cold snap on the night of Jan. 7-8. The interior of the house almost always stayed between 68 and 72. It got as low as 62 early before dawn on the coldest mornings.

The chart also shows when there was sunshine and how much, and the temperature of both the inside and the outside of the heavy adobe wall between the greenhouse and the interior, which stores heat when the sun is shining on it and slowly radiates it into the rest of the house. It shows when the fans to distribute heat through the building were running. (For more about interpreting this data display, and what it tells about the functioning of the Balcomb building, look at this chapter's Supplement.)

The chart only shows the results of the measuring program during the two weeks it covers, but it was the persistence of those results over three years of data gathering and study which earned the Balcomb house its high technical status.

Measured performance is a vital part of understanding sustainability in buildings, or anywhere. There are indeed other vital things. Sustainability is a matter of good judgment, well-grounded feeling, and practiced intuition, as well as of appropriate measurement. However, measurement is essential if you want to understand how and why a building is working well or failing, and if you want to learn how to design one successfully.

Here's the plan of the house. The photograph earlier emphasizes the sloping roof of the south-facing greenhouse. The plan emphasizes the

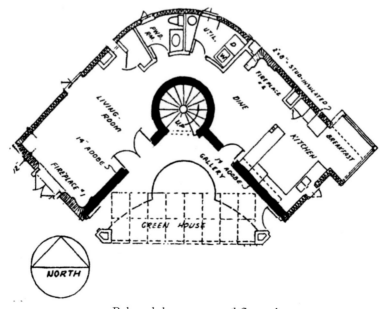

Balcomb house, ground floor plan

diagonal adobe walls on each side of it and around the central staircase. The house proper folds around the greenhouse. There are two floors— the living room is half the ground floor; the dining room and a kitchen with a breakfast nook occupy the other half, and a powder room and a utility area are tucked into curve above the passage that connects them. There are three bedrooms above, reached by the circular stair in the center of the building and a balcony on the greenhouse side of the massive adobe walls.

The two-story, 20 ft tall adobe walls, 14 inches thick at the bottom and tapering to 10 inches as they rises, provide a major thermal sink between the greenhouse and the house proper. The abundant Santa Fe sun heats the greenhouse, but cannot heat the living areas directly. Instead, the boundary wall absorbs heat during sunny periods and gives it up again when the greenhouse cools at night, as well as passing it slowly through the wall to provide nighttime heat to the living quarters.

In the winter, heated greenhouse air is drawn off at roof level and carried in ducts down to heat the living room and dining room floors from underneath, with wide, flat rock beds under each room to store and slowly release heat the way the greenhouse wall does. The rear walls of the house, facing northeast, north, and northwest respectively as they curve from right to left in the plan, are heavily insulated and have a substantial exterior "berm," 4½ feet of earth piled deep against their exteriors The living area of the house has very small temperature swings day to night and season to season; 89% of its heating requirements are supplied by the solar features, so the cost of purchased heating energy is far lower than it is for a conventional house in Santa Fe; and the "thermal mass" of the house (the materials that store and release heat, mainly the greenhouse inner boundary wall and the below-floor rock beds) can supply up to two days of heat during the occasional cloudy cold spells. Thermal mass serving this storage or balancing function became a key feature of passive solar design, whether integrated inconspicuously in Balcomb's fashion or sitting in plain view as a massive wall or floor.

We will see that the Lovins house behaves quite similarly, although data from that building is much more qualitative. The Lovinses did not have the ready access to measuring gear that Balcomb enjoyed, nor did their goals prioritize careful measurement to the extent the Balcombs' did.

In fact, the Balcomb house also had more than measurements to offer. Sara Balcomb's paper leads with qualities, not quantities: "What a passive home offers its occupants is a delightful new kind of freedom and comfort."[23] Freedom from depending on external fuel infrastructure and its bills, and freedom from worrying about physical and financial shocks to such a basic need as staying warm. Freedom from a status quo in which "the health and comfort of people has been held hostage to the politics of nations." The house provided the comfort of "… a natural warmth. There are no drafts, no hot spots, no dry air blowing through the house. . . . We have found that we simply take our comfort for granted, never having to worry about cold feet, dry skin, drafts, or chills." Beyond that, she wrote, "our family thoroughly enjoys the additional benefits of a sunspace, roses and gardenias in bloom in mid-winter, the pleasant aroma of fresh greenery, the sound of water splashing in a small fountain, and fresh fruits and vegetables all year round."

These benefits go well beyond typical engineering notions about good function. We will see their like in the Lovins house. They get outside the flattened approach of econo-mystical planning and engage the full dimensions of the lives to be lived in sustainable houses. Sound, smell, and taste come into the picture; leaves and flowers, water, seasonal patterns of growth all have places. Though Balcomb didn't mention them herself, other commentary noted the appeal of natural materials. For example, a profile in *Mother Earth News* said, "To an adobe fancier— and the allure of an earthen home 'growing' out of the land is very real to many folks—the Balcomb house falls somewhere between shelter and art."[24]

Sara Balcomb also valued how little attention this house requires of its occupants: "Our own home requires no action on our part aside from the once a year opening and closing of one vent in the sunspace. [Closing the vent directs hot greenhouse air down into the rock beds, and is the winter setting; opening it sends the hot air out of the house entirely, as one wants in summer.] One of the best things about our home is that it conserves energy—my energy." Engineering measurement can tell us whether the valve operates as intended. But it can't say much about the depth or intensity of the value of having such minimal requirements to the operators of a house.

In this house under these owners, there's a marriage between low and high tech, laboratory science and garage invention, the expertise of the Los Alamos national laboratory and local aesthetics and initiative, with results of lasting significance.

Superinsulation

Efficiency was the other half of the soft path for buildings, and the third of the main streams of research. The exemplar here, the 1979 Eugene Leger house in East Pepperell, Massachusetts, has little of the curb appeal of Santa Fe's Unit One. Its important contributions all lie under the skin.

Its builder also remains unknown to a surprising degree, given the influence this modest looking, modest sized house has exerted on soft path building. The few scraps of personal information available do not

Eugene Leger house (from architecture.ideas2live4.com)

give the impression that Leger himself was modest at the time. Joseph Lstiburek, an active engineer, consultant and longtime commentator on progressive building, had this to say about him in 2008,[25]

> What a character. An American original. A cross between James Cagney and Emeril Lagasse in the body of a building official. How many Chief Building Officials have you ever met that have designed and constructed a unique structure that changed the world?

Leger himself, in one of his few published items, shows plenty of self-confidence:

> In 1980 I announced that the double wall was an unnecessary method that was adding thousands of dollars to the cost of superinsulated houses.[26]

The confidence here is not only in the tone, but also in his willingness to tell his peers that they were fixating on the wrong aspects of the house he was being widely celebrated for designing and building. Interestingly, Leger and all commentators agreed that the unobtrusiveness of the building itself was high among its virtues.

Leger lived and worked in northeastern Massachusetts, in an area of once but no longer prosperous small cities, outside the Boston area's complex of universities and technology-centered industry. He designed and built houses, as part of that very large part of the American housing industry that has nothing to do with architecture. For a period, he was a chief building official (i.e. building inspector) in Merrimack, New Hampshire, just across the Massachusetts border from Pepperell. There is every sign that he was a practical, intensely competent, self-sufficient American man with an opinionated manner, the sort of person other people people value or tolerate because his insights are profound and his personal energy and willingness to take risks in pursuing them are so unusual.

The functional appeal of the Leger house is easy to state: it stayed warm in a New England winter at a heating cost 90% lower than what was typical for houses of the time. It didn't need a conventional furnace. Yet it looked like a conventional house inside and out, a rectangular box with rectangular rooms of exactly the sort that were going up in subdivisions all across the country, and it was built as a commercial venture, with no outside sponsorship or financing. That was enough to capture the attention of progressive builders. Compare its appearance and its setting with those of the Saskatchewan house, typical of the period's experimental, overtly solar projects.

(Whatever its appearance, the Saskatchewan project was widely known to people looking for much better energy performance in houses. It certainly influenced Lovins, who says that its goal of combining solar and superinsulating approaches was inspiring, a definite benchmark in the personal path that led to the Snowmass building.)

Attention quickly became admiration as people learned how Leger had done it. He had simply seen that combining several known efficiency ideas would allow a qualitative leap—eliminating the furnace. No furnace reduced construction costs by several thousand dollars, which helped to balance the cost of the efficiency improvements significantly. This was a major conceptual insight. That big a reduction is only possible when one goes far enough with efficiency. It seems paradoxical, but doing a lot can end up costing less than doing only a little. This phenomenon eventually turned up in enough different contexts to become one of Lovins' most frequent themes, under the banner of "tunneling through the cost barrier."

Leger's recipe basically combined much more insulation than usual, and much greater care in sealing the building against unwanted inflows and outflows of air. The former involved a new, thicker wall structure and multi-layer windows; the latter required radically fewer openings in the shell, with multiple small consequences for plumbing, wiring, and the construction of the shell itself.

Sunlight was not a prime feature. Leger partly came out of a part of the American alternative building movement which regarded the sun with suspicion, not pleasure. Of course they thought there should be some windows, as in all houses. But the sun could easily overheat a room. The windows which let sunlight in also let large amounts of heat out, and getting ample sunlight put big constraints on how a house could be placed on its site, to the detriment of views, existing trees, and road access. It also seemed obvious to many people at the time that places like Massachusetts wouldn't ever enjoy enough sun in heating season.

As the 1970s unfolded, such disenchantment no doubt also drew nourishment from increasing distrust of the counterculture's willingness to discard conventional wisdom as well as conventional habits. But to many people the environmental crises of the decade still called for new departures, away from business as usual in housing as much as anywhere else. There was fertile ground waiting when researchers at the University of Illinois came forward with their "Lo-Cal" house proposals, starting in 1976.[27] The core idea was to dramatically improve the insulation and air-tightness of houses, and the Lo-Cal group coined the term "super-insulation" for it.

Their proposed increase in insulation was indeed dramatic—over twice as thick as normal practice. And their proposals were merely designs, only backed by paper estimates, not built and measured projects. Many people in this basically conservative industry were uninterested. But in those tumultuous times, others, including Eugene Leger, took heed. Some were organizations, such as the provincial government of Saskatchewan, which combined Lo-Cal ideas with active solar heat collection in the Saskatchewan House. Some were pioneering individuals like R.P. Bentley of upstate New York.[28] Leger stood out: his insight was both radical and easy to imagine implementing.

The notion of dispensing with a furnace was not in the Lo-Cal proposal, and did not emerge right away. Why should it have? Card-carrying engineers, adventurous architects and self-taught inventors all knew that houses in cold climates lose heat, which has to be resupplied somehow. It seemed obvious that meant furnaces. However, the energy crisis was motivating fresh looks at ways to minimize losses. As some investigators tried estimating the practical effects of various adjustments to insulation levels, window sizes, rates of air leakage and so on, they realized that a house's occupants were generating heat in significant amounts. Lamps, water heaters, stoves and other appliances, and radios or televisions all produce heat when they're turned on. They have a primary purpose other than heating, but all the energy that flows into them quite soon turns to heat. Light gets absorbed, mechanical motion is drained by friction, electrical impulses heat the wires they flow through. Indeed the mere presence of warm-blooded animals in a building generates heat: human output ranges between 60 and 120 watts per person, depending on activity level. The Lovinses' bull terrier, Nanuq, would have been in the 50-100 watt range. Higher wattage devices, like 1,200 watt toaster or water heaters with 4,500 or 5,500 watt elements, generate correspondingly more.

Heat from these other sources contributes to the total needed for indoor comfort just as much as as heat from a furnace. If you want to know how big a furnace a house needs, you start with an estimate of how much heat the house will lose in a day, using climate information and some specifics about the house's construction. The furnace doesn't need to supply this full amount, however. What are called "internal gains" from appliances, lights, and occupants' metabolism already supply part of what's needed. The furnace just needs to be big enough to supply the rest.

In conventional houses, internal gains made only a small contribution to keeping the place warm. In the Lo-Cal designs, humans and their gear weren't any more active, but the extra insulation and airtightness made heat losses so low that internal gains could take care of a large fraction of what was needed. From there it was a short step for Leger and several others to realize that it was within reach for a house to get all its basic heat requirement from the occupants and their activities, and not to need a normal furnace at all.

Airtightness turned out to be complicated. Over the timespan covered by this book, its status among progressive builders has gone from an unknown to the flavor of the month to bogeyman and then coming part way back. It's not only important for household energy; it also has a primal connection to human health.

Every house needs fresh air coming in and stale air going out to keep its occupants alive. In traditional houses, right down to the 1970s, this happened without special provision. Doors, windows, and the structure itself were all loosely fitted enough for both fresh and stale air to generally move as one would wish, with no needed for specific arrangements.

One consequence of the OPEC crisis was the realization that loose construction meant large heat losses. Heated inside air was getting out, taking its heat with it. It was being replaced by cold outside air, which needed heating. The amounts of heat were quite large, with as much as 30-40% of a house's total heat loss due to air moving out of and into the building. A good part of the success of superinsulation in reducing energy lay in shutting down multiple air leakage paths and confining air intake and outflow to chosen vents and ducts.

For example, Eugene Leger not only made windows and outside doors well-fitting, but also fully sealed the door and window frames into their openings in the walls. He arranged plumbing and wiring to need no wall penetrations of their own. The entries blocked direct air flow with vestibule designs, in which one door was typically closed before the other was opened. Fresh air for this modest building came through a single window-mounted ventilation unit in the family room which also used the outgoing air to partially heat the incoming.

This was all very well, and valuable in the long run, but it doesn't take much reading or hearing about environmental fixes to realize that each fix may well reveal or create some further problem. DDT kills harmful insects but weakens the eggs of valued birds. The introduction of cane toads to Australia in the late 1930s was an attempt to control a plant pest without pesticides; it ended in the toads multiplying, largely unchecked, without measurable impact on the pest. Making buildings much more airtight led to new problems, too. The mid-1980s saw the emergence of "sick building syndrome," in which worrying numbers of office and residence occupants experienced headaches, asthma, sinus irritation, lethargy, and other symptoms that disappeared when they left the building. Although the syndrome was quite amorphous, and some questioned its reality, blame was quickly directed toward the much tighter structures that builders and designers had embraced to save energy only a few years earlier.

Since the 1980s, there have been several other waves of concern about one aspect or another of indoor air quality—off-gassing from paints, carpet adhesives, or insulation; toxic mold; radon gas; and rot caused by trapped moisture. Tight buildings obviously have the potential to aggravate any problems like these, so dealing with them has been one active area of green building work, deploying a broad range of ideas. The main solution to the need for fresh air in a tight building has turned out to be energy or heat recovery ventilation (ERV or HRV). This gets more discussion later. For now, the main point is that fresh air is no longer a problem for low energy construction.

One striking feature of most discussions of the Balcomb house is the expression of people's pleasure, satisfaction, or even delight in the experience of being in the house. This actually occurs in all the solar adobe houses I know about, and in fact in most passive solar houses of all kinds. The complete absence of any such comment in the writing about superinsulated houses is equally striking. There is discussion after discussion of how they are put together, and how much fuel or electricity they use, and what functional issues arose, and how these were addressed. Opinions about these matters are often strong, and can be strongly expressed. But I have yet to encounter an interview or report of a visit or reminiscence by a builder or owner that mentions what the experience of living in a superinsulated house is like except sometimes to mention in passing how much a given house looks like conventional houses, as if that were obviously a good thing. This inattention or disregard of or indifference to the experience of life marks off the superinsulation stream of development most clearly from the solar stream.

Looking normal, needing no special attention, being a house like any other except for very low energy bills has definitely been an animating goal for the efficiency stream of housebuilding. The summary report on the Lo-Cal House states this in typical fashion:

> The objective of this research program was to design a house with minimum energy needs for heating and cooling using standard building materials and methods.[29]

One can read all of the reports and commentary on superinsulation without encountering anything more connected with life lived than this. That work was legitimate, much needed, well managed, solidly grounded, and in fact wildly successful in meeting its goals. But as Lstiburek remarks,

> And then…nothing happened.[30]

Though the early 1980s saw some thousands of houses built using the insights and methods of the superinsulation pioneers, their methods did not become widespread and their insights faded from from view as that decade wore on. He goes on to say,

> In Canada, the R-2000 program became a boutique program that was pretty much ignored by mainstream builders. In the United States, after the Leger House, pretty much nothing happened there either.

Today, most housebuilding in the US is markedly more efficient than in 1970, thanks to a slow but steady stiffening of the requirements in state and local building codes. But it has all been done in small steps. There still hasn't been much if any adoption of the qualitative leap through which the right assemblage of efficiency ideas removes the entire need for a furnace.

The way forward for wide adoption of the radical possibilities offered by the efficiency stream turned out to be through Germany. The Lovins house had a role in getting that to happen, in which its aspiration to be a benchmark, its connection to larger goals than everyday functionality, was vital.

Supplement: Some building science stepping stones

When general readers glance at the chart showing sample data from the Balcomb house, they're unlikely to see more than squiggles with some degree of order; professional readers may recognize the ink pen traces from a 1970s chart recorder. For either group, these two weeks of data can come to show very clearly how passive solar design does its quiet

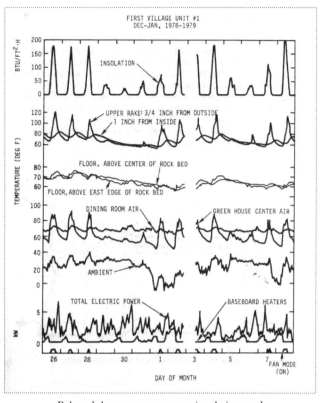

Balcomb house temperatures, insolation, and
electric power use: Dec. 26, 1978 to Jan.8, 1979.

work. It takes no math, just some background and some interpretation,
which I will provide, one line at a time.

What significant messages about the Balcomb house are lurking in these
carefully plotted lines?

The goal of gathering this kind of multi-channel data is to build a
coherent comprehensive account, rather like a chamber music ensemble
building a complex experience of sound out of carefully executed
individual lines. In this case, the account concerns the physical interaction
of this house with its thermal and solar environment.

(1) Days and hours (and the fan)

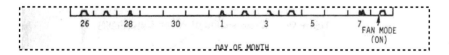

The line along the bottom of the chart tells one which days generated the data: December 26 through January 8, a total of two weeks. The chart-maker(s) also use it to show when the fans which assist heat distribution in the house were on. The fan mode bumps have different widths, which means the data is finer grained than day by day. A reasonable guess is that it's hourly (and one can actually verify that this by counting the number of zig and zags the wiggliest line lower down on the chart makes in a day). Each day's 24 hours, then, run from midnight to midnight between the thin vertical tick marks here.

 Thus on December 26, we can estimate that the fan came on a bit before mid-day and stayed on until evening. Back on the whole chart, we can see that the 27th and 28 saw much shorter run times, and there were none at all on the 29th, 30th, and 31st.

(2) Outside temperature

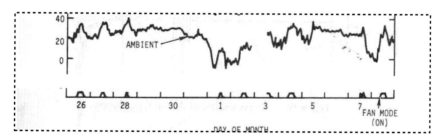

This line shows the hour-by-hour outside temperature over the two weeks being tracked here. ('Ambient' means 'of or relating to the immediate surroundings of something'.) The scale markings on the left give degrees Fahrenheit, so this is where we can see the temperature got up to 40° F a few times, and was below zero for most of Jan. 1 and 2, with another cold snap on the night of Jan. 7-8. The blank, most of Jan. 3, is a gap in all the data on this chart: the instruments seem to have been turned off.

One often talks about irregular data like this in terms of averages, but the Balcombs, the technically savvy inhabitants, discuss the building's performance largely in terms of temperature swings. This may partly come from the difficulty of extracting an average from the wiggling line of a chart record like this, but it may equally come from their householder's sense of what matters. A spell of overheating is not cancelled, in lived experience, by a period of chill, even if the mathematical average of temperatures is in the comfort zone. One wants a good degree of stability, like the preferred porridge in the Goldilocks story, neither too hot nor too cold. At the same time, a certain amount of warmer/cooler variation may well be enlivening, if the swings are not too great. (For the record, Sara Balcomb does report in passing that the average outdoor temperature in this period was 23° F.)[31]

(3) Temperature in the dining room

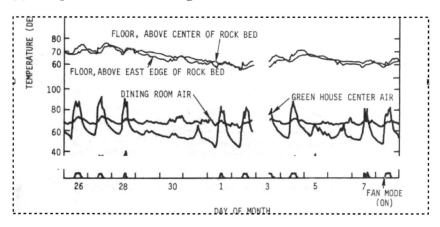

This is the set of measurements that show how well the house dealt with the generally low and briefly very low temperatures outside. Dining Room Air is perhaps most important. It varies up and down in the band between 66 and 72° F, except for the early hours of Jan. 2 and Jan. 8, when it got as low as 62 or 63° F. Outside, as we have seen, the air was mostly in the 20s, with two very cold spells in the two week period.

By the way, I got those numbers the way anyone could from this chart, by eyeballing, that is, by visually estimating where the highs and lows would fall along the given scale from 60 to 80 degrees. I put a straightedge between the two 60 degree tick marks on either side, to help keep my eyes on track. It's helpful that Sara Balcomb's paper confirms my readings for the December days, but it wouldn't have been essential. Professionals know that eyeballing is always required with analog instrument readings, between whatever the finest markings are. It introduces some variability in readings that digital readouts eliminate, but one should be mindful that modern science and engineering were largely built on analog measurements, so they are clearly precise enough to get a lot of good technical work done.

Zig-zagging more wildly above and below the dining room air line is the line for Green House Center Air. It's doing what one would expect from the design of the house. When the sun is out, the greenhouse will collect a lot of heat, and its air will get hotter. When there's no sun, it will cool off a lot, because the big sloping glass surface above it doesn't insulate well. The chart shows this happening for air in the center of the greenhouse. Up at the top of the room, the peak temperatures are probably even higher than the 93° F or so I estimate for the peaks on the line for "center air." If you compare the outside temperatures and the greenhouse temperatures, you can see that even on the nights when it's below zero outside, the greenhouse only cools to about 45° F.

That's because the greenhouse air can also receive heat from the massive rear wall whenever the air is cooler than the wall is. This wall-to-air transfer keeps the greenhouse air from cooling all the way to the outside level at night, and gets the cooling during the several days of very cold weather to be slow and steadily downward, rather than diving as fast as it does outside.

This pair of lines allows a first conclusion, perhaps the most important one. The house is maintaining comfortable temperatures in the downstairs living quarters, and even on the coldest nights the greenhouse is staying well above the point where the plants would suffer.

(4) Available solar heat

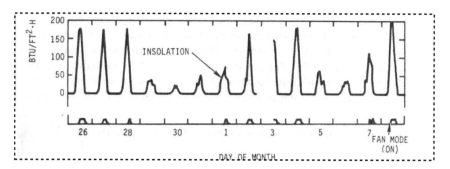

The top data trace shows the "insolation," the amount of solar heat arriving at the building's location during each hour. ("Insolation" and "insulation" are not the same.) Right away, before looking at any details, we can picture the sunshine history of these two weeks. The first three days had steady, good sun, with solar heat zero for several hours after midnight (we're going from midnight to midnight each day), then rising to a mid-day peak, and falling quite symmetrically to zero as night falls. The next four days got much less, with the peak on Jan. 30 down by 80% or more from the sunny days. The sun itself didn't stop shining, and the building didn't move; it must have been cloudy weather. It's no surprise, if you look back at the temperature trace, to see that the outside air didn't warm up on these days, the way it did on the first three.

The sun came back on Jan 2, 3 and 4. (The data gap on Jan. 3 shows up here again, as it does on all the traces, but there's enough of it to see that there was a lot of sun.) Finally, another cloudy spell on Jan. 5-7 ended with return to good sun on Jan. 8, the last day of this data run.

The most important technical detail for using this trace is the scale on the left edge. The amounts range between 0 and 200, but you have no idea what this means unless you understand the unit of measurement, and that it has several wrinkles. It is written as BTU/FT²·H, clearly an abbreviation. These are just marks on the page, not incantations, and they have the virtue of fitting onto the display and perhaps saving a little time for experts. Unfortunately, they also serve as obstacles to citizens' understanding and involvement, but it isn't hard to get comfortable with them. H stands for hour; FT² stands for square foot; the slash / stands for "per" (which gets attached to the item to the right of each slash); and BTU stands for British Thermal Unit, an amount of heat.[32] So the abbreviation can be read aloud as "BTU per square foot per hour." I actually encourage my students to say abbreviations like this aloud several times. It sounds trivial, but it helps with a key problem. People hate sounding stupid, and even the confidence that you're pronouncing a technical phrase properly is a surprising help, if you're a beginner. (Go ahead, try it.)

Fine, but what does it mean? What do square feet have to do with measuring heat? And why do hours get into the act? If we're measuring solar heat, why not just use the standard unit for heat, a BTU? These important questions take us into some important features of solar energy, of the kind that we know in a way, just from ordinary life, and yet rarely focus on.

Why not just use the heat unit? The short answer is that: we want a measure of how much sunlight is available to people with solar houses. The sun radiates heat in all directions. A relatively tiny amount, though it's enormous in human terms, falls on the Earth. That heat is well measured, but the householder and designer don't need that number. They want to know what they have to work with, not what comes to the whole Earth. The amount of solar heat that one square foot of exposed surface receives is a useful form for them. As far as the sun and the weather are concerned, that square foot could be the surface of anything. Glass, grass, stone, water . . . the same sunshine and solar heat arrive for all of them.

A house occupies a lot more than one square foot. Depending on when they were built, US houses average between 1600 and 2700 sq. ft. (The average size has grown steadily since the 1940s, by the way.) As a house designer considers some definite size, she or he can readily figure out the total solar heat available simply by multiplying the solar heat per square foot by some number of square feet. The house size may or may not change during design, but the solar heat available for each square foot of its area does not. Thus heat per square foot (abbreviated BTU/FT^2) has become a standard way to provide solar data for houses.

As to hours, they are in the act because the amount of usable solar heat available at a given place also depends on how long you collect it for. In the hour around noon on a good day in New Mexico, as much as 360 BTU may arrive at each square foot of roof or flat plate collector. But more arrives the next hour, and the hour after that. The hourly amounts differ, but the total grows and grows. There is no definite maximum or total; the sun keeps on shining and shining. What designers need to know is the hourly rise and fall of available solar heat, day by day and season by season, so it's standard to provide the heat per square foot arriving in each hour (leading to the full abbreviation $BTU/FT^2 \cdot H$). This is called "insolation," and can be in a table of hour by hour numbers, or as a line on a graph, as in the Balcomb data.

(Several additional wrinkles affect how much usable solar heat comes to a building, such as its orientation toward the Sun's path and the angles of the surfaces it's reaching, but this line of data on the chart is only showing its basic availability and how that's varied over time.)

(5) Is the available solar heat a lot or a little?

One question I haven't posed yet, though you may have: is that Santa Fe insolation a lot or a little? Almost everyone has some intuition about this, from imagining standing outside in full sun in the Southwest. But if intuition were enough, one wouldn't go to the considerable bother of making numerical measurements of the situation.

There are two good reasons for doing it. First, this kind of measurement helps keep designers honest, especially with themselves. Avoiding self-deception is one of the central goals of good technical work. The great physicist Richard Feynman put it this way: "For a successful technology, reality must take precedence over public relations, for Nature cannot be fooled."[33] We need to know whether our new gadget is working better today than it was yesterday. Is it working better than existing gadgets; is it even working better than having no gadget at all? The all too human temptation is to fudge the answers toward what one wants, hopes, or expects. That afflicts scientists and engineers as much as anyone, and carefully conducted measurements are one guard against it.

Good measurements also allow different people's work on physical things to be coordinated and merged, making it possible to get better results than they could achieve individually. This is a question of degree, of course. Coordination of human effort is very old, and can happen without any numerical measuring. Ships can be built, extensive irrigation systems constructed, armies maneuvered. But good numerical measurements have drastically expanded the possibilities, and made an almost infinite number of things we take for granted possible, right down to things like the way any light bulb from any manufacturer will screw into any socket in America.

There are important uses of solar heat that depend on having enough, though the available numerical quantity of solar heat is obviously not the only thing that has animated people over the centuries to let sunlight into their buildings. In keeping the Balcomb house warm through the Santa Fe winter, one is working against one of the deepest imperatives in Nature, the flow of heat from hotter to colder places. The average temperature in Santa Fe during January is about 30° F. If one has the indoor spaces around 70° F, heat will flow from the warm interior to the cold exterior during every hour of the day and night. The rate will not be constant, since heat flows faster when the temperature difference is larger, at night for example, and more slowly when it is smaller. But it will always be flowing out of the building, so unless heat is supplied from somewhere like the greenhouse, the house will get colder and colder.

How fast the heat flows at a given temperature difference depends on what the house puts in the way. All building materials resist heat flow to some degree, but the flow of heat from hotter to colder can't ever be stopped entirely. Each part of a building—walls, windows, roof, foundation—typically has several layers and/or segments, all of which allow heat flow in different amounts and in a variety of ways. For present purposes, the most important thing is how much heat gets lost altogether. The chart doesn't show this. There would be too many variables to track. However, there was already a good theoretical understanding of the physics of heat loss by then, and experts like Balcomb could make confident estimates. During the two weeks recorded on the chart, his estimate was that a total of 8.6 million BTU moved from the inside of the house to the cold outside

Now we have something to compare the insolation numbers on the chart to, and they look very small, down in the zero-50-100-150 BTU range, compared to 8.6 million BTU in losses. This is a house claiming to be largely heated by the sun, but there are only seven or so good solar days in this record. It looks way short of what's needed.

But it isn't. To understand why, we need to look at the information that the chart shows in a different way. The insolation data shows how many BTUs of solar heat were arriving at a square foot over the course of an hour, and each segment between two tick marks on the line with the dates represents 24 hours.

I've made an expanded version of the insolation data for December 26 with 24 small tick marks across the bottom, one for each hour. It has the same vertical scale as the Balcomb's graph, but I have replaced their continuous line with a bar for each hour that shows how much solar heat arrived during that period. If we connected the tips of the bars, we'd have the same continuous line from their data log that we started with.

Just as before, we can see that the peak hour brought something like 170 BTU/FT². But this new way of visualizing the situation makes it plain that the hours just before and just after brought nearly as much. To find

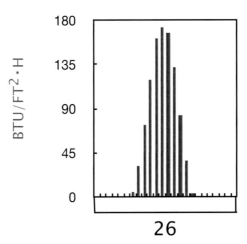

the total solar heat arriving on the 26th, one would have to add those amounts, and the amounts for all the other bars, as well.

If we do this addition of all the bars for the 26th, we get roughly 985 BTU arriving for each square foot exposed to the sun. The Balcomb house has 1400 exposed square feet, 1000 for the living quarters and 400 for the sunspace. It turns out that at 985 BTU for each of them, the house received a total of 1,379,000 BTU on the 26th—1.38 million BTU.

Now it seems much more believable that the losses of the two weeks (8.6 million BTU) could be replaced by the solar heat available during that time. About six good days like the 26th would do the trick, and there were actually seven, plus the equivalent of at least an eighth day if we lump the seven cloudier days together.

(6) Heating of the mass wall

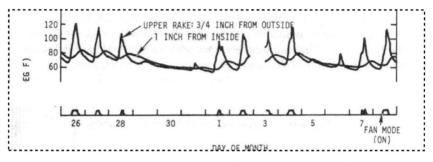

This is the most complicated process in the system. The pair of lines tells us the temperature at two different places in the upper part of the massive adobe wall that separates the greenhouse from the living quarters; "outside" refers to the greenhouse side, "inside" to the living quarters side. Recall that the wall is about 10 inches thick at its upper level. Both traces are consistent with what we've seen about air temperatures. The greenhouse side gets very hot on sunny days, with the adobe, which receives solar heat directly, peaking above 100° F. A little eyeballing of the vertical alignment (helped by a straightedge) shows these peaks happening several hours after mid-day, another consequence of solar heat continuing to arrive hour by hour until sundown.

The indoor side of the wall is quite warm, according to this record; it gets up to 80° but it's never hotter than that. On sunny days, this temperature rises and falls in a regular 24-hour rhythm which lags the greenhouse rhythm by about seven hours (eyeballing again). This validates a key design idea about massive walls: their interiors heat slowly, layer by layer; the inner layers do not receive much heat from the day until the outer layers have heated up significantly. The same goes for cooling: the outermost layer gets exposed to night sky and cool air, which start cooling it around sundown. As soon as it's cooler than the next layer in, heat from there begins to flow back out. This makes the outer layer's cooling go slowly. Having heat start moving back toward the outer surface doesn't stop the flow of heat inward, however. It flows toward any cooler zone, and the inside layers of the wall are still much cooler than the mid layers.

The upshot of this complicated dance appears in the wall's temperature record—a spiky rhythm near the greenhouse surface, and a rounder, delayed rhythm near the indoor surface. Thermometers more in the middle of the 10 inches of adobe would show rhythms intermediate between these extremes.

(7) Electric power usage

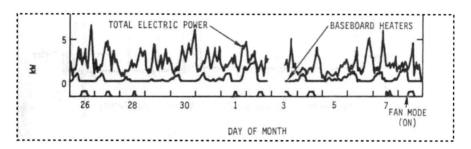

The last data stream I'll discuss shows how the house was using electricity. It was fully connected to the local grid, for lights and appliances and most importantly for water heating. It also had baseboard electric heaters in every room, as backup heat set to come on if the room got below 64° F. The Balcombs monitored the baseboard heater separately, as you can see in this area of the chart. One could roughly estimate the total heat they provided in this period using the bar chart technique from above, but it would be laborious. Luckily, Sara Balcomb gives the total, which came to 253,000 BTU for the two weeks. This is about 3% of the total estimated heat loss, so it's clear the electric heaters were not the mainstay of comfort.

Of course, the electric power that went into lights, toasters, electric typewriters, and every other use all ended up as heat, just as in the Leger house. The biggest single contribution like this during during this period was provided by heat lost from from the water heater (785,000 BTU); most of the rest made motors of various kinds go round, and what that didn't include, like electric light, bounced around the building, heating whatever absorbed it a little at a time. Adding up the energy delivered in all the jagged ups and downs of that line (which is what your household electrical meter does, in effect) gives us 2.6 million BTU, which is about 30% of the total heat loss.

This allows us to draw the second major conclusion about this house's thermal performance during this time: solar heating provided 70% of the house's needs. Another 27% was provided as a side effect of other household activities, and only 3% came from energy specifically purchased for heating.

---

[4] Macy, Joanna. *Despair and personal power in the nuclear age.* New Society Publishers, 1983.

[5] See the 2012 report of the Blue Ribbon Commission on America's Nuclear Future for an overview. The report is archived on the Web at http://cybercemetery.unt.edu/archive/brc/20120620211605/http:/brc.gov//

[6] Lovins, 'Wonder in the Bewilderness". *Harvard* magazine. September-October 2011

[7] See John McPhee. *Encounters with the Archdruid.* Farrar, Straus and Giroux, 1977

[8] AB Lovins, "Energy Strategy: the Road Not Taken?". *Foreign Affairs* **55**, p. 66 (1976); available free at https://rmi.org/insight/energy-strategy-the-road-not-taken/

[9] The most visible renewable sources of the time, during the mid 1970s, were small-scale wind electricity and solar thermal collectors, which indeed had very modest technical requirements. The recent enormous expansion of wind power, and the emergence of solar electricity as a widely usable, low cost option for utilities have both called on quite sophisticated structural, electrical and industrial engineering, so the issues about centralized decision-making have appeared in new forms.

[10] Laird, Frank N. *Solar energy, technology policy, and institutional values*. Cambridge University Press, 2001.

[11] Kenneth Brower, *The Wildness Within: Remembering David Brower,* p. 197 Heyday; Berkeley; 2012

[12] Lovins, interview

[13] Image sources: Saskatchewan—http://design.theownerbuildernetwork.co/files/2013/07/1977-Saskatchewan-House-Regina-Canada-Winter.jpg ; Leger—http://design.theownerbuildernetwork.co/files/2013/07/1979-Leger-House-East-Pepperell-Massachusetts.jpg; Balcomb—Balcomb, S. (1984). Living in a passive solar home. *Energy and Buildings*, 7(4), 309–314.

[14] This recalls the way in which the first automobiles were modeled after horse-drawn carriages: how else would one convey people at that time? The qualities truly intrinsic to the car (safety, comfort, adequate power to handle substantial extra weight, needed vision outward, and so forth) only registered and shaped its changed design over time.

[15] Anthony Denzer. *The Solar House: Pioneering Sustainable Design*. Rizzoli, 2013.

[16] Wilson, Chris, *Pueblo Style and Regional Architecture,* p. 188. Van Nostrand Reinhold, 1990.

[17] "Living Proof: First Village, Santa Fe, NM". *Progressive Architecture*, April 1979

[18] Unit One qualified for an $8000 Federal solar heating and cooling demonstration grant (in a program that awarded an average of $7000 per dwelling unit to a nationally distributed set of projects). *Mother Earth News* quotes the total cost (land plus building) at $104,000. ref Mother Earth news interview]]

[19] Wayne and Susan Nichols, "A Second Generation Solar Village", undated conference report

[20] Denzer, ch. 10, "The 1960s: Creative Activists"

[21] Perlin, John. *Let it shine: the 6,000-year story of solar energy.* New World Library, 2022. Chapter 18, "Solar Heating in Early America (1200-1912)" gives one account of solar design in pueblo buildings.

[22] Balcomb, S. (1984). "Living in a passive solar home". *Energy and Buildings*, 7(4), 309-314.

[23] Sara Balcomb, *ibid*

[24] Unit One: A Solar Adobe Home. *Mother Earth News*, September/October, 1979

[25] Lstiburek, J.W. (2008). "Building America". ASHRAE Journal, 50(12), pp. 60-65.

[26] Leger, E.H. (1988). "Superinsulated Homes". *Environmental Science & Technology*, 22(12), pp.1399-1400.

[27] Schick, W.L., Jones, R.A., Harris, W.S. and Konzo, S., 1979. "Details and Engineering Analysis of the Illinois Lo-Cal House", Technical Note 14. Urbana, Ill.: Building Research Council, School of Architecture, University of Illinois.

[28] A good contemporary review is by Shurcliff, W.A. (1986). "Superinsulated houses". *Annual Review of Energy*, 11(1), pp.1-24. Bentley took out a patent on his approach (Thermal efficiency structure, U.S. Patent 3,969,860).

[29] Schick et al, *ibid.*

[30] Lstiburek, *ibid.* He goes on to say, "We do have the Building America program, but we're not building a lot of efficient houses. We say the houses are efficient, but they are not, when compared to the groundbreaking projects of the 1970s."

[31] Sara Balcomb, *ibid*

[32] In this book, I generally use a different energy unit, the kilowatt-hour (kWh). 1 kWh is the same amount of energy as 3412 BTU.

[33] R. P. Feynman, "Appendix F: Personal Observations on the Reliability of the Shuttle," Report of Presidential Commission on the Space Shuttle Challenger Accident, volume II, p. F5.

4: Imagining, Barn-Raising, and Surviving

With the help of some professionals and a big volunteer crew of amateur
builders, we then built it.
Not knowing this was impossible made it possible.

—Amory

Generating the design

First came the couple and their ideas, then came the professionals and
the volunteers. Amory and Hunter naturally dug right into the question
of what house they wanted on their newly acquired land, and naturally
they had both ideas and confidence about talking them through. A series
of notes and diagrams from the fall and winter of 1981-82 show classic
middle-class rationality at work: "What do we want in our house? Let's
make a list." Reading down a page of notes from that moment, one finds
"big kitchen, pantry, mudroom entering greenhouse, East eating patio
inside outer wall?, library/workspace, master bedroom, . . ."

They were revolutionaries in the policy world, but neither their temperaments nor their strategy in selecting the location for their new organization inclined them to develop aa assertively countercultural daily life. One key advantage for them of locating in Snowmass was the possibility of ongoing access to the top layer of US decision-makers through the nearby Aspen Institute. Those people would hardly drop in comfortably at a commune. But the personal, family dimension was even more important.

Amory and Hunter had met, married, and then lived largely on the road ever since 1978. Paula Quirk's house in London was their nominal base, but their work was speaking, consulting, and advising. Their life required constant travel; both of them have said that they basically lived out of a large, battered suitcase called House. Finding a place and making a nest was a central goal of their return to the US. The travel, the speaking, and the advising would all continue, but they needed a real base, with a big kitchen, a mudroom, a master bedroom and storage walls. Later, there might be children. They would certainly need space for Hunter's mother, Farley Sheldon. They had lived with her in Los Angeles in 1981, and looking ahead it was likely she would relocate to be near them. And there should be a "crittery"—at least a stable, probably stalls or pens for pigs, chickens, or the like. They hoped that the place could grow a good deal of its own food.

Three quarters of the page of notes goes to this list, and to a rough diagram of how the items might fit together. Its most prominent element is a large greenhouse area, occupying the whole south face of the plan. Immediately outside is a garden area; the entry to the house is through the greenhouse; the greenhouse label has a note—"w pond + hot tub". Hunter was clear from the outset that there would be plants in this house, and that life there would frequently be carried on among them.

It's not until the last two inches of the sheet that overtly "green" moves come into view. Marked off from the previous items by a line, there is another list—"solar still?, hot tub water heater, domestic water heater, ΦV space (short for "photovoltaic space, using the Greek phi), batteries, ac/dc wiring, biogas?, gray water, food storage icebox". These are infrastructure items, or services, as the building industry calls them. Plumbing and wiring, hot water supply, electric power supply.

The notes indicate a plan or hope to handle these through the soft path, but at this stage, the thinking only extends to moves which would be out of view, hidden in walls, floors, or closets. That changed before many months passed, but invisible services were a natural enough starting point. The house was to be seen as the Lovins statement on what the soft path would be like on the street, or in a subdivision. They also needed to have it feel welcoming and friendly to their hoped-for associates in the Aspen world. Conventional design kept services as much out of sight as possible; lights without wires, faucets and drains without pipes, and a furnace in the basement were the norm.

In fact, great deal of the soft path activity of the 1970s had been dealing with the fittings and facilities, the wires (and power plants), the pipes (and wells and septic systems), and the furnaces (rooftop collectors and their plumbing) in ways that kept them out of sight. Efficient unobtrusive performance was the logic of Gene Leger's Massachusetts house and the other projects in superinsulation that dominated efficient building in the late 70s and early 80s. It's no surprise that Amory and Hunter, new to house design, started in the same way.

However, it wasn't long before the other stream of soft path action, the stream represented by the New Alchemy Arks and the Balcomb house in Santa Fe, showed its influence on their planning A second drawing, done a month or two later, shows "an egg surrounding a greenhouse," in a phrase of Hunter's. The general outline definitely looks more like an egg, and the greenhouse now has a large funnel shape, squarely in the middle of the plan. The rest of the house is firmly divided in two, with kitchen, dining area, and bedrooms clustered on the west side, along with an area marked "library 'social side' (conversational/conference)". In this sketch, one crossed the garden area on a small bridge and reached a "library 'study side' " which holds a number of "work pods", a defined workspace for Amory and Hunter, and a great deal of bookshelf.

This spatial organization was informed by knowledge of the Balcomb house, and it was also dramatically influenced by Amory and Hunter's decision in April 1982 to found the personal think tank they quickly named Rocky Mountain Institute (now called RMI). Up to then, the main auspices for their work had been granted by Friends of the Earth, which had not paid much but had provided the basic bona fides which even gifted and energetic advocates need. But when David Brower, its founder and figurehead, was fired, that central line of support was gone, and Amory and Hunter needed to look elsewhere.

Moving to a different non-profit was possible; so were university jobs. But as Amory puts it, "We were both self-employed and didn't particularly want to work for any of the NGOs, firms, or agencies we knew about, but we felt we could be more effective with a handful of colleagues than just as Mom and Pop." The result was the notion of RMI, a notion that found itself instantly merging with the building project. The Lovins' base would house a workplace as well as a family life.

Their new egg-around-greenhouse image established a degree of separation between work and family, a physical demarcation without much physical distance, that suited both Amory and Hunter well. The greenhouse became an axis around which both clusters of activities and meanings, family life and professional community, could revolve. The green life close at hand would be good for the soul and possibly for the dinner table; it would also remind the authors of analysis and policy what they were really after, above and beyond the tactics of controversy.

This plan, two wings along the sides of a substantial greenhouse, descended directly from the Balcomb's plan in Santa Fe. Their house would be bigger than the Balcomb's 2400 sq ft: an early note of Amory's guesses 3800 sq ft, and the final building is a little over 4000. The functions of the two wings would also differ from the Balcombs' wholly residential pattern, but the greenhouse would serve as a passive solar furnace and heat balancer, just as the Balcombs' did.

The specific arrangements evolved somewhat as the design matured in early 1982 in consultation with Steven Conger, a young architect with the Aspen Design Group, a local firm, who had just graduated from Yale and wasn't even licensed yet. The egg sketch has a two-story portion on the west side, with bedrooms and bathrooms on top of the kitchen/dining area. By mid-May, these had moved sideways, further west, and come down to ground level. The third in the sequence of drawings, Steve Conger's pen and ink rendering of the final design, shows that final arrangement as well as a unified approach to shapes and proportions that gives a feeling of thoughtful yet relaxed coherence.

The house was now an East-West line of rooms rather than an egg. The greenhouse remained the dramatic center of the plan, the more so as its glazing had been defined as a 30° slope rising well above roof level. The site rises from east to west, so the interior changes level three times, by several steps each, as one goes from the library/office area at the east end, through the garden and the kitchen/dining/entry level to the bedrooms which were now fairly secluded at the west end.

The serpentine walls were a response to Amory and Hunter's request for more organic shapes than those in conventional houses. Steve recalls them having just read *Black Elk Speaks*, which is somewhat scornful about the white man's tendency to "live in boxes."[34] In fact, the walls curve in two dimensions, but not in the third. They rise straight up vertically, maintaining the same curves all the way up. It is as if the earth had been a mold, cut in this specific serpentine outline, and the volume of the house had been created by pushing its material straight up through it. This extrusion was critical to the construction method they chose.

The walls were to be massive, 16 inches thick, composed of two parallel six-inch layers of stone and steel-reinforced concrete sandwiching four inches of rigid foam insulation. They are almost four times as thick and many, many times as heavy as the walls in typical houses of the time, wood-framed and lightly insulated.

In these walls, the two main streams of 1970s alternative building, passive solar and superinsulation, are physically married. We have seen how different in spirit these two kinds of building were at their origins, and by 1982, there had been a good deal of dispute between the two schools as to which was the true path to eco-salvation. Amory's stance was, "Let's do both." The walls would be part of the unbroken, well-insulated shell advocated by the superinsulators, and would be carefully joined to roof, floor, windows and doors to eliminate leakage. They would be massive, too, as advocated by the solaristas, to serve the stabilizing function seen in the Balcomb house, tempering daytime solar heating by storing much of it and carrying it into the night hours when heat was needed.

It's not obvious from the final rendering, but anyone inside the finished building is always very much aware of the way the greenhouse area merges completely with the other living spaces. At the Balcomb house, the greenhouse is folded in the arms of the two wings of living space, so to speak, but it's clearly separated from both of them by the massive adobe wall. You don't see it from those spaces, or move through it in going between them. It's really separate from the house proper in terms of structure and circulation, even though it is intimately connected in thermal terms.

Amory and Hunter's egg sketch would have led to something similar. The greenhouse had become more fully integrated with the rest of the house, but it was still bounded by a mass wall on each side. The final design goes much further toward integrating the spaces. The greenhouse glass is carried by a large cantilevered arch that rises well above eye level for people inside. You see straight through to the plants, and can walk straight to them and through them if you want to. There is no barrier. Some thermally stabilizing mass is still there, in the concrete of the arch, but a good deal of that function has been given to the outer wall. Its thick stone and concrete are not just for appearance; they work to provide thermal comfort.

Opening the greenhouse area like this relied on a major technical advance in windows. Large windows lose heat quite readily, and what is a greenhouse but a structure made of large windows? In the Balcomb house, heat loss is reduced significantly by using double glazing. Even so, the temperature swings enough between day and night for the greenhouse air to get down into the 40s toward the end of the coldest New Mexico nights. As it happened, one result of Amory's endless reading and networking was that he happened to know of a new kind of double glazing, in which a specially coated plastic film was stretched between the two sheets of glass. The coating lets visible light through, but reflects radiated heat very completely. This means that sunlight can readily shine in during the day, but heat cannot shine out at night. These "superwindows" keep the space inside the greenhouse much warmer, and this allows it to be thoroughly integrated with other spaces.

The building's thermal performance was also improved by earth sheltering, another thread in the alternative building explorations of the 1970s. The long north side of the building is banked up to roof level with dirt for almost its whole length. The goal was to use the earth itself as a buffer against high or low outside air temperatures, especially the very low temperatures of Rocky Mountain winters.

In getting all this to work well, the details matter, but the central technical point is fairly simple: superinsulation reduces a house's heating needs sufficiently for well managed solar collection to handle them, even in a climate as demanding as Snowmass's. The house/office would need no fuel-burning furnace.

Steve Conger's final rendering is a good starting point for understanding what the house's inhabitants (and its architect) hoped the feel of the house would be. Attending to it lets us imagine what activities or choices or experiences it might support or hinder, what would be the character of the place. Charles Moore, a noted architect and theorizer of the 1970s whom Steve Conger mentions as a direct influence, put the issue this way:

> The ways that a house lets you move, with grace or confusion, the shelters it puts around you, the things that it brings to your attention, all establish a substratum of meaning that accompanies the life you live there.[35]

One thing comes forcefully to our attention in the rendering: the surfaces have roughness, leafiness, fields of grass-ness: they have emphatic textures. The walls are palpably stone, and rough, not dressed or fitted stone. As far as thermal storage is concerned, there was no need for the stone to show itself, or for the walls to be stone at all. Concrete would have done just as well for mass and for structural solidity, and been much easier to build, so choosing to use the stone and having it be highly

1739 Snowmass Creek Road, final rendering (1982) by Steven Conger

visible were both choices about the "substratum of meaning" meant to accompany the lives lived here.

The same forthright emphatic natural textures are present in the house today, as a glance at the walk-through photos and others through this book will confirm. The stone evokes solidity, age, kinship with the cliffs and screes of the vicinity; its variegated color is perhaps a reminder that Nature is complex, and contacting it certainly a reminder that the world can resist us and even discipline us with abrasions and contusions if we don't respect her.

The photos also show the other prominent visible materials—the strong-grained oak of the roof beams and decking, the occasional unmilled beetle-killed tree trunks serving as columns, the variety of foliage in the greenhouse and in frequent pots, the smooth concrete floors of the main living/working areas, the contrasting unevenness of the steps down past the greenhouse. Together, they provide a visual and tactile experience very much in the spirit of the Mountain West, where houses have rugged materials, an earthen color range, tough fabrics and clothing, pictures of mountains and mountain valleys, rivers and animals, trophies and mementoes of successful hunting and fishing. Here, though, the trophies on display are international awards and translations of Lovins' books into foreign languages. The big game has been conceptual, and the successes have been in moving and persuading people, not in physical prowess.

The same is actually true of the CEOs and captains of industry in the area. Their local houses often have similar decor, and many of them display trophies their owners really caught or killed, but the real triumphs of these leaders are corporate. The Mountain West atmosphere of the houses is there to provide a certain kind of welcome to their peers. It projects the comfort of relaxed affluence and a desire for visitors to be at ease in surroundings with a familiar feel. Connecting with such people and engaging them in the soft path was one of the key reasons Amory and Hunter were locating in the area. The ensemble of meanings in their house was intended to be compatible with those relationships.

In its provisions for movement and shelter, the other ways Moore tells us a house establishes meaning for its users, the design plays several interesting games. The changes of level from east to west mark changes in privacy, and go with striking differences in degree of enclosure. The office area at the east end has a lofty ceiling and a tall wall of library books facing an equally tall wall with two tiers of windows across an undivided workspace floor with a continuous ribbon of desk around its edge. The Lovinses' bedroom/bathroom zone is at the opposite end of the house, all the way to the west, up the three modest but definite level changes. The last set of steps takes one to a narrow hallway which is not long but definitely conveys that one is entering a private space. The two rooms there, which were originally conceived as master and second bedroom, are not very large, and the stone of the walls and oak of the substantial window frames are very present. The house is narrowest here, front to back, and the serpentine of the south wall naturally generates an enclosing and sheltering curve for both these rooms.

We saw in the first walk-through how the house turns entering people away from this private zone and toward the dining/living/kitchen area. Everyone—visitors, co-workers and inhabitants alike—tends to gather there, in a relaxed but carefully furnished space, whether for a real sit-down or just for a moment passing through to the office. The unobstructed view into the foliage of the greenhouse, the sound of its running water, and the clear ability to move right in there at any time all connect you with light and a sense of sky and space. The dining table, kitchen counters, piano and comfortable seating look at this from under the shelter of the dark oak beams and decking overhead. In a low-key way, this fits with the so-called "prospect and refuge" notion that people find it appealing to be in places which shelter or conceal them while giving extensive views out.[36]

The plan shows the same serpentine at work here as in the private zone, but the house is deeper here, front to back, so the the serpentine simply makes a gentle distinction between the living and sitting areas without making places in either area out of view from the others.

Compared with the first sketches, the final design's space for intimate family is much reduced. There is still a second bedroom, a private bathroom and a personal storage space in that wing, but there is no family room or private sitting space. Family activities have to overlap with the public and semi-public activities associated with RMI and Amory and Hunter's roles as soft path leaders. Perhaps that showed foresight; the ambition to bring the world to soft path thinking was as strong as ever for the Lovinses in 1982. With RMI as their organizational lever and the Snowmass house as a noteworthy fulcrum, the demands on their time and energy could well be all-consuming, and their professional activities and their personal lives were often pretty much indistinguishable.

Conger's professional rendering was done in the spring of 1982, before construction started. It was the lead image in a four-page brochure announcing the "Lovins Research Center/Bioshelter/House Project." Inside were a double page architect's plan of the building and a detailed summary of its parameters, features, location, soft-path provisions, and role as shelter for Rocky Mountain Institute.

The eventual building stayed largely true to this image, and to the brochure's plan, though there were changes in a good many details. (If you compare them carefully. you can even see that the rendering and the plan are not completely consistent with each other.) The roof looks like a field of grass in the rendering, and the original intention was indeed to plant it for grazing by the potential pigs or chickens. That was set aside early; expectations of the greenhouse as a significant source of vegetables and fish gave way over time; adobe floors were ruled out by the building inspector as "not proven durable" and smoothed concrete took their place; and the locations and space allowed for certain functions were adjusted. We will look at some of those changes when we take up the building's history of use, but none of them materially affected the nature of the house and the life and work that went on there. Its character, and its success, depend on the large design moves— the greenhouse and its glazing, the walls and their thermal qualities, the arch, the workspace, the semi-communal living/dining area.

Construction

"Amory and Hunter Lovins and a diverse crew of talented volunteers are building a multipurpose structure in Old Snowmass, Colorado during the summer and fall of 1982." So began the text of the hey-there brochure announcing the project to the world. The building would be "one of the most beautiful and technically advanced new buildings in the country," and it would be built by volunteers. It was, but it wasn't only built by volunteers, nor was it finished before the end of 1982. The story of what followed that optimistic announcement is instructive.

Why volunteers? Neither Amory nor Hunter had built anything bigger than a breadbox; their architect was just beginning his career and had limited construction experience; and a failed project would give a black eye to every soft path advocate. It seemed clear that the project would almost certainly go much faster, pose fewer risks, and might even be less expensive if professionals did it. Why use volunteers? The question is good. The possible answers are several, and they are tangled, so talking them over will wait until the following chapter, Day One, where we look at what house and what situation Amory and Hunter had when the dust settled in early 1984.

For the time being, the only thing to be said is that the harmless looking phrase, "if professionals do it," conceals the crucial assumption that there are professionals who can in fact do what is intended. Amory was convinced this was a bad assumption, because there actually were no professionals available who already knew how to do what his design needed in structure and equipment, and none who would accept his and Hunter's active involvement in working things out as construction progressed. The alternative was to line up "a diverse crew of talented volunteers." Right or wrong (some of each, as it turned out), the decision went that way. Amory and Hunter would be the unlicensed general contractors, and they would find a suitable mix of brawn, brains, skills, perseverance, and resourcefulness through their connections in the world of pragmatic environmentalists[37] and their appeal to the students who thronged avidly to their campus talks.

Barn-raising

As Steve Conger imagined it, and Amory and Hunter found persuasive, construction would take the summer of 1982, and the house would be occupied in the fall. It did not work out that way. The eventual certificate of occupancy is dated January, 1984, eighteen months later, and interior finish work continued for another six. Chris Cappy, the invaluable paid "director of crew logistics," who supervised the construction itself from beginning to end, divides the story into three phases: Barn-Raising (May–October 1982), Valley Forge (November 1982–mid-February 1983, and Adult Supervision (mid-February 1983 onward). I will outline the story and then turn to what lessons or insights it may convey.

There were three obvious sources of the barn-raising spirit—Amory and Hunter's limited assets, their charisma, and the construction method they and Steve Conger had chosen. The Lovinses could expect a flow of income from speaking and consulting, but they had very little capital, so a way to keep out-of-pocket costs down was very welcome. They were able to set up a $120,00 loan, which was real money but well short of what a house of the proposed size would typically have cost in Snowmass/Aspen at the time. $550,000 - $650,000 would have been more like it, if it were to be done by a regular contractor. (The 2024 equivalent would be roughly $1.6 - 2 million.) So the prospect of low labor costs was very appealing.

Their popularity on campuses gave them likely access to enthusiastic beginners, willing to be paid in adventure instead of cash. Steve Conger, inspired by Frank Lloyd Wright, had suggested a construction method suited to beginners. It was slip-forming, which conceptually is simplicity itself: the walls would be made of concrete; the wooden forms to hold the concrete in place while hardening would be just 20 inches tall instead of the full height of the wall; and the wall would be made 20 inches at a time. When one layer had hardened enough, the forms would be moved upward, into position for the next layer to be laid on top. The photograph gives an idea of what this looked like in practice.

The low-rise forms would be easier to make and much easier and safer to handle than forms the full height of the walls. The pressure of 20 inches of liquid concrete would be much easier to contain than that in a full height form, so their forms could be lighter. In fact, Steve Conger had actually already worked with slip-forms on another residential project in the area, so he, at least, had some field experience on that aspect of the project. And the serpentine shape created no conceptual problem for this method. One just made curved forms for the curved segments. They could be used and then moved up 20 inches at a time, just like forms for the straight segments.

The fit between funds, hands, and concept was good. Of course it was too good to be true in the way construction played out. Vision met reality, starting that June. The normal projection is that vision loses out to reality. What happened here was more complicated and interesting. Instead of collapsing, the vision did what visions can do; it reshaped itself around the realities it encountered and continued to lead a way forward. In the end, there was the house/office you have already walked through, a shelter and stage for living and working over the next decades, an icon for sustainability, and a cluster of potential lessons we are exploring.

The first stage of barn-raising was assembling the crew. Slip-forming is a fairly labor-intensive approach, but a supply of volunteer laborers was at hand. They would need knowledgeable direction, but those prospects were favorable. Amory and Hunter were established, persuasive, high profile advocates of the soft path, natural magnets for both theorists and practical people looking to make the future brighter. The task was to get commitments for a broad enough range of skills.

A tentative crew list, dated April 28, 1982, gives an indication of how it went. RMI's formal existence consisted of nothing more than its registration as a non-profit with the Internal Revenue Service and the Colorado Secretary of State, approved two days before. Construction was supposed to begin in late May, just a month later. Two-thirds of the tentative crew were based outside Colorado. Amory and Hunter's network was clearly being tapped, and some process of invitation was at work. There are 38 names; 19 of them have accepted and have given firm dates for their participation. Most of them were committing to most of the summer, though two or three are down for quite short periods and one is listed as "off site". (He was presumably available for consultation by phone or mail but not doing any physical construction.) The other 19 were in various states of less definite involvement.

Two luminaries appear, Wes Jackson of the Kansas-based Land Institute and John Todd of the New Alchemy Institute. Both were national figures, at least in the world of energetic, pragmatic counterculture initiatives. Neither planned to be around for more than a few days, and so would not literally be crew members, but their auras could be expected to add to Amory and Hunter's in the glow of excitement and significance around the project. Several of the longer-term workers building the Snowmass house recall the feeling that they were there to change the world, and people like Jackson and Todd, as well as later drop-ins like David Brower, were important reinforcements to that feeling. In that sense, they deserved their listing.

The tone of the April list was definitely pragmatic. Each person got a short skills/background tag indicating the contribution he or she might make. There are builders, contractors, carpenters, masons, plumbers, electricians, concrete people, framers, cooks. Six, including Amory and Hunter, are tagged as "helpers" or "learning". They actually needed some beginners, qualified by commitment rather than expertise, or they risked misusing the experts' time on the inescapably repetitive work of erecting and roofing this many square feet. There were five women, counting Hunter. In proportion to the total, 13% was perhaps a little more than usual for 1982, and three (counting Hunter) were on the list in a solidly professional sense. But the project was not notably ahead of its time in women's involvement.

The large contingent of students who followed Amory and Hunter west after their visiting professorship at Dartmouth were not on this April list, made before the university term ended. There are no surviving documents to show who arrived when and stayed for how long, but something like eight or ten Dartmouth students, a third of the enrollment in their spring class, made the trek. Students also appeared from Bucknell, Boulder, Oberlin, and other colleges where the Lovinses had talked. Memories differ somewhat as to numbers, but there were somewhere between 25 and 35 volunteers for most of that summer. Some lodging was at a rented mobile home a short walk down Snowmass Creek from the site. There was room inside for Amory and Hunter and at least 6-8 more; the rest tented outside.

Jock de Swart, the paid construction foreman, brought an insta-water heater and built a shower. Aged 35; born and raised in Los Angeles; son of an adventurous, well-known regional sculptor and painter; Jock brought a combination of organizational and manual skills to the project. He had started a small non-profit as a clearing house for possible environmental solutions. He had founded and run a for-profit business designing and installing solar systems. These were solar thermal systems —flat-panel solar collectors, storage tanks, piping and pumps—so he was handy in a general way, though he had never run a project as big as the Snowmass house and had no experience with passive solar design. His thoroughly genuine, openhearted approach to people and his deep commitment to positive action for the environment were actually the most important things he brought to his role, organizing and dealing with this collection of unpaid enthusiasts.

A typical day on the project began with general breakfast at the creek house, and with Jock doing a whiteboard talk outlining the day's work for the different teams. In the early going, it was clearing thistles, detailed surveying of the sloping site, laying out the floor footprint, digging the trench for the water supply. Then came building forms and gathering stone by hand from a neighboring hillside.

The stones came straight from the hillside, a ton or two at a time. They moved about 200 tons of stone in the end. In Snowmass, weathering makes plenty of rubble of the local sandstone, especially through the freeze-thaw cycle. Rocks in every size from boulders to sand are banked up to form all the lower hill slopes. Some of the crew would go over every day with a pickup truck and some sheets of corrugated sheet metal, the kind used for farm sheds. They would arrange the sheets in a line running up the hill, cast about next to them for stones that could be handled easily and were roughly flat on one side; those would get tossed onto the sheets to slide down to the pickup. Then they had to be picked up again and heaved into the truck's bed. It was all hand work, and it was often hot at 7,100 feet in Colorado in midsummer. No excavators, no conveyor belts.

Difficulties and resolutions

The masonry was to be tackled in three sections. First the center walls (for the kitchen, dining and living room); then the east walls (for the workspace end); finally the private bed/bath area on the west. The photograph early in this section looks over this last section at an early point in the slipform work. The view is from the northwest corner, from a point up on the hillside which eventually was merged with the back wall by using fill dirt to make the berm against it. The nearest serpentine formwork is set up for its third rise, and the rectangular frames where windows will go are visible further back where the serpentine ends. To the left is the curved wall of one of the circular "pods" added to the design by Steve Conger to allow for services and storage. This one eventually housed the bathroom for the private part of the house.

The four pods at the back of the greenhouse, the one perched at the very western end, and the two inside the private zone, were one more complication. They all had the same circular form, with the same radius, but each of them still required its own set of forms, because they had different door openings. The greenhouse arch also needed a unique set of forms, though that work was done well after the summer. There was also steel reinforcement ("rebar") to tie the successive pours firmly together. And there were window and door frames to build around; this did not happen at convenient places. So the number of different forms required was quite large; in all, the project needed something like 20 of them.

The slip-form system was being asked to do several things beyond its simple core concept. The walls were stone and concrete, not concrete alone, so the stone had to be carefully placed and the concrete had to be worked around it by hand. The walls were actually a sandwich, two layers of stone and concrete with a slab of rigid insulation down the middle. A notch had to be cut every few inches in the insulation slab to allow it to curve as the walls did. The photo from the earlier view of construction, gives an idea of how complicated, yet precisely aligned, the setup needed to be, and it doesn't show the form ties, thin aluminum rods running between the two sides of the forms. They were needed to keep the weight of newly poured concrete from bulging the forms outward and allowing the concrete to run out before it set up enough to support itself

The outer and inner surfaces of the walls also had to cleaned of stray concrete after coming out of the forms. The second clip shows this being done. Field collected uncut sandstone of this kind is never more than very approximately flat, and a degree of roughness was important for the Mountain West aesthetic of the building. So there was plenty of chance for patches of hardening concrete to end up on the visible faces of the stones after the forms were pulled off. For speed of construction, one would have left it there, but for this kind of building it was important to chip any stray concrete away, leaving it visible only in the joints, like mortar.

Progress was slow and laborious. The few paid participants, most notably Chris Cappy, Jock de Swart and Charlie Manlove, a jack-of-all-trades problem solver and organizer, were keeping the somewhat chaotic process moving forward. The volunteers were having a ball. There was no pay, but they were living a dream, changing the world, getting evening lectures from Amory's expert friends, who came through to give advice. Jock told me, "Everyone was in love with Amory; it was like Arthur and the Round Table." Work was the main thing, but there was some volleyball with the monks at the Trappist house five miles up the road. Some Sundays people went to the monastery for contemplation, and there was at least one climb of Mt. Sopris. Hunter and Amory took the whole crew to the Midland Tavern for beer and spaghetti every week.

There were also heated debates. As the walls got up to window level, the question of how to handle the frames became pressing. There was a major disconnect between the details drawn by the architect, the practicalities of slip-forming, and concerns about heat loss from thermal bridging. This occurs wherever there are places in which a building's structure doesn't allow the blanket of insulation to be continuous. For example, the vertical 2x4s in conventional framing, the studs, are thermal bridges. They are needed; insulating materials are not nearly rigid or strong enough to make a wall. But the wood of the studs does not insulate well, so each if them is a way in which heat can pass through the wall to the colder exterior more easily.

The major issue at the windows was whether the glass should align with the insulating layer in the middle of the wall, or be set further toward the outside. The architect urged them all strongly to choose the second alternative. It definitely improves the aesthetics of the window/wall ensemble and prevents accumulation of snow or ice on the outside sill. However, it allows a depth of some inches of interior cold surface around each window box, adding to the heat losses at every opening. which distressed the participants who were committed to optimizing the building's efficiency as the heart of the project. In the end, Amory went with the architect, and some of the volunteers left the project in frustration.

Looking back, a number of key people were not sure they would choose slip-forming again for this kind of job. One or two are quite sharp about it. But right now, we place ourselves mentally in the middle of things, the system chosen, the job under way, the challenge being to make it work as well as possible.

One departure from the barn-raising approach came in mid-August. It was time to pour the north wall, which would be over 19 feet tall in places, and banked on the outside with earth. Chris Cappy urged that they should pay to have this done by a concrete contractor, on the grounds that it could be done quickly with tall forms, that such forms would hold enough weight in liquid concrete to be dangerous if they failed, and that a company with experience and suitable equipment was therefore the safe and sensible choice. Amory and Hunter readily agreed. They were self-confident, and they believed in the potential of volunteers and community collaboration, but they recognized their limits.

September came, and the project was very far short of its anticipated and hoped for completion. Jock de Swart needed to leave, partly for outside personal reasons, and partly because he had recognized that the job was overwhelming him. His place was taken by Larry Doble, "noble Doble," a brother-in-law of Steve Conger's and a civil engineer. He had arrived somewhat by chance when the foundation was not yet complete, and he stayed through winter, through the completion of the walls, the forming, pouring and unveiling of the greenhouse arch and the placing of the roof timbers and decking. His extensive experience with building bridges was invaluable in setting up the formwork and reinforcing steel for the arch.

As the construction foreman, Larry organized the students into teams of four to six, and had each team working one of the forms. This allowed them to develop a rhythm and sense of coordination with each other. He was also calm and effective, quite tolerant of the students' wider lives (he says, "a lot of pot got smoked that summer"), but tough and clear when it came to the work. One student calls him the Yoda of bridge-building.

Cold weather in these mountains starts in September and gets serious in October. The crew reached a low point on a day which never warmed enough for the concrete to set properly, so a whole day's work had to be stripped out and the slumped concrete had to be cleared up and scraped off the lower areas of the wall. The question of continuing or putting construction on hold for the winter had to be raised. There was a way to keep going: one could enclose a current work area in plastic sheeting and run a propane heater inside it to keep the temperature up. This would be expensive, anti-green, and inelegant, but it would allow work to continue. The alternative was to simply wait for warm weather.

Amory was convinced that continuing was essential, despite the bad conditions. Halting would disperse the crew, which would reduce monthly costs but would require a whole new effort to reassemble a crew in the spring. Meanwhile, interest payments on the loan would keep coming due. At that point, interest rates were very high compared to more recent times. The rates for construction loans ranged from 15% to 20%, so the cost of delay over the late fall, winter, and early spring would be considerable. Costs were already an issue, because the crew had needed to be fed and housed ever since June. The economists' mantra, "There's no such thing as a free lunch," describes the situation precisely. No summary of accounts has appeared, but the cost of food and basic supplies, together with rent on the creekside mobile home, was on the order of $5000 a month. It was clear that the $120,000 they'd borrowed would by no means see the project through. The non-volunteer staff, like Chris Cappy and Charlie Manlove, were increasingly worried.

Several interested professionals who were not explicitly on staff but had been helping with information, advice, and problem-solving were equally worried. Sometime in January, Cappy began talking with them quietly about making a new plan, with realistic timetable and budget for getting the building finished. In late February this group sat Amory and Hunter down for a serious talk about shifting much more of the work to professionals. The walls and roof structure were nearly complete, thanks to the volunteers having slogged on in the cold, but there was much still to be done—windows, roof insulation and roofing, and all the so-called "trades" work of plumbing, wiring, flooring, painting, and so forth. Under the new plan, there would still be volunteers, but considerably fewer of them, and they'd be more fully under the direction of experienced tradespeople. Amory and Hunter would concentrate on raising money through continued lecturing and pursuit of grants, and leave the general contractor role to be shared by Cappy and Manlove, the latter handling technical questions, and the former concentrating on public relations, external arrangements of all kinds, and the big picture.

There were still construction dramas to be dealt with, such as the dust devil that passed directly over the site in the middle of the roofing work. It ripped off the sheet of EPDM, a synthetic rubber, that was to provide a waterproof membrane over the roof's insulating tiles and oak beam structure. The tiles went, too, scattered widely over the hillsides. Both tiles and sheet were recovered and installed, but there was no way to inspect the entire sheet for rips or punctures, and indeed the roof later did leak somewhat, though not in ways that went beyond stains and irritation. The 2006-09 renovation replaced the roofing entirely but the underlying structure was in good shape.

Generally, though, the process of construction lost its mythic quality and became usefully conventional. The mythic stage had firmly established the physical form and feeling of the building. There was no going back on that. The bulk of 1983, the second year of construction, went forward in a workaday manner; it was essential given the situation, but it was no source of lessons for innovations in sustainability or building practice. The additional unanticipated year culminated in a dated document that marks the official end of construction. The Certificate of Occupancy, issued January 9, 1984, was Pitkin County's declaration that a structurally safe, adequately plumbed and wired and generally code-compliant building now existed at 1739 Snowmass Creek Road.

---

[34] The Lovinses were not assertively countercultural, but they were quite aware of that sphere and moderately receptive to its moves.

[35] Moore et al. *The Place of Houses* (Holt, Rinehart and Winston, 1974), p. 143

[36] This idea originated with geographer Jay Appleton, whose *The Experience of Landscape* (1975) has been durably influential among architects and landscape designers.

[37] This fine phrase comes from Andrew Kirk, *Counterculture Green : the Whole Earth Catalog and American Environmentalism* (Kansas, 2007)

5: **Setting Sail, 1984**

The normal Hollywood treatment of this story would center on construction, and the ongoing struggle for survival against the odds: the sunlit naiveté of the launch, the going getting tough, the tough getting going, enduring the snow, surviving the bankers, and then—the final shot of the sun setting behind a finished palace of curved stone walls and sloping glass. However, the soft path is not about arriving. The sea voyage metaphor is a good one for the Lovins project, but the intent behind having a house was to sail in it—to have it be seen and used, lived and worked in, visited as a place in which some American lives, personal and professional, were unfolding. The construction was a saga in some ways, but it was only about building the boat. Now it is time to look carefully at what sort of boat it was.

The most prominent aspect of the soft path was its emphasis on energy efficiency and renewable energy. Technical effectiveness in these two areas was critical to its success. But what kinds of efficiency and what forms of renewable energy were needed? Lovins' most significant insight was that the answers should start with users and their needs instead of technical alternatives and their comparative capacities.

Starting with users opened a way for their experience of the building, their pleasures, satisfactions and delights, to have a role from the beginning in shaping and organizing the place. It wasn't going to be enough to have them move in and do the interior decorating. This is a profoundly important (and challenging) principle for developing genuine sustainability, but even the Lovinses were only partly conscious of it at the time. In his seminal *Foreign Affairs* article, Lovins put forward five characteristics of soft technologies. Two, or perhaps three, of them are about the importance of end users in evaluating the alternatives.

> — They rely on renewable energy flows that are always there whether we use them or not, such as sun and wind and vegetation: on energy income, not on depletable energy capital.

> – They are diverse, so that energy supply is an aggregate of very many individually modest contributions, each designed for maximum effectiveness in particular circumstances.

– They are flexible and relatively low-technology—which does not mean unsophisticated, but rather, easy to understand and use without esoteric skills, accessible rather than arcane.

– They are matched in *scale* and in geographic distribution to end-use needs, taking advantage of the free distribution of most natural energy flows.

– They are matched in *energy quality* to end-use needs: a key feature that deserves immediate explanation.[38]

The focus on end-use needs was one of his revolutionary moves as an energy analyst. Up to the mid-1970s, the energy sector had conceived its task as making its supply reliable, secure and above all adequate to an endlessly growing demand. Obviously, national prosperity depended on having enough coal, oil, and electric power, and the industry believed that this demand would increase steadily. The details of demand did not require study; they were taken for granted, and would simply be worked out in markets, boardrooms, and shop floors through the private sector's millions of daily micro-decisions. If anyone had asked about engaging with demand and altering it, it would probably have been felt to be unwise, inefficient, and generally improper for the energy sector to intervene in or even look too closely at such things. Its job was to ensure that lights would always come on when the switch was flipped; gasoline would always gush from the hose at filling stations; and steel mills, refineries, assembly lines, and the rest of the economy's production and distribution apparatus would function at whatever pace was desired.

Until the OPEC crisis of 1973, energy analysts and planners during the long period of growth since the end of WW II had overseen a system which produced "abundance in the short and medium terms and technological fixes in the long term," in Frank Laird's summary phrase.[39] Laird's masterful account of solar energy's struggle for footing in national policy highlights the way planners and decision-makers took endlessly growing demand to be like a force of nature, enormous and impersonal, rather than a process amenable to adjustment, much less control.

The 1970s rattled all these understandings. OPEC threatened abundance; more and more people found nuclear energy problematic as a fix; and economic growth itself was showing its seamy sides. Unsurprisingly, many rallied to shore up the status quo, but the door was opened for deep questioning.

Lovins' fundamental insight about the importance of considering and starting from end uses is easy to state. He put it this way in *Foreign Affairs*:

> People do not want electricity or oil, nor such economic abstractions as "residential services," but rather comfortable rooms, light, vehicular motion, food, tables, and other real things.

His revolutionary move was to make this quite commonplace observation into a primary reference point for judgments and decisions about providing energy. One would work back from end uses, looking for the most efficient ways of meeting them, rather than working forward from the mine, the well, or the power dam, and looking for ways to make the most of their production.

Under the name of "integrative design," this viewpoint has remained a cornerstone of Lovins' work. As this book unfolds, you will catch glimpses of it at work, in two distinct but connected ways. By starting with end users, it encourages fresh thinking about what is really needed and how to provide it simply. Simultaneously, it helps one recognize that users have multiple wants and needs—physical, cognitive, emotional, collective—and rewards the finding of ways to meet several with a single step. The massive cantilever arch in the Snowmass greenhouse is Lovins' favorite example. A look back at the walk-through photos in Chapter 2 will show it active visually, not just structurally. It also houses cooling vents and lighting and stores solar heat. Doing some of this is quite common in architecture, much less so in engineering, and it is very rare in both arenas to make end users the genuine starting point for design.

A first consequence was to reframe assumptions about the need for distribution. The received understanding had been that useful energy needed to originate in large-capacity, centralized plants or places. Then, of course, it had to be spread out with pipes or power lines or roads or rail lines to the widely dispersed users. How else would energy get to them? But when the rebellious mood of the 1960s and 1970s revived interest in solar and wind energy, people were considering and beginning to use energy in forms that nature already delivers to the doorstep. Being off the grid, or having power supplied at the scale of neighborhoods instead a sprawling regional scale became thinkable.

Sorting out the possibilities of rethinking and transforming distribution has proved a lengthy business which is still far from over, 50 years later. Lovins has been a key actor in those debates, which engage corporations, governments at all scales, political parties, chambers of commerce, banks, and legions of engineers and lawyers. But he put the insight to work personally by basing his thinking about their house on what their actual needs were, and how they might be met in the building itself. Some outside links to the energy system came later.

What energy was for

We already know, in general terms, what the Lovinses wanted their house/office to shelter and support—private life and a small institute. But what would "comfortable rooms, light, vehicular motion, food, tables, and other real things," in the language of the *Foreign Affairs* article, imply for the two of them? What provisions for these things were in place after the builders had left and the dust had been swept and mopped away? In this chapter we look at how the important first two items in that list of needs were provided by appropriately chosen and deployed soft technologies. We will see in the next chapter that the soft path also had important consequences for the feeling and experience of living in the building.

One page of Lovins' hand-written notes from early in design shows him looking at the planned pattern of life in the building in this way, task by task.

He's estimating the size of the photovoltaic array the house would need. For this, the most important data is the expected electric power demand, so he lists the electric-powered items, with their wattages (W) and likely hours per day (h/d) of use. Indirectly, he's outlining the pattern of activities the house and its gear should support.

Rough el. balance / demand :

		h/d	kW-h /d
lights	test – work 2 × 1750 lumen (42 lumen/w) = 2 × 83 w	av 5	.83
	scan-o 10 × 1100 lumen (61 lumen/w) = 10 × 18w (gu'l)	av 3	.54
	scan-off 3 × 550 lumen (61 lumen/w) = 3 × 9 w (outdoor)	av 10	.27
	IIfluor 3 × 6000 lumen (85 lumen/w) = 3 × 71 w (K, shop, lib)	av 2	.43
typewriter	138 W	5	.69
a-a hxs	say 2 × 35 w + 1 × 85 w — check data	24	3.2
Lanier	CPU + screen 600w + quiescent print 70 / 14A@117 vAC starting surge on printr, 26/A total breaker	5	3.0
	printer running = extra 59 w	1	0.06
waterfall pump	say 15' head × 1/4 cfs @ .7 eff 39 = ~ kW	12	4.68
solar dhw pumps/ctls	say 120 w	4?	0.48 ?
K. appliances (small)	say 10 kw·h/y (Norgard)		0.03
freezer	240 kw·h/y (Schlueter lit.)	—	0.66
vacuum cl.	say 50 kw·h/y (Norgard "normal")		0.07
washing machine	say 200 kw·h/y (Norgard "stingy")		0.55
TV, radio, clocks, sewing mach.	200 kw·h/y 1200 c/t TV "medium" Norgard		0.55

16.04 ~
0.67 kw·av ~5-7 A @ 117V

5855 kw·h/y
~488 kw·h/mo
@ 6¢/kw·h = $32/mo.

no —
space-htg
water-htg
clothes-drying
cooking
lgtng   say 220 w/m² × .1 = 22 w/m²
⟹ 30 m² cells

Most entries are obvious—lights, pumps, and kitchen appliances—but some are less so. "Typewriter" meant an electric typewriter, a nearly universal tool for writers by then, now of course long supplanted. "Lanier" refers to the typewriter's successor in Lovins' work, an early stand-alone word processor the size of a small sofa.

The most telegraphic entry, "a-a hxs," stands for "air-to-air heat exchangers." These are the key to keeping air fresh in a cold climate without running up huge energy costs heating air drawn in from outdoors. They were also critical to managing humidity, since some of Amory and Hunter's personal end uses implied a large greenhouse with fishpond and small waterfall, integrated with the living space.

Most of the list is what one might expect for a house/office. The lights and pumps and appliances provide resources for cooking and eating, some level of work in the outside world, household management, leisure, socializing, grooming. These things are thoroughly typical of middle class American life.[40]

The one unusual item in the Lovins list is the pump for a waterfall to serve the planned system of fish tanks in the greenhouse and provide the clear sound of falling water at a considerable distance. This hardly represented a major lifestyle departure. The merging of home and workplace was unusual for the 1980s, a return to the old pattern of living above the store. But there was no intent to go about life in radical difference from American norms. The importance of the place would be in how these things got done, and specifically how they could be low impact and yet satisfying and indeed pleasurable.

The note at the very bottom left might be startling:
no—space-htg, water-htg, clothes-drying, cooking, refrig.

However, the "no" only means no outside electric power. Lovins had those end uses on his mind, but he didn't assume that the only ways to meet them were the conventional ones. The space would definitely be heated, hot water would be available, clothes would get dried, cooking and refrigeration would happen, but this would all be done without using outside electricity, because at that time electric power was the most problematic of all forms of energy supply, given the environmental disruptions of mining and burning fossil fuels and the growing concerns about nuclear power. Now, 40 years later, it makes sense to electrify completely in many places, because of how well the soft path push for renewable energy has done with sun and wind. That doesn't mean that there should now be one standard pattern for sustainable design; starting with users and their needs still makes sense.

Making the energy budget

The next question the page of notes tackled was how much energy each of the listed uses really needed. There were all the planned electricity uses, and Lovins wanted to know how big an array of solar cells it would take to supply them. This was one part of a larger question—how much energy of all kinds would the house need, and would there be enough of it? The era of cheap and abundant energy had been able to ignore this question, but the energy savers, solar enthusiasts and policy reformers of the 1970s could not avoid it. It remains important now, because energy, though increasingly renewable, is neither cheap nor really abundant.

Energy needed budgeting, just like household income and expenses. The notes are an electric energy budget for the planned house. Unlike budgets about household finances, which usually have to treat income as fixed and expenses as trimmable, Lovins started with a tally of uses. The work was to see how large an energy income would be needed to serve them. Or rather how small an energy income could be arranged for them.

The steps in the exercise are worth following, because they illustrate the blend of hard data and educated guesswork which is unavoidably at work, visibly or out of sight, wherever soft technologies are used.

The starting point is the rating of each power-using device in watts. Each listed item has a note about this—some lights at 83 W, some at 18 W, the typewriter at 138 W, and so forth. There is also an entry for each item in a column headed "h/d", which stands for hours per day. He needed to know how long each item was likely to be used each day. The wattage alone only tells you how rapidly or quickly an item uses energy, not the total amount it uses; the difference is very like the difference between speed (how fast you travel) and distance (how far you travel). Professionals highlight this difference by using different words for the two, "power" for the first (how fast), and "energy" for the second (how much).[41]

The electric meter is one place where the distinction is enshrined. The watt and the kilowatt are units of power, and relate to how fast the meter goes around at any moment. (In case you're uncertain, a kilowatt is 1000 watts.) The meter is there to measure energy, though, so what it actually counts, and what you get billed for, is how  many turns altogether it makes in a month. The common unit for energy (and billing) is the kilowatt-hour, the amount of energy used when a one kilowatt device runs steadily for one hour. Of course, you probably never have a device using a thousand watts that runs steadily for exactly one hour. When a 750 watt heater (0.75 kilowatts) runs for 80 minutes (1.33 hours) you get billed for .75 kilowatts times 1.33 hours, or .9975 kilowatt hours.

Lovins' "h/d" column is about energy, not power: he needs to know how many kilowatt-hours his solar array would have to produce each day, so he multiplies the power rating of each item in kilowatts by the estimated hours per day of use, and out comes the last column, "kWh/d"; the total is shown as 16.04 kilowatt-hours per day.

In making estimates like those, the wattages are solid and uncontroversial information. They're stamped on each item's nameplate or retail packaging, after all. Daily hours of use are much more approximate, because of the inevitable variability occasioned by weather, visitors, health, travel, or professional demands like grant deadlines.

There is an important point here about estimates of all kinds. If you combine a precise number and an approximate one in making any kind of estimate, you get an approximate result. That result is worth having, but you have to remember that it only indicates a range of possibilities, not an exact amount, no matter how precise the precise parts of your estimate were. Estimating is always a blend of data and educated guesswork, like a number of other things in sustainable design.

The biggest single item in the kWh/d column is the waterfall pump, at 4.68 kWh/d.

> The number comes from multiplying its relatively high power demand (390 watts) by its relatively extended hours of use (12 hours).

Other items on the list need much less power or run much less. They are also of obvious practical importance. The pump's job would only be to circulate fish tank water, and to do it audibly, through a series of small cascades. In fact, the cascades involve pumping the water higher than just keeping the fish alive would require, and demand extra daily energy that is going to have to be provided by extra solar, which was quite expensive at that point. They were on a tight budget and borrowed money from the beginning. Why is the waterfall pump there at all?

Its presence is very significant, because it reveals the importance of whole lives lived in the Lovins' planning. I can't emphasize too much or repeat too often that sustainability should not just be a matter of reducing harm. We need to "envision the enduring prosperity of all living things." The waterfall pump was part of the design simply, and essentially, because Amory and Hunter wanted the sound of running water in the house. In narrowly functional terms, this sound wouldn't add anything. The fish would gain the same weight with silent water circulation. But the multi-sensory presence of water was a key ingredient in the whole experience of living in the house, and the energy required for it was absolutely worth having.

Non-electric energy

Let's go back now to the list of no's: "no—space-htg, water-htg, clothes-drying, cooking, refrig." Recall that "no" for these items meant no outside electric power. They would still happen and they would still require energy, but it would not be from the grid and its centralized power plants.

All these "no" functions involve the flow of heat, mostly getting it into something (shower water, food, clothes, the whole interior), sometimes getting it out (refrigerator). No notes survive which give Lovins' own estimates for these thermal uses. For getting a sense of the relative amounts of energy involved, we can use estimates from various sources.

Cooking: The Lovinses intended to cook with propane, as I mentioned. One big reason had to do with efficiency. You can cook with electricity, and the proportion of the electrical energy that goes into actually making ingredients hot, as opposed to heating the stove, the oven, or the kitchen's air can be very close to 100%. Its efficiency can be very high in that sense. But making electrical energy at the time usually required burning fuel, and there is a profound physical limit on how much of the energy in a fuel like coal, oil, natural gas, or propane can be converted to electric energy.[42] It takes very special efforts and very large power plants to convert even as much as half the heat from burning a fuel into electric power.[43] The industry average is more like 30%.

It would have been nice to use solar heat, but cooking is the one function in the "no" list which needs higher temperatures than solar can readily provide, and it generally needs it at times of days when direct sun is not available. So the Lovinses went to propane.

> Using propane would require relying on an outside, conventional energy supply, but the 1982-84 project never aimed at total independence from conventional energy. It's important to recognize that sustainability does not equate to self-sufficiency, and self-sufficiency doesn't guarantee sustainability. (The building did become self-sufficient as far as energy was concerned in the 2006-2009 renovation, and then actually aimed at exporting some solar to the grid to displace a little of the region's fossil-generated production.)

Essentially all the thermal energy in the propane flame can go to cooking, though it's not very efficient about getting that heat into what's cooking. Most pots and pans let a good deal of heat slip past them, and more heat flows out through the thinly insulated walls of ovens than goes into the food.[44] It does heat the house, so it's not a total loss. More efficient cookware and appliances are available, at a price, and the Snowmass house tried some of them in later years, but they didn't exist then. Cooking with a lid on the pan saves a surprising amount of energy, and they did that.

Cooks and kitchens use widely different amounts of heat, but a very average gas kitchen might use about 2 kWh a day.[45] If you use gas, your bill doesn't show how much you used in kWh; it is only used for electrical use in ordinary life. However, because of the very fundamental fact that energy cannot be created or destroyed (which is sanctified as the First Law of Thermodynamics), there are fixed ratios in the conversion of energy from one form to another. A given amount of electrical energy supplied to a heater always generates a specific amount of heat, for example. This means that units of measurement defined for one form of energy can always be converted to units defined for the other forms in standard ways. The choice of units is a matter of convenience, and I use kWh for all forms of energy here because it makes it much easier to compare their amounts.

Water heating: Here the sun came into play again, but this time as a provider of heat, not electricity. Flat-plate collectors, the leading solar technology of the 1950s, got space on the roof to serve the house's showers, sinks, and hot tub, via a 1500 gallon storage tank sized to handle two weeks of cloudy weather. That was a reasonable reserve for Snowmass, which has abundant winter sun and few extended cloudy periods.[46]

Storage had long been a stumbling block for solar thermal systems. Tanks large enough to store heat for long periods of use are expensive, and so is the insulation needed to keep a lot of water hot for long times. Lovins had spotted a kind of technical loophole, however. Water naturally stratifies by temperature when it's undisturbed. Warmer water floats; cooler water sinks. If water to use is only heated from the top of the tank, it can be usefully hot even if most of what's lower in the tank is cool, so a thermal collector does not need to heat the whole tank before useful hot water is available to a house. In addition, the efficiency of the solar collector can be increased if it's fed by the cool water from the bottom of the tank, because there will be more transfer of heat if the difference between the temperature of the water and the temperature of the collector's surfaces is larger.[47]

Putting local weather together with the stratification idea allowed the storage tank to be much smaller than conventional wisdom would have allowed. This brought the cost down to tolerable levels, and flat plate collectors became the house's system, supplying something like 11 kWh per day for hot water uses.[48]

A propane-fired on-demand heater provided backup for the occasional times when some combination of clouds and high use of hot water exhausted even the two-week tank. It would almost always be inactive, but it would ensure that dishwashing, laundry, and bathing could continue even during prolonged bad weather. (Lovins later estimated that backup supplied 1% of the house's annual hot water energy.[49])

Drying clothes: The design used the same sunlight that heated water to dry clothes, a good deal more straightforwardly. A south-facing window in a small roof enclosure let sunlight directly into a laundry space below. Solar-heated air gathers in the upper part of this space and an arrangement of hangers, cords and pulleys allows laundry to be pulled up there to dry. As long as the sun is shining, this simple solar input supplies perhaps 4 kWh per day even in January, about one-third of what the much more complicated water system does.[50]

Staying warm (a.k.a. space heating) With our heads down in the notes about energy needs, it may or may not have been obvious that we've ignored a very large elephant until now. The biggest category of household energy use in the US was then, and still is, keeping warm. In the United States as a whole, two-thirds of household energy use in 1978 went to space heating. Everywhere in the country, except perhaps at sea level in Hawai'i, heat is needed for indoor comfort at least a few nights a year. Most places have a multi-month heating season. At Snowmass in the 1980s, 7100 feet above sea level, only June, July and August had even mid-day temperatures in the normal comfort range. The area has warmed somewhat since then, but nights and evenings are chilly or outright cold all year round.

The Lovins house dealt with this by remaining a full-on passive solar design, but one that was thoroughly married to superinsulation. The center of the solar design was the large greenhouse, flanked on the east by RMI workspace and on the west by social space and private quarters. The large window areas let sunlight stream in, and the massive walls smooth out the variations between day and night, cloudy and clear. That heat is retained by tight construction, thick insulation, windows that let light in but obstruct outgoing heat flow, and heat recovery ventilators (also called heat exchangers) that keep much of the heat in outgoing air inside the house. The effect is to shrink the heating needed, even in winter, to Eugene Leger's goal: the house has no furnace.

Traditionally, in European houses and in houses built by their American descendants, staying warm in in the winter and cool in the summer were handled quite directly. If you were too hot, you could open the windows; if too cold, you would close the windows, of course, and then could stoke up the fire, and perhaps reduce activity in rooms far from it. The advent of central furnaces led to the invention of more indirect controls: furnaces were inconveniently located in basements or the like, for reasons of cleanliness. They could not change output at all quickly, and could not supply different flows to different rooms by themselves. Inventions like mechanical dampers could address the distribution of heat and increase or decrease its overall flow, and mechanical or electrical thermostats could activate them automatically. Controls like this appeared first in industrial settings, such as chicken incubation houses, as early as the 1830s, but long before the energy crises and responses of the 1970s, thermostat controlled central heat was standard in American houses.

Basically, this system was just a much cleaner and more convenient version of the traditional one. You purchased a furnace adequate to the largest expected demand; you turned the thermostat up or down to suit yourself, rather than fooling with the windows or the wood stove; and the furnace and the radiators or hot air registers did the rest. The national network of suppliers routinely provided any needed amount of fuel. The ideal was actually that heating and cooling would happen invisibly, yet with complete effectiveness.

The possibility of doing without a furnace was one of the inspired insights of the counter-cultural 1970s. It called for a different philosophy. Householders would not be able to answer the swings of weather or inclination by simply turning a dial. Solar and superinsulation design took a new direction: the house as a whole would deliver controlled heat. Careful insulation would isolate the interior from outside conditions much more effectively; sunlight would supply heat, and massive walls would temper the differences between day and night, sunny days and cloudy ones. The general ideas were already known; what was new was relying completely on them. It was a profound shift, because walls, insulation and glazing are structural, not adjustable like windows or a thermostat. They are permanently fixed during construction, yet they needed to deal with decades of future variability somehow, providing a steady level of thermal comfort without any adjustments by the occupants.

This was a brand new and critical design challenge. A house is not an industrial product that comes stamped with a wattage; the sun may be reliable in its courses, but clouds and cold air are not; and what makes people feel warm enough varies a good deal. How could you know it would work?

You couldn't know the future. Instead, you'd have to trust some statistical measures of how much heat the Sun would provide, hour by hour, day by day, and trust some estimates of how much heat the house would lose hour by hour, day by day. The designer, helped by an engineer with expertise in estimating solar-input/heat-loss balances, would juggle the plan, revising thicknesses of insulation, amount of south facing glass, and so forth until an estimated balance was achieved. In 1982 such statistics were already solid enough for the Lovinses to be confident that they would be warm all year.

> One advance since then has been the development of well-tested, relatively easy methods for making the heat balance estimates Lovins and the engineering minded passive solar researchers who preceded him had to do roughly and with large safety margins.

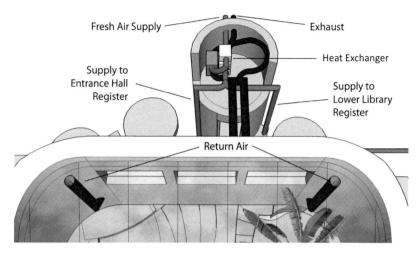

Fresh Air Supply — Exhaust

Supply to
Entrance Hall
Register

Heat Exchanger

Supply to
Lower Library
Register

Return Air

Location of heat exchanger and ducts for incoming (green, "supply") and outgoing (blue, "return") air, seen from above the main green space (note banana fronds)

More staying warm (a.k.a. the fresh air issue): A last but very important consideration for staying warm concerns fresh air. Houses need fresh air coming in and stale air going out. Traditionally, loose construction, chimneys and wind and breezes got this to happen without special arrangements. Incoming air was cold in winter, of course, but you stoked the fire or turned up the thermostat and all was well. When saving energy became a major goal, designers first pressed builders to make much tighter houses; when they realized that this reduced the exchange of stale and fresh air to unhealthy levels, they began installing air-to-air heat exchangers. The basic idea is to channel incoming and outgoing air streams into adjoining ducts, so heat from the warm outgoing air can pass through the duct wall to the cold incoming stream. Substantial transfer of heat is possible. You can shift 70% to 90% or more of the heat that would otherwise be carried out of the house to the incoming stream, reducing the amount of energy you need to heat the building air significantly.

A heat exchanger like this was in Lovins' thinking from very early on. In fact, the finished building had several. One large rotary unit served the main space, drawing in stale air from the top of the greenhouse enclosure, where warm air floated up, and delivering fresh air through two ducts opening on the east and west sides of the main living/working space. One issue with centralized ventilation of the kind you need for these heat exchangers is how to get full circulation of the building's air. The linear plan of the house, with narrow access to the west side, made it likely that air in the family spaces would be too static if the big main unit was the only exchanger, so there was a smaller through-the-wall rotary unit in the main bedroom at the west end. Three even smaller units were installed in the two bathrooms and the kitchen stove hood, to ensure that these local sources of humidity and odor would definitely be under control.

My rough estimate of the net effect is that the building has an average heat loss of 150 kWh per day in January, the coldest month in Snowmass. (This combines the losses through the walls, floor, windows and roof with what the ventilation/heat exchange system doesn't succeed in retaining.)

How much energy is needed in all

Drawing these different end use amounts together, we can total up the energy needs of the house as it was finally designed and built.

Electric power use (rounded)	17 kWh per day
Cooking use (propane)	2 kWh per day
Hot water use (solar)	11 kWh per day
Laundry dryer use (solar)	4 kWh per day
Space heat needed (solar) (in January)	150 kWh per day

The point of these numbers is simply to give an idea of relative amounts. All are quite rough, and some reflect national averages, not the Lovinses' own usage. But you can see that cooking use is certainly quite small compared to electricity use (lights and office gear), and both are very small compared to the need for typical midwinter space heating.

Where energy came from

When the Lovinses moved into the building, neither electric power nor propane came from the site. (Nor did food, the energy supply for the occupants' bodies.) The electricity came from the Holy Cross Rural Electric Cooperative, as it did for everyone else in the area; the propane came from the bottled gas company. The food was from supermarkets and food stands in the ordinary way.

There is a simple side to these facts, and a subtle side. The couple hoped and expected to be able eventually to generate a good deal of their electric power from solar cells on the roof, and a good deal of their food from the greenhouse and animals raised on the place. It was simply the case that neither of these arrangements was in place yet. They hadn't had enough money to buy the cells, and the charm of contributing to their groundbreaking project had not led enthusiasts to donate it. After some early efforts food production became marginal; solar cells did eventually appear. Both outcomes emerged from the ongoing life in the place.

The subtler side of this has already been mentioned. Self-sufficiency was never a primary value for Amory and Hunter Lovins. Their plan was never to lead a life disconnected from the energy transactions of society. It wasn't a disadvantage or disappointment in their eyes to be cooking with commercially produced propane. Much later, they didn't see it as a problem to send a good deal of the place's solar electricity out to the grid, rather than storing it on site in batteries. Their goal was always to make good use of renewable energy, according to the situation, not to make exclusive use of it a matter of principle.

In fact, of course, the really important on-site energy supply was solar heat. As our table of comparisons shows, heat was by far their biggest energy need. As Eugene Leger had realized, running the lights, keyboarding, showering, walking about, digesting food, even sleeping all contribute to the internal heat of a building. Energy gets mobilized in various forms for many purposes in buildings, but in the end it's all heat, and the amounts can be considerable. They had even allowed his modest Massachusetts house to dispense with a furnace.

In Snowmass, all the activities using electric power, hot water, and heated air (for drying) would also help to heat the house, to the tune of 34 kWh per day, according to our estimates. Moreover, the body heat from the two principal inhabitants would add perhaps 3.6 kWh a day.[51]

> Body heat alone can be enough to deal with deep winter cold if the heated zone is small enough, like the space inside a good sleeping bag, When Rocky Mountain Institute grew, each additional person would contribute their body heat while present, coming to maybe another 0.6 kWh per day each.

The total energy input from ordinary activities before any employees arrived came to roughly 38 kWh a day.

> If you think about these numbers a little, it becomes clear that they must be very approximate. Body heat production goes up and down drastically between light and strenuous activity; different cooking patterns could easily have the range on twice or half as much; and the lights and other electrical gear will be on differing amounts on different days.

So what does adding the above estimates give you? The full answer is somewhat extended, but boils down to, Not nothing. You do get some real information. You mustn't use it blindly, but it is real.

> The estimates are very rough, but this is where respect for what they do offer and their limits comes in. If the number says we're close to a target, that's all it tells us. It doesn't say exactly how close we are, but we can legitimately think that small measures will make up any difference. And if it tells us we're far from the target, we know that we'll still be far even if the numbers are somewhat different, so small measures won't close the gap, and we'll have to find big ones.

For the Lovinses in Snowmass, the internal sources of heat only covered about a quarter of their need for space heat, reducing it to something like 111 kWh per day in January. Could they have gone even further, as far in this respect as Leger? Perhaps. But there would have been a heavy price to pay in shutting the house away from view of the Colorado landscape, which counted heavily in their decision to locate in Snowmass. And in this location, they were able to bring the sun into the balance.

As I mentioned, you do this at the design stage with statistical averages. A very rough estimate, using the kind of information Lovins had at the time, shows the sun supplying 150 kWh per day in January, the least favorable month.[52] This is 30% more than our estimate for the remaining heat needed; so our estimates of average supply and of average needs and uses could all be off by a good deal without our ending up with a significant shortfall.

The average available solar heat in the Snowmass winter is favorable news for soft technology advocates who want to build there, but reliable solar heat requires more than favorable averages. It isn't the average level of the sea in a storm that sinks boats. It's the height of the wave crests and depth of the troughs that matters.

There's the same sort of critical difference between the average insolation and how much solar heat you have at any given moment, or during a week, or over a month. The energy arriving from the sun is continuously changing direction; it disappears at night and in storms; it can be much weaker during long cloudy spells—the sun is not a heat source that can be controlled whenever you like with a thermostat dial or engine throttle. The passive solar approach, pioneered by people like the Balcombs and used wholeheartedly in the Snowmass house, uses a building's mass to deal with the problems. You soak up excess solar heat with concrete floors, stone walls, exposed brick, even interior pools of water. This so-called thermal mass keeps the building from overheating in full summer sun, but it's even more important that it makes a store of heat available for nighttime or cloudy periods. If the building's air gets a little cooler than the warmed up mass, heat flows out of the walls and floors and keeps the room's temperature in bounds.

Getting thermal mass right, which means having enough of it and having it exposed enough for heat to flow easily in and out of it, takes skill. Lovins had the skill and did get it right. The big sloping greenhouse roof and the other south-facing windows let in enough solar heat, and the thick walls with their sandwiched insulation kept enough of it in for the building to function as planned, from the beginning.

[38] Lovins in *Foreign Affairs*, 77

[39] Laird, *op.cit.*

[40] A good reference for activities in buildings is the American Time Use Survey, an annual survey since 2003 by the Department of Labor in which 25,000 members of US households list their activities over the preceding 24-hour day, weekday or weekend. This covers both in-home and out-of-home time. US Bureau of Labor Statistics, American Time Use Survey. https://www.bls.gov/tus/

[41] 'Energy' and 'power' are both common words, used almost interchangeably in ordinary usage. This unfortunately blurs the quite important distinction between how much and how fast, but both the ordinary (blurred) and technical (sharp) usages are very well established. All you can do is keep straight at each moment whether you're in a general or a technical discussion Confusingly, 'power' can also just mean 'electricity.'

[42] How one can know this, and how it can become one of the most certain things known about the physical universe, is a fascinating story, outside the scope of this book, but well within the grasp of general readers willing to follow a carefully constructed non-mathematical train of thought. Morton Mott-Smith's *The Concept of Energy Simply Explained*, originally published in 1934 but still available as a reprint (Dover), provides an outstanding introduction.

[43] The highest achieved efficiency so far is 53%. Suppes, G.J. and Storvick, T., 2006. *Sustainable nuclear power*, chapter 7. Elsevier.

[44] http://www.greenbuildingadvisor.com/blogs/dept/energy-solutions/efficient-cooking

[45] A rough estimate is all that is appropriate here. H. Richard Heede's *Homemade Money* quotes 750 kWh/year, which is about 2 kWh/day.

[46] Chapter 12 introduces the ingenious statistics that can give confidence to the decision about how much storage to have.

[47] Hollands, K.G.T. and Lightstone, M.F., 1989. "A review of low-flow, stratified-tank solar water heating systems." *Solar Energy*, 43(2), pp. 97-105.

[48] Estimate based on prorating US Energy Information Agency (EIA) data for average household energy uses in 2009.

[49] Aris Yi, Samuel Ramirez, Michael Bendewald. "Banana Farm 1.0" (Factor Ten Engineering Case Study). Rocky Mountain Institute, 2010.

[50] Insolation estimated from the area of this window (25.5 sq ft) and January average daily solar energy absorbed.

---

[51] A standard architectural engineering reference quotes 75 W for a person sitting, walking or doing light activity. This comes to 1.8 kWh/day for a person spending all day in the building. This contribution to the energy balance is very small compared to others, so the exact amount does not matter very much (Data source: Stein et al, *Mechanical and Electrical Equipment for Buildings* (Wiley, 2006).

[52] More about assumptions and data source are in endnote 155 (in Chapter 12).

6: **Reflections on Visions, Costs and Feeling**

As the owners changed their roles from lead contractors to inhabitants, they knew that dealing with the technical challenges of supplying energy through soft alternatives was only one dimension of their success or failure. There are two broad questions to address in evaluating other aspects of the project. Did its creators achieve what they wanted? And did they achieve what *we* would want, that is, did the building work in ways we, as onlookers and members of the general public find valuable?

This calls for an old-fashioned kind of discussion—an appreciation. The Oxford English Dictionary (a wonderful place for older meanings) says "appreciation' can mean "The action or an act of assessing the nature or quality of something or someone; judgement, estimation" (entry 2.a) and "Clear or correct understanding; perception, recognition, esp. of subtleties or complexities" (entry 5). There are definitely subtleties and complexities about this house and its design, involving meanings and experience as much as the metrics of performance.

A full appreciation should wait until we have seen the house/office accumulate some history. But some questions and some observations present themselves already.

The vision met reality and got it to help

The first striking thing is that they managed to complete the building, substantially the one designed and displayed in the 1982 brochure. The building was there, in stone and concrete and glass and wood, and it embodied the design of two years before. The massive serpentine walls, the big central greenhouse area, heavy insulation in both walls and roof, superwindow glazing, earth sheltering on the north side, and air-to-air heat exchangers were all present. The plan was unchanged except in minor ways: the shifting of a stockroom doorway to allow more book shelving in the office area, simplification of the entry wall and the solar drying loft, the addition of a small circular, sky-lit "pod" at the very west end of the private quarters, and a few other items. A number of less important green-building features had dropped away; water filled columns for additional thermal mass, a three-season sleeping area on the roof, and gray water heat recovery. The greenhouse plantings and fish were not in place yet, nor were the solar collectors for domestic hot water. Generally speaking, though, this was the promised building. In spite of the dramas of the volunteer crew period and the time and cost pressures of the "adult supervision" period they had brought it into being.

As mentioned previously, estimates for the final cost of the building ran between $550,000 and $650,000 in dollars of the time, depending on whether land, landscaping, and financing costs are included. The building was big, but it was built to house a consulting business as well as a home, and in any case custom homes of that size were common in the area. A good local contractor building a custom house the size of the whole building but conventional in structure would have charged something like $533,000 for direct construction alone.[53] By this measure the cost was not unreasonable. It was clearly much higher than they'd hoped, but its having been completed anyway, substantially as originally designed, suggests the power and persuasiveness of the vision behind it.

As I've said before, when certain visions meet what everyone takes to be reality, that reality changes. Confronted with unexpected obstacles and difficulties of many kinds, including inexperience, workforce turnover, and winter weather, the vision for 1739 Snowmass Creek Road got reality to reveal new avenues for continuing forward toward an unchanged goal.

Destination or milestone?

The completed building certainly clarifies some things about the Lovinses' intentions. Many things about the design and its construction show that they didn't expect or want it to become a literal standard. The place refuses to fit in either of two pigeonholes in American culture for unusual buildings. Housebuilding in this country is overwhelmingly conventional. One builds what has been built before, with minor adjustments useful in marketing. Two kinds of departure are recognized. They could be called Everyone Should Do This, which presents and urges a new standard to replace the old, and I've Only Myself to Please, which almost belligerently asserts the individual's right to go off on his own (usually his own, not her own). The Lovins Snowmass house/office is neither of these.

They did hope the building would have wide influence, but once again we are at the difference between a milestone and a destination. The goal at Snowmass was to point toward new ways to live in the affluent world, and the strategy was to show that a number of unlikely seeming things were possible. You could have a house without a furnace high in the Rockies. It could be as comfortable as any affluent householder could desire. The sun could power a business, not just a home. You could be distant from primary nuclear targets and still be actively connected with the world of influence. You could construct most of a landmark building with volunteers. You could let the sun in without letting the heat out. Renewables and efficiency—the soft path—could do the job. Each of these statements ran against considerable conventional wisdom, but the completed physical structure demonstrated them all.

In a transformed world based on soft technologies, would everyone live in the Rockies? Would everyone combine home and office? Would everyone have stone walls with serpentine curves, very small private quarters, cylindrical storage closets? No, no and no. These were choices made by this particular couple; they were not at all required by the new technical approaches used, superinsulation and passive solar design. They were choices originating in the wish to lead a certain kind of life in the place.

Other elements such as the south-facing orientation were indeed required. But they could be brought into a design in many different ways. A building could be blockier, could be two stories tall, could have quite a different balance of private and public spaces, could be much smaller, could have quite different masonry, and could still exhibit much the same thermal behavior. The great arch didn't need to be held up by a tour de force of cantilever construction. Its mass is very helpful, especially at the top, but similar mass could be provided by one horizontal and two upward sloping beams, supported by columns at the two upper corners. The point is that someone seeking this level of thermal performance isn't constrained to stick at all close to this design. It's not a standard in that sense. A visiting Thai architect took the integrative approach back to Bangkok, with its opposite climate (hot and wet), with equivalent success.[54] This is very important. Integrative design, i.e. starting with real end users and their setting, will generate buildings that suit preferences, climates, cultures and general circumstances in real ways.

It was important, actually, for this building to be unusual. Rocky Mountain Institute, the Lovins vehicle for exerting influence, needed to become a brand, and a unique building would help them do it. Their ambition was radical, their personal styles were eye-catching and ear-catching, and settling for a generic physical home would have significantly undercut their ability to catch and hold attention.

At the same time, the building needed to feel desirable and achievable. It could not be I've Only Myself to Please. The hope was that there would be many visitors, many journalists and camera crews, and many write-ups, profiles, interviews, video clips and photo essays, so the place would also have be pleasing and inspiring to streams of outsiders. In particular, they wanted a building that would seem suitable to the stream of top decision-makers passing through Aspen that they hoped would be visiting and coming to consult with RMI there. It needed to be a fulcrum around which larger-scale thinking and acting would pivot.

The one-line message of the building, then, would be neither Everyone Should Do This or I've Only Myself to Please. Instead, it needed to be Yours Can Work This Well.

This is a knife-edge position to adopt. It counts on potential followers combining a solid grasp of the underlying principles with a lively ability to imagine and materialize them in diverse, personally suitable ways. Architects are trained to do this sort of thing with structures and spaces, but not with services like heating. Builders are not, by and large, inclined or encouraged to explore aesthetic or engineering alternatives, and the general public, their customers, aren't usually educated to be able to do either. Moreover, the technical departures, such as superwindows, heat exchangers, and thermal mass were not yet widely familiar to any of these groups. Thus the influence of the building depended on much more than the brilliance of the Lovinses' analysis and rhetoric. Its part in the development of green building from 1984 to the present depended on the interactions between the new possibilities it demonstrated and the habits, and shifting incentives and constraints, at work in the building sector during that period.

> As it happened, another one-line message, a good one for a think tank, was also present. To industrialists and other visiting decision-makers, the building turned out to say, somewhat sotto voce, "if the Lovinses could think this up for themselves, imagine what they could think up for you and your enterprise." That was a longer message, and more indirect, but perhaps just as influential in bringing them the kind of ongoing attention and influence they aimed for as the one about the building itself.

The cost question(s)

What about the cost? The place is big, it's unusual, it has a lot of glass. All those things spell expense. It was built by volunteers, or at least the shell was; even though they weren't paid they had to be fed and sometimes housed, and relying on them meant construction took longer than usual—much, much longer. Surely that added to the expense. Perhaps this all puts the project into the special, easily dismissed class of private visions, along with Hearst Castle, Bucky Fuller's Dymaxion House, and the Batcave.

This is an important question. Actually it is a sheaf of questions hiding in a single phrase. If you come to the house hoping it is already your dream home, the question of whether it's too expensive is simply about whether you have that much money. Others may come looking for a house of the future, a generic free-floating dream of possibility rather than their own quite particular dream. The World's Fairs specialized in visions of this kind, and their descendants in this generation are speculations about a colony on Mars. For such visions, the question may really be whether the cost is fantastical enough. Having it be too low or too reasonable might be disorienting, bringing the house out of Disneyland, so to speak, and into one's actual world, uninvited.

It's more likely that one might ask that question about its cost in the seemingly no-nonsense mode of econo-mysticism, in which one sets dreams aside and asks, "Are the decisions likely to pay off?" as we imagine mortgage bankers do. In this mode, one mentally treats the house as one more item in the realtors' Multiple Listing Service database —an option for sale with so many square feet, such-and-such a list of amenities, a paragraph of enticing characterization—and tries to imagine what a buyer who knew only those things might it find reasonable to offer. Then one not only wonders if the total cost is too high, but also if the same market appeal could have been generated more cheaply.

The Lovinses had a ready answer to this last version of the question: a house of the same size in the area, and built to a similar level of "custom" layout and finish, would have cost about the same. They also had reassurances of a general kind to offer visitors or questioners from further away: the Aspen area had high costs; the future would reduce the costs of special building items as production increased; the house had much more built-in furniture than usual; and so on.

Straightforward information like this does not always persuade straightforwardly. It raises further questions. How can the costs be normal, when the place is far from normal? If unusual features don't cost more, why don't they get used more often? It helps when a powerful concept can be used in explanations, and Lovins articulated just such a concept—the idea of tunneling through the cost barrier.

This was mentioned above in the context of Leger's Massachusetts house. He showed that enough extra insulation and enough tighter construction, which both cost significantly more than usual, could allow the house to dispense with the substantial cost of a furnace.

The Lovins house followed this lead. The superwindows, extra insulation and heat exchangers added something like $19,000 to the bill, but having no furnace and not needing ductwork for distributing a furnace's heat saved an estimated $20,000.[55] On balance, providing for the the house's heating cost slightly less than conventional heating equipment would have. It's crucial to recognize that this only happened because the passive solar and superinsulation elements were taken far enough. If the

Lovinses had quailed at a $19,000 bill and cut back on the thermal features, they would have needed a furnace, too. It might have been smaller and thus somewhat cheaper than usual, but the ductwork would still have been needed, and the cost premium would have been substantial. Conventional thinking would then have put the energy saving features in the nice-but-costly zone, which usually makes them candidates for elimination.

"Tunneling through the cost barrier" describes a possible solution in this kind of situation. For a designer wanting to save energy, there is a barrier —the steady increase of cost with every extra inch of insulation, every step up in window performance, and every provision for heat exchange. Skepticism about the costliness of energy-saving approaches rests on awareness of these added costs, but add enough inches, improve the windows enough, and get good heat exchange, and you reach a point where the furnace can be taken off the project budget, and the total cost drops drastically. You are on the other side of the cost barrier. It can be cheaper to do a lot than to do only a little.

In addition, the owner of a well performing low energy house can also enjoy very low running costs rather than paying normal amounts for furnace fuel every winter. Unfortunately, many people don't think much about the full life cycle costs when they're looking at a house or shopping for a car. They're focused on the sizable purchase price. If there were a way to set up these cost figures side by side for comparison, we would have a sensible way to deal with the question of whether residential energy saving pays off. In fact, there is such a way.

A sensible cost question

Comparing your purchase cost and your running costs is not straightforward, since they operate on very different rhythms and time scales. Purchase costs only require attention when you're buying or selling, dramatic but quite isolated events years apart. Running costs murmur for attention every month or even every week, or just get taken care of automatically. However, most people are familiar with one way to translate purchase cost into an ongoing rhythm—contracts like auto loans or mortgages. The standard mortgage converts the very large one-time cost of buying a house into a monthly series of equal payments over a lengthy span of time. Each month, you pay the bank back a small piece of the money you've borrowed along with interest on the money you still owe, and after thirty years you have paid off the whole loan and all the interest and own the property free and clear. There are many variations, but this is the plain-vanilla version.[56] If household finance is whitewater canoeing, mortgages turn giant waterfalls into long rows of stream-bed rocks and their surface waves. A standard mortgage can be within reach of a family that's making ends meet each month with something left over, while accumulating anything like the full value of a house would take them decades.

Undertaking a mortgage is still a major step, though. Having found a place with sufficient appeal, and found that paying $250,000 for it will actually mean coming up with $1000-2000 a month in mortgage payments, the buyer takes a deep breath and prepares to commit to this serious but achievable drain on monthly income. The psychology of this moment often biases people against any unconventional "extra". Suggesting something like adding better insulation for $10,000 sounds like a great deal to pay compared to the monthly installment. Our image of a challenging but manageable whitewater run now seems to have a possible waterfall. But this is mixing up first cost and running cost. The insulation will be as much a part of the house's fabric as its roofing or plumbing, so one should set its cost alongside the full house cost for comparison. That would make the picture look quite different: the insulation would make the house 4% more expensive, which is a real increase but nothing like the 1000% ratio between the insulation's extra cost and the monthly payment.

The sensible next step would be to ask how the monthly payment would increase if the insulation were added to the mortgage. In our example, the monthly payment would go up by $50-90, again real enough but now well within the scale of other normal monthly expenses. The mortgage system would once again have translated a big one-time payment into terms that can readily become part of the flow of family income and expenditure.

It could do this, but often doesn't. Neither the buyer, already feeling stretched, nor the broker, anxious to make a sale, nor the banker, nervous about the unusual, care to push into "extra" items.

The mortgage system could take a further, quite transformative step by starting to include the owner's monthly expenditures for energy in its calculations. Ability to carry monthly costs is already a key factor in bank decisions about offering mortgages, and energy, especially for heating and cooling, is a notable factor in a household's monthly costs. Buying an energy-efficient house reduces those costs every month. That makes it easier to carry the mortgage, or possible to carry a bigger mortgage. Certain US lenders actually do this. The first so-called "energy efficient mortgages" were offered as early as 1980, and they continue to be an option with some lenders (but not very many) down to the present. It is instructive and sobering that good ideas like this do occur to relevant actors in the building sector, but fail to spread. There are indications that such failure can come from people not wanting to look too unorthodox to their peers, instead of from hard-headed analysis of risks and returns.[57]

Without an energy efficient mortgage of some kind, any extra features that might save energy leave buyers wondering if they have the money and if the projected savings from the extra features will be high enough to be worth it. We're back confronting the full waterfall rather than the gentler rapids, and it's no surprise that many turn away.

People's willingness to invest in unconventional features can also be affected by their thinking about long term market value and resale potential. Many Americans move often, so they aren't going to be in a house long enough for savings on the energy bills to add up to much. Perhaps adding solar panels or extra insulation would increase the resale value of the house enough to justify the investment, perhaps not. Some unusual feature like having serpentine walls instead of straight ones might enhance the first owners' life in the new house a great deal, but make it awfully hard to sell later. Those who see calculations like this as the primary things to worry about in considering a house are likely to have a jaundiced view of the Lovins's, and a real estate appraisal ten years later actually concluded that its unusual layout reduced its value as a family house. It wouldn't have been a success as an investment property.

However, the proper investment question for resale-oriented people is a different one: could one profitably build a house of mainstream character profiting from the possibilities for passive solar heating and a superinsulated envelope that the house demonstrated and publicized? The rough equality with area construction costs showed that the approach wouldn't be disqualified by expense.

Expense is only half the equation in building or buying houses, of course. The other half has to do with appeal, and appeal is a doubly or even quadruply slippery matter. There is what truly appeals, what the industry thinks will appeal, what appeal is constructible, and what kinds of appeal buyers will settle for. The econo-mystic perspective on house buying is centered on selling eventually. Never mind what lives are lived in the house between now and then. What value will the market allow at that future moment? This vests authority about design decisions in unknown future persons, so the only workable strategy is a generic one: avoid the unfamiliar and join a self-reinforcing consensus as to what an appealing house is like.

It's true that a house is their biggest capital asset for most families who own one, and its market value does matter. What it's worth whenever it's sold has large consequences for people's finances and their lives. Unfortunately, the econo-mystic mindset often expands this important concern into being the only concern about the value of the property, obscuring or greatly diminishing the value of how life might be lived in the building. The Lovins house offers a different path. It invites visitors to concentrate on the experience of living. Never mind the business of selling me years from now, it says, and allow the sunlight, the rough stone, the lush plantings to speak to you in the present. Let what you hear include the additional murmur that the place is doing its small part in making a sustainable world. And let your unavoidable consciousness of cost issues be soothed by the thought that much less money than normal is flowing out of this house because less heat is flowing out and more sunlight is flowing in.

The experience of the place: one person's meditation

Unfortunately, most actual visitors to Amory's house can't concentrate on experience much, because they are moved along at a good clip by Amory or an RMI staffer pointing out its many features. My own repeated visits to the house during the writing of this book have allowed me some spells of being there at whatever pace I chose, opportunities to meditate more extensively on the various dimensions of experience that can be present in a house, and to sense ways that they show up in this one. I kept returning to a marvelous thought from an influential theorist, Christopher Alexander. He centered his thinking on what he called "wholeness", a term that has appealing auras but begs for definition. He provided or evoked this in several ways over the course of his long, productive career. Good for our purposes is the following, from 1987:

> The whole is coherent. It is truly whole, not fragmented, and its parts are also whole, related like the parts of a dream to one another, in surprising and complex ways.
>
> The whole is full of feeling, always. This happens because the wholeness itself touches us, reaches the deepest levels in us, has the power to move us, to bring us to tears, to make us happy.[58]

This departs from the common approach to definition quite a lot. My laptop's dictionary, for example, says wholeness is "the state of forming a complete and harmonious whole; unity."[59] Alexander's poetic, evocative phrasing is clearly after something more. First, he highlights coherence. A building which is whole should have parts which all make sense together. It's no random assemblage that happens to stand up and keep the rain out. You should be able to sense that the parts truly belong together, and there may be many ways this happens. "Complete" and "harmonious" bring to mind legitimate but conventional ways. Suggesting that the parts of a building might relate to each other like the parts of a dream opens a much wider doorway to variations in layout, placement, and materials, even very unconventional and unexpected ones.

One example is the Vietnam Memorial in Washington, D.C. In black, not white stone, it descends below ground level, not rises above it, the names it records are given by date of death, not by alphabetical order, and the stone is polished to reflect the faces and gestures of those who come to read and even touch the names. All these departures from convention generated intense controversy at first, but it was not long before the memorial became one of the most sought-after points in that city of memorials, with the recognition that these choices in the design reinforced and deepened each other.

But coherence by itself is not enough. We all have encountered buildings which are coherent, but impersonal. We call them cold or mechanical or inhuman. The parts make sense together, but they do not engage with the human processes of their occupants, or they do engage with them, but only with the purpose of dehumanizing them—in prisons, for example. Alexander insists that the buildings we want can and should move us in deep and genuine ways. Feeling is essential. We all do know buildings which are welcoming, or warm, enlivening, uplifting. Or sobering, humbling, challenging, calming. They connect in some profound way with human life. This is what Alexander means by feeling. A building that is whole is full of this kind of feeling.[60]

The success of the Vietnam memorial comes from its ability to call up feelings. They vary widely, from personal grief to reawakened sense of brotherhood or trauma to pride or distress at what the nation did at that difficult time. Visitor after visitor testifies to this. Few buildings have this profound an effect on those who visit or inhabit them, but Alexander presses us to look for feeling in the spaces we design, and to make the most of clues for achieving it.

Equally strong but quite different coherence and feeling are present in the American high school basketball court. I mean the room as a whole —wooden floor, hoops and backboards, stands, electric scoreboard, very high roof. These are spaces of pride but no pretensions to design. They are generic, not unique; they speak to just one part of the lives they intersect; their own life has more hours of dozing than wakefulness. When a game is on, however, or even when it is just practice, they are places of intense feeling, and they are places that intensify feeling. Excitement, hope, tension, resolution, achievement, dismay can all be present, and the ways sound reverberates in the place, light gleams off the floor, the floor thumps and squeaks under players' feet, the hoops focus attention and effort, and the seats crowd everyone together all make Alexander's wholeness vividly present.

Alexander saw little sign of this in the efforts at green building going on around him. Impersonal engineering seemed to monopolize designers' attention. Clearly one could use less energy in providing basic shelter, but in his judgment this was being done by turning buildings into machines. The Saskatchewan House (chapter 3) is one example. He would say its ponderous south-facing facade, monopolized by solar collectors, is only interested in capturing the largest possible amount of solar energy. It does nothing to contribute any support to the ongoing lives of its occupants. There is justice to this charge, and much sustainability-oriented design at that time and since has suffered from this shortcoming. But the Lovins house/office does not. Its key arrangements for sustainability—the ways it takes in sunlight, tempers and distributes it, and husbands its heat against the demands of the severe climate outside—make the building much more whole, more coherent and full of feeling, than a conventional building would have been.

Meaningful order[61]

To begin to appreciate coherence in the Lovins building, let's go back to where we began—standing in the entry space, with a very solid door just closed behind us, a long bench in front of us with a heap of orangutan dolls at its left end, four or five small steps going up to a closed door on our left, and a shadowy passage on our right leading toward a flash of green and sunlight.

What's in immediate view definitely has one kind of order. It is tidy and well kept. But I'm looking for something deeper, attending to what messages and feelings arise from the structure and spaces, above and beyond tidiness. I need to be alert for ways in which that order might be surprising and complex, and for ways in which the experience of the place might move me.

The message here at the entry is, Go right. There's something to your left, but go to the right. That's where the opening is, that's where the light and foliage are. This is not a usual message. In most houses the entry message is "Keep going ahead". There is a hallway that takes you straight back, perhaps by a stair that takes you straight up. But here in the Lovins house the depth is to my right, and the darker passage followed by the bright but unusual space at the end indicates that any order in this house is a complicated one.

If the first practical test of order in a building is whether one gets lost or stymied in finding one's way, a second is whether the building's activities support or clash with each other. The physical organization of a building can be meaningful in various ways. In churches, synagogues or mosques the position of altar, pulpit, ark, or mihrab provides a natural center of attention. That arrangement of the physical space predisposes the congregation to sense the spiritual order of the world, as understood by each tradition. Theaters and legislative assemblies have similar strong arrangements for focusing attention. Sometimes a house organizes its occupants' attention around gazing out at a striking view, or focuses it on a wide-screen television, the synthetic version of one.

These are meaningful spatial and experiential orders, but they are not the only ones. Another familiar one is the family circle, organized around the hearth in many traditional cold-climate houses and around a breakfast island in many recent suburban layouts, or scattered around a family room. Even a swimming pool can be the primary source of order for a house's circulation. Amory and Hunter's house has a definite organization of this kind, centered on the greenhouse. It's intensified by the absence of barriers. The light and the foliage draw one in from the entry.[62] They are just as present to you from the office area, and from the dining/living/kitchen space. The sound of water can be heard quietly but definitely everywhere in the building except the private quarters. At the same time, the green space is arranged with paths and chairs as an additional living space for the house. It's not a separate realm; its character is distinct but influenced coherently by the life and work in the spaces around it.

This order is rather like the solar system's, with Amory, Hunter and the rest of RMI orbiting like the planets and asteroids, or visitors like a swarm of comets from far beyond, and the green space holding all these trajectories in their proper paths. It provides a strong pervasive center in the physical and symbolic order of the building, like the sun.

The different components of the extended main space convey different feelings. The wall and roof ensemble are vertical and horizontal, squared up and massive in the work and dining/kitchen areas; the greenhouse combines sloping overhead glass, earth in irregular beds, and stepping stone pathways. But the greenhouse animates every space it adjoins, while the other spaces, though present, do not generate drama or tension for the greenhouse.

This is not surprising. The greenhouse was conceived all along as a world of its own, not cut off from the rest of the house, but definitely distinct from it. Its appeal to Amory and Hunter was its immediacy, its literal grounding of their words-and-charts work of analysis and persuasion. The latter was (and is) vitally important, but it is not life itself. Naturally, then, any energizing of space flows more strongly from greenhouse to office and dining/living than the other way.

Connecting and inhabiting

The center of this building's human activity is the dining table, a phrase which is really a shorthand for the whole arrangement of spaces, furniture, and fittings in that part of the house. Set at a crossroads of walking routes, with easy access to the kitchen, plenty of visual contact with the greenhouse, and ongoing awareness of the activity in the office area, the dining table usually has one or more people at it. They may be eating and talking, may be working, may be taking a break, but the main currents of life in the building are always present there.

It's set up to be a busy place, a criss-cross of close working relationships, with visitors of all kinds from dignitaries and donors to fellow wonks and touring vacationers. There are rushed hours before grant deadlines, lunch and snacks, informal negotiations, evening parties. The dining table provides a hub for all these human comings and goings and pauses. The space around it continually reminds one of the concepts and practices all these people are exploring and developing. Sunlight is all around and there's the latest efficient lighting at night; vegetation is close at hand; stone and other real materials are there; the sound comes from bubbling water, not air conditioning.[63]

The feel of the dining table and the areas around it exemplifies the elusive but important way in which some spaces encourage or allow you to inhabit them. This is something deeper and more engaged than simply using or occupying them. Bloomer and Moore's "taking [a place] to be our own in satisfying ways" is one good way of putting it.[64] The dining table gets inhabited. People can stretch or sit up straight, converse or find some silence, hold forth or listen in, have a meal or a drink of water. The stay may be long or short. The place is truly and naturally welcoming in this way.

Other parts of the house/office are not for all comers. The small private quarters are definitely private. The materials and their shapes are much the same as elsewhere, but the spaces are more compressed, and there's no provision for foliage. The way in is tightly constrained. This area feels self-contained, even confined, in contrast to the expansive character of the more public zones.

The office area's character is different again. This space connects its inhabitants in very direct spatial and physical ways to what they know, believe and think. A dominant feature is the very tall and long bank of books, reports and resource materials, completely covering two walls. Amory's forte as an analyst was to command this material in great breadth and depth; this was also the work of Rocky Mountain Institute, and the giant library wall was both a demonstration of the institute's reach and a constant reminder of the need to continue it.

The unusual shape and configuration of the workspace was definitely not institutional. Edged by the ribbon of workstations, with its rhythms of piled paper, keyboards, office chairs, screens and carelessly dressed

staffers, this area looks more like a trailhead than a hub. It's where well-paved knowledge ends and trekking into territories of untamed information begins. Though the space is crowded, the work is always done by individuals and small teams. It is rarely relaxing. Progress is sometimes exhilarating but often slow and uncertain.

One doesn't readily think of inhabiting a trailhead. More generally in American culture, inhabiting a workplace smacks of pathology. "He lives at the office" is a description of a distorted life, even if it's a very well paid one. Ever since the rise of the factory and its white collar equivalent, the office, work is usually a place at which one gives up many hours a day and a good deal of one's self. The rest of life happens elsewhere, at the other end of the commute.

Amory and Hunter's vision for RMI was different. It shared the spirit if not the literal practices of the older world of artisanal masters, journeymen and apprentices, living under the same roof and plying their trade together. In some ways, it also prefigured (by 20 years)s the work-play-work places made famous in the early 2000s by Google and other digital leaders. Joining the family residence to the institute work area by a kitchen/dining/living area and large greenhouse was definitely an attempt to reintegrate the personal and professional elements of experience for the institute's people. It played out unevenly. On the positive side, there were days when skiing totally trumped desk work as an RMI priority, and there were parties in the work area, though no weddings. Less positively, there was rapid growth, which spilled increasing numbers of staff into more conventional workspace at the old Windstar building a mile away, and private life for Amory and Hunter fragmented. The vision of complete integration of work and the rest of life did not fully come to pass, and it turned out to have some drawbacks, but the building offered its occupants an unusual opportunity to enjoy the benefits and pleasures of inhabiting rather than merely occupying it.

The circulation path behind the greenhouse, from dining/living down the somewhat irregular stone steps, past the cylindrical storage and bathroom pods to the office area, offers another strand of experience. The 4-foot change of level creates a gentle drama of difference between the two ends, accentuated by the increasing space overhead as you goes down, because the beams and decking of the ceiling do not step down with you. The way is wide and straight enough for each end to stay in touch with the other visually and aurally, while the distance and the changes in level and headroom keep the two zones distinct.

This is completely in accord with RMI's intended work pattern in the building—a trailhead for hunting and gathering in the wilds of policy linked with a hub for person-to-person connection and support. Neither the RMI vision nor the building's design aim at tension in this linkage. The work may be tense at times; the building offers good space for buckling down to deal with it, and there is also good space for tempering it or keeping it in its place. Resonance is a far better term than tension for the goal of the building, and indeed for the result.

Edges and transitions

A provocative utterance from Christopher Alexander calls for a radical deepening of our ideas about what entrances, trailheads, and boundaries of all kinds can mean:

> The thing we called wholeness—the feeling, or the intuition, of what the wholeness is—*always extends beyond the thing in question*. If we speak of the wholeness of a person, we may be confident that this wholeness is felt through that person's connection with the world. It is not possible to be whole by being isolated from all that surrounds you.[65]

This conviction got Alexander to pay unusual attention to boundaries and edges, regarding them not as mathematical lines marking abrupt qualitative distinctions like the ones between inside and outside, public and private, or domestic and foreign, but as zones of transition in which such distinctions overlapped or blurred together. In his view, boundaries are places in their own right, where experience can be good, bad, or indifferent, and the designers and and inhabitants of buildings should do what they can to give them wholeness.

His starting insight is simply stated:

> The experience of entering a building influences the way you feel inside the building.[66]

Something similar is true about leaving, or about moving from room to room. Leaving the intimacy, good or bad, of home is an experience that influences the way we feel while going off to work. Coming in from the weather is accompanied by a strong feeling when it's fierce outside, but the transition from being exposed to being enclosed is a real shift in all weather. Indoors, the closing or opening of window blinds, the slam of a bedroom door, perhaps a throb of muted music which speaks of someone nearby but not right here, and many other moments are experiences in which the presence of a boundary is significant. Alexander asks us to notice things like this happening, and to design with these feelings in mind rather than only thinking about how to deal with physical facts like rain or cold.

The entry space of this building aims to encourage a certain feeling of anticipation in visitors, a sense that something unusual and attractive lies before them. In his role as a visionary analyst of energy affairs, Lovins had already drawn on an instinct for showmanship and an ability to shake up his audiences' assumptions in aid of new directions in policy. The entry to his house works to the same effect through its unspoken messages about direction and discovery. Expect things here to hang together in unexpected ways, it says. You'll find it happening down the passage to your right…

This was done spontaneously, without knowing Alexander's work about boundaries, and perhaps Lovins was not fully conscious of its potential effects of visitors when he was designing the house. In a paradoxical way, such an individualized, even idiosyncratic move has better chances of achieving wholeness than something more generic, in the way that dealing directly with a person is more complete and deeper than dealing with someone role-playing that person.

Edges and boundaries have effects, for good or ill, on many common concerns like health, safety, and comfort. Walls, windows, doors and other features of a house help define boundaries and give them form; they keep everything from happening everywhere all at once. We don't want to dissolve them, and we don't want to strengthen and rigidify them too much. Getting the building's help in handling them well is an important step toward a good life.

The Lovins house/office has a variety of boundaries in play, many quite conventional, some less so. At the most conventional end, all the bathrooms have doors, all the toilets have lids. No unsettling changes there. Those concerns are well contained in the customary ways.

Less conventional is the treatment of the roof, walls, and windows, the boundaries between the inside and the outer world. The heavy insulation and airtight construction are largely hidden away, but they do change what you experience indoors. The building is unusually quiet, as the extra mass in the walls, extra thickness of the roof, and extra layers of glass and film in the windows all reduce outdoor sounds a great deal, compared with normal construction. Moreover, the inside surfaces, especially the glass, don't cool down in winter or heat up in summer as much as normal. They stay closer to the overall indoor temperature. This turns out to help thermal comfort in a subtle way. Being near a hot or cold surface makes one feel hotter or colder, even if the air temperature is the same in both cases. This may well make these surfaces even less noticeable than before.

Visually, however, walls, windows, roof, and sloped greenhouse glazing catch your eyes. A newcomer to the building might not have much sense about how they affect one's sense of the place over time, but certainly wouldn't mistake their kind of presence for anything generic. The people working in the place, long-term or temporary, do know one important thing they announce—the building's ability to save energy. The flows of heat and light are fundamental connections across the boundary between between inside and outside, and the visual reminder of what the building is doing invisibly to handle them carries important meaning to the inhabitants.

The floor is a different matter, and somewhat problematic. It's basically a series of concrete slabs, one at each of the three levels. As mentioned earlier, they decided during construction not to insulate underneath them, and when the building was finished, it turned out that the floors were colder than they wanted them to be.

These reflections on aspects of lived experience in this building are mine, not those of the inhabitants. And they arise from thinking about it now, not from actually standing in the building when it was first finished. The relevance of this, you recall, is to widen the field of view as we consider what lessons the place has to offer. Sustainability is more than a matter of reducing some environmental impacts. It is about making a world that a sufficient number of people want to sustain. And so it is about the quality of lives lived. Finding ways to tease apart, discuss, debate, understand the qualitative aspects of life is then a vital part of the search. Readers should respect their own reactions to the dimensions of experience I have brought forward—order, connection, inhabitation, boundaries. You may find others of equal importance, and you may differ from my sense of how the Lovins house embodies these. As we step out in directions shown us by visionaries like Amory, the key is for us to have a wide enough field of view, to make buildings that we actually care about and which will repay that care.

---

53 A rough estimate for custom houses in the Aspen area at the time was $130 per square foot (in 1983 dollars). With the building at 4100 gross square feet, that would have made $533,000 the construction cost.

54 Boonyatikarn, S. (2004). Sustainable Architecture: Experiences from Thailand. Shinawatra University Thailand. Available at https://citeseerx.ist.psu.edu/ under 'Experiences from Thailand'

55 Numbers from Yi et al (2010). Rather smaller amounts leading to the same conclusion appear in the early journalism about the house. The quoted estimates were done as part of a careful case study of the house for the RMI Factor Ten initiative, and seem more complete, even though they were done close to 20 years after the fact, and include a quite rough allowance for the labor of installing ductwork.

56 Mortgages of this kind now provide such an established reference point for middle-class life that few realize that they are only a couple of generations old, an invention of the post-World War II period. Until the 1930s, home mortgages were typically short term (three to five years), limited to 50% of value, and ended with a balloon payment. The New Deal saw the outlines of a new system, based on the Federal Housing Administration (FHA), but it was not until the late 1940s that it thoroughly took hold, largely through local banks backed by a national system of mortgage guarantees, with mortgages covering 90% or so of value with terms of 30 years. See Lea, M.J., 1996. "Innovation and the cost of mortgage credit: A historical perspective." *Housing Policy Debate*, 7(1), 147-174 gives detail about financing; for wider background, Jacobs, J.A., *Detached America: Building Houses in Postwar Suburbia*. (University of Virginia Press, 2015) is useful.

57 Beamish, T. D., & Biggart, N. W. (2012). The role of social heuristics in project-centred production networks: Insights from the commercial construction industry. *Engineering project organization journal*, 2(1-2), 57-70.

58 Alexander, Christopher. *A New Theory of Urban Design*. Oxford University Press, 1987.

59 New Oxford American Dictionary, 2021

60 In pursuit of specific ways that coherence and feeling can be supported in the built environment, Alexander and his co-workers developed an extensive "pattern language" of spatial and activity relationships. Each pattern describes a particularly successful way of resolving some tension that arises between activities and/or physical structures and spaces. Alexander, C., 1977. *A Pattern Language: Towns, Buildings, Construction*. Oxford University Press.

---

61 For this phrase and several others in this discussion, I am indebted to thoughtful writing by Kent C. Bloomer and Charles W. Moore in *Body, Memory, and Architecture* (Yale University Press, 1977), though the focus here is quite different from theirs. It is also different from Alexander's. In trying to pin down the notion of wholeness, he concentrated on specific physical characteristics of buildings (see *The Nature of Order*, Vols. 1-4 (Center for Environmental Structure, 2002-2004) whereas I am working with the meanings they convey, such as order or boundary.

62 In the first year or so, the light was there but not the greenery. The plants came quickly, though, and the effects described have been longstanding.

63 This space meets very well the recommendation in Alexander's *A Pattern Language*: "Create a single common area for every social group. Locate it at the center of gravity of all the spaces the group occupies, and in such a way that the paths which go in and out of the building lie tangent to it." (Common Areas at the Heart, Pattern 129)

64 Bloomer and Moore, in *Body, Memory, and Architecture*, p.105

65 Alexander, Christopher, et al. *The Battle for the Life and Beauty of the Earth: a Struggle Between Two World-Systems*, p. 88. Oxford University Press, 2012.

66 Entrance Transition, Pattern 112, in *A Pattern Language*.

7: **Some 1983 Choices and What Became of Them**

With the county building officials satisfied (January 1984) and the owners moved in, the Snowmass building quickly assumed its function as the fulcrum for shifting the world, a base for actualizing the hard path critique/soft path proposal through Rocky Mountain Institute's studies, analyses and publications. The range of action was wide. Energy, economic development, water/agriculture, security; electric power utility boards, state governors, the Swedish Academy of Sciences, the *Wall Street Journal* and other news media—such were the topics and venues for RMI's national and international activity in the first six months of 1984. In contrast to the conceptual sweep and major consequences of this work, the Snowmass building was a still point at the center, the location of day to day work, the site of board meetings and official visits, and the destination for a steady flow of visitors. The building's own key function as demonstration project began, quite suitably, even before all the details were finished. Visitors getting a tour, and there were something like 2500 in the first year, or journalists doing on-site interviews, and there were at least 20 of them that year, would quite properly get the sense of a project in motion, a future unfolding.

Over the next twenty years, literally tens of thousands were shown the place, and dozens of media pieces were made about it; national and international political and professional figures came to meet one or both of the Lovinses.

These years saw the building acquire history. This included a slow accumulation of wear and tear which led to a major renovation starting in 2006. Nothing collapsed, nothing failed. It's just that time and entropy are at work on energy-saving, environmentally sound buildings, as they are everywhere. That wasn't surprising. Sustainability needs sustaining. If the first vital stage of sustainable building is about creating structures and services that have a chance of being sustainable, a next and equally vital one is figuring out how to keep that going, which means learning how to mix renovation, adaptation and rebuilding over the long haul. The

Snowmass building has now been around for over forty years, long enough to open some windows onto this second stage. Performance has been good, but renovation became important eventually, and there were indeed still some things to take care of right away.

In the later months of 1984, the building and grounds acquired their botanical components. Much of the outdoor landscaping was completed that summer, and the greenhouse got its soil and plants in the late fall.[67] The literal greening of the building came most of a year later than the legal certificate of occupancy. Fitness for habitation, as defined these days, has many physical requirements. Water, light, sewage, structure and so on have to be positively provided, but the biological aspect of a legally inhabitable building is all about absence and prohibitions. No rodents, no molds—that sort of thing. US culture has well developed ideas about the basic physical factors that make for health and well-being, but at least in the building sector, nature is still regarded largely as a threat. Just recently, there have been the beginnings of a wider understanding, for example in the work of Terrapin Bright Green,[68] but much more will be needed before designers, builders, owners, and regulators generally accept biology as a constructive partner.

Hot water was another early item. On day 1, the project had no solar panels. There were definite plans for the building's baths and sinks to have water heated by rooftop solar collectors, and there were more distant hopes for getting electricity from an array of photovoltaic solar panels. The collectors did go in before too long, in November of 1984, and duly provided hot water thereafter, retiring the backup propane heater to genuine backup status. Photovoltaics did not arrive until 1990, and then they only covered a portion of the building's load. The sun's major contributions to the building's energy needs came from its passive design features. Those didn't rely on pumps, inverters, valves or switches, collectors, or panels. The sun was a vital energy source for the building, but not through devices that required power or provided it. For basic comfort and habitability, all the building needed was to be open enough to the sun's light, closed enough in the right ways to keep the resulting heat in, and enough of a thermal sponge to store extra daytime heat for dark times. So it was quite fitting for it to open for business, and to open itself to visitors, months before the collectors were installed.

Visitors' Guides

To help with the stream of natural questions from all these visitors, the Lovinses wrote the first of a twenty year sequence of Visitors' Guides in 1984.[69] For the first ten years or so, these were accompanied by a handout on where to get building components or equipment items highlighted in the visits. The evolution of the documents provides quiet indications about how the building did its work of demonstration, as well details about how the building's equipment evolved over time.

The 1984 Guide has five pages of general explanatory text, followed by a plan of the building spread over two facing pages and showing the locations of 27 items or points of interest in a tour of the whole building from east to west. The price is printed on the cover ($1.00), and a full page each is devoted to the key people of the design/construction phase and to the suppliers or donors of services and equipment. RMI was making a fast take-off, but it was nowhere near having comfortable finances, so asking visitors to pay for the cost of printing the eight half-legal size pages of the Visitors' Guide was a matter of course, as was a constant process of tactfully soliciting donations and thanking donors. There was no venture capital providing startup money here.

The original Where to Get It handout was even simpler—two typed pages combining supplier addresses, explanatory comments, and scraps of advice in a tone that could be described as chatty-with-footnotes. There were nineteen items. Several are part of the ensemble of passive solar/superinsulated components that make up the building shell. Glazings, insulation, air-to-air heat exchangers—where to get such things was critical information for visitors inclined to borrow the concepts; it was also critical to the Lovins approach to avoid one-of-a-kind or custom-fabricated equipment in the building. The first physical steps on the soft path needed to be available to buy, but it was early days, and people would be grateful for help in finding the suppliers.

Plan in 1984 guidebook. Captions repeated below in same vertical order.

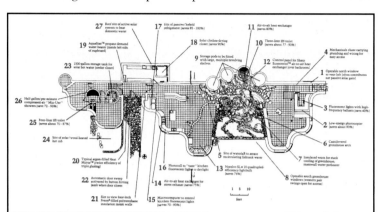

27 - Roof site of active solar system to heat domestic water
19 - AquaStar™ propane demand water heater (inside left side of cupboard)
23 - 1500 gallon storage tank for solar hot water (under closet)
26 - Half-gallon per minute compressed-air "Min-Use" showers (save 72-93%)
25 - Four liter Ifö toilet (saves about 70-87%)
24 - Site of solar/wood-heated hot tub
20 - Typical argon-filled Heat Mirror™ (twice efficiency of triple glazing)
22 - Automatic door sweep activated by button hitting jamb when door closes
21 - Slot to view four-inch Freon®-filled polyurethane insulation inside walls

17 - Site of passive/hybrid refrigerator (saves 95-100%)
18 - Solar clothes-drying closet (saves 90%)
9 - Storage pods to be equipped with large, multiple revolving shelves
16 - Photocell to "tune" kitchen fluorescent lights to daylight
14 - Air-to-air heat exchanger for stove exhaust (saves 75%)
15 - Microcomputer to control kitchen fluorescent lights (saves 70-90%)

11 - Air-to-air heat exchanger (saves 80%)
10 - Three liter Ifö toilet (saves about 77-90%)
12 - Control panel for Sharp Economini™ air-to-air heat exchanger (over bathroom)
5 - Site of waterfall to aerate recirculating fish-tank water
13 - Norelco SL*18 quadrupled efficiency lightbulb (saves 76%)

4 - Mechanicals chase carrying plumbing and wiring for easy access
1 - Operable north window to vent loft (often contributes net passive solar gain)
3- Fluorescent lights with high frequency ballasts (save 40%)
2 - Low energy photocopier (saves about 90%)
6 - Cantilevered greenhouse arch
7 - Insulated vents for stack cooling of greenhouse; mass-wall water preheater
8 - Operable south greenhouse windows (western pair swings open for access)

The majority of the Where to Get It items are fittings for the life inside the building—lightbulbs, refrigerators, toilets, showers, water heater, photocopier, wood stoves. Their relevance is partly obvious, partly subliminal. Obviously, a soft path life is more than keeping out the cold. One needs to see, eat, bathe, relieve oneself, work, and so on, and one wants the gear involved to function sustainably. We have seen already that the softness of the soft path is about needing little energy to provide these things. It also helped, in advocating for the soft path, to provide possibilities that it was easy for the audience to think about adopting themselves; that goal calls for small scale items as well as major investments or features that could only be considered if you were constructing a new building. Reducing heat losses with massive walls or air-to-air heat exchangers is all very well, but shower heads and lightbulbs are easier for most people to grasp mentally. Their functions are more tangible, and our experience turning on a light or stepping into the shower is more direct than something like a subtle change in the way a building's air is heated. Talking about smaller, more immediate household things can provide stepping stones to the larger, less visible ones.

Most of the 1984 Where to Get It items reappeared in version after version, but locating them doesn't require special instructions from a visionary any more. Today, they can easily be found with a simple Internet search. The vision had pointed in a direction that American commerce could and did pursue. Suppliers have changed, some terminology has changed, but the key items are readily available in the marketplace. Today's makers and suppliers are mostly unaware that their products were once exotic. Amory Lovins and his house/office were only part of the national process which has produced this change, but they exerted a key influence on its early stages.

The items have typically matured as products, which is to say they have been elaborated into a variety of performance levels and versions suitable for special niches. The "heat mirror" film in the superwindows came in three varieties in 1984, five in 1986, and seven in 1988. By 1991, manufacturing insulation was switching away from using chemicals that widened the ozone hole, without any loss of performance. Well insulated pet doors became available in the 1980s; March 2018 saw an online review of "Best Insulated, Weatherproof & Energy Efficient Dog Doors" listing four competing brands. One key item, perhaps the least romantic of the essential ones, was the air-to-air heat exchanger. These are now called heat recovery ventilators or energy recovery ventilators, and a recent check found 37 brands offering 413 models of varying sizes and features. Our economy doesn't stay with plain vanilla, no matter how tasty; "28 Flavors" is the American way. The good thing about this is that soft-path items that once were new or unfamiliar enough to need a Where to Get It handout are now ready at hand, in multiple versions.

A few items did not reappear as the versions progressed—insulated vents and shutters, decorative doors, a submersible utility pump, an active solar system, "Min-Use" showers. Most went on working down to the renovation. The original active system, providing solar heated water for showers, sinks, and kitchen is fully functioning today, having needed only a pump replacement or two over 35 years. Absence doesn't indicate problems in these cases. I'm sorry, personally, that decorative doors fell off the lists. The doors are there in the building, and are decorative; mentioning them as something you might want to get if you were interested in sustainability was a quiet reminder that the success of the building involves its hospitality, not just smooth functioning. My guess is that they did not fall under the announced topic for the Where To Get It list, "resource-conserving building materials and household appliances." Perhaps they also opened the door for unwanted debate over aesthetics. The texts of the Visitors' Guides do continue to point out tables and other doors from time to time for their decorative value. I'm sorry that Where to Get It didn't include more ways to get people looking for artisanal and craft elements as well as purely functional ones.

The greenhouse

If I were guiding a tour, I'd start with the greenhouse, because of how central it is to one's experience of the place. Curiously, what's in it receives a much more broad-brush treatment in the Visitors' Guides than the various energy efficient devices. The 1991 Visitors' Guide highlights 46 features of the house for attention, of which only one is in the greenhouse ("Waterfall to aerate recirculating fish-tank water"). In the Guide's explanatory text, aside from mention of the banana tree (see below) and "our Hawaiian tree fern," the plantings get only this description:

> The greenhouse provides excellent semitropical growing conditions year-round. Its terraces support a wide variety of trees and smaller plants, protected from pests by a half-dozen kinds of biological predators.

Animals get their own brief mentions; there are "two green iguanas" as well as "decorative carp and many edible fish such as catfish and bluegills, plus occasional tilapia and, in the lower tank, freshwater clams and crayfish."[70] The rest of the greenhouse section, over ten times as many words, describes physical considerations and arrangements, such as arch structure, heat collection, humidity control and irrigation. The tone, content, and proportionate attention of this coverage was much the same from 1984 through 2003.

Somewhere between 2003 and 2007, something happened to make plant life seem more important, and it became present in a whole new way in the 2007 (post-renovation) Visitors' Guide:

> Starting in August 2006, Aaron Westgate has led a major greenhouse renovation to improve soil health, broaden plant biodiversity, increase edible crop production, and improve esthetics. EDAW landscape architects David Sacks and Greg Hurst, with advice from Cheyenne Botanic Garden director Shane Smith, chose and arranged specimens to yield a year-round succession of fruits, vegetables, beauty, and fragrance. . . . The soil was rejuvenated with compost, horse manure, coconut coir, and worm castings, and a diverse spread of beneficial cover crops was planted: clover and peas to fix nitrogen, buckwheat to add carbon, and deeply rooted vegetables such as carrots and beets, which break up the hardpan subsoil with their aggressive taproots. Computer-controlled drip irrigation was installed to improve water efficiency and ensure reliable irrigation of our prized tropical crops. New specimens are now being planted, and the replacement banana trees are growing more than an inch a day, aided by tropical mycorrhizae from Fungi Perfecti and liquid worm poop from TerraCycle. The new jungle is starting to grow out rapidly during 2007.

The difference in attention is quite dramatic. This shift is another major illustration of the fact that visionary work is about paths, not end points. In 1984, the house pointed in a direction; in 2007, the house had moved that way, and went on pointing toward further possibilities. Several quite local things largely explain the Guides' cavalier treatment of the greenhouse before 2007: Amory's primary background is in physics, not biology; the lead in plant and animal aspects of the 1984 household was Hunter, not Amory. Their marriage weakened over time; Hunter moved out in the late 1980s and the couple explicitly separated about 1991. That meant that after the first five years or so, developing more sophisticated arrangements in the greenhouse or adding more detailed information to the guides wasn't likely to happen.

What is really instructive is that the Lovinses made their solid commitment to wrap the building around a greenhouse, and to have it integral with the house, without the fine-grained justifications that went with the house's other features. It wasn't there just because Hunter wanted to have it, or just because it would help heat the building. The couple shared the intuition that having sunlight pour into the heart of the building and make things grow there was at the core of what they were doing, and that was enough for them in 1984.

Actually, a theoretical justification of the sort that Amory's own work relied on, based on research showing the value of those things as contributions to the experience of living in the house, was not available in 1984, or for some years after that. The new focus in the 2007 Visitors' Guide is a fair indication of when enough research and demonstration projects had accumulated for a left-brain treatment of the biology of the greenhouse to be workable. Although farmers, foresters, gardeners and researchers have paid close attention to growing plants for thousands of years, the 1980s saw the rise of a quite new wave of investigation and initiatives in the United States. It originated from the turbulent merging of social activism with environmental concern which we have already seen generating the alternative building movement in the 1960s. It happened that homebuilding had a developed portfolio of practices and engineering knowledge which that period's yearning for transformation could quickly put to work in a burst of experiments with solar energy, alternative materials, and amateur initiatives. The moment was memorably marked by the *Whole Earth Catalog*, first issued in 1968. We've seen how this conjunction of technical knowledge, practical methods, and transformative hopes, boosted in urgency by the OPEC crisis, continued in the 1970s and led among other things to the Lovins house/ office, with the Balcomb and Leger houses as landmarks along the way.

Something similar happened in agriculture, but it was delayed by about 20 years. The 1960s saw plenty of interest in self-sufficiency; there were innumerable individual and small-group tries at raising vegetables, chickens, food fish, and so forth. However, growing things at that time was primarily a matter of conventional farming, gardening and agribusiness, three disparate though overlapping spheres. Their basic goals were worthy enough—subsistence, personal satisfaction and profit, respectively. But imagination in all three spheres was largely confined to small modifications of the world as they found it.

It was not until the 1980s that a real convergence of knowledge and practice that pointed toward the possibility of transformative changes in the food system began to happen. Agroecology emerged as a field of interdisciplinary science; there were innovations in marketing like community-supported agriculture (CSA), and widespread concerns about the nutritional quality and climate impacts of conventional agriculture. The 1992 Rio conference (officially the United Nations Conference on Environment and Development) is a key mid-way landmark. The convergence went on gaining strength through the 90s and is continuing.

Growing things in the Lovins house was on a tiny scale compared to the regional food systems of interest to the UN conferees, or even the modest farms marketed through CSA's. Hunter did grow vegetables, and there were fish, and pigs from time to time, but the Visitors' Guides from 1984 through 2003 show that the growing of plants and animals was not really a showcase activity for the place, except in one respect. From early on, two or three specific inhabitants were highlighted—two iguanas for a while, that tree fern once or twice, and in most years after 1990, the banana plants, which became a mainstay. First there was just one banana plant, a gift from a departing intern, bought from a local nursery under the impression it would stay small, never fruit, and simply be a somewhat unusual thank-you. To Amory, always delighted by the unexpected and always on the lookout for ways to dramatize his conceptual insights, it was wonderful that the plant transcended all these expectations. As he wrote in the 2003 Guide, "as soon as it tasted the twelve-year-old horse manure it was planted in, it went bananas.[71] In the first year and a half it grew to seven meters and gave five bunches of fruit." The greenhouse has had six banana plants since then, yielding a steady flow of crops, over 80 by now. Bananas are now a favored prop when Amory presents himself in a talk.

Amory Lovins and recent banana crop

The point about bananas and iguanas has not been about alternative agriculture; they have served as light-hearted but basically serious testaments to the building's ability to maintain a semitropical indoor environment through the rigorous winters of the Colorado Rockies. From 1984 to 2003 or so, the mere presence of plants like bananas or tree ferns and animals like iguanas was what mattered. The details of growing them were not particularly important.

The changed content and tone in the 2007 Guide reflects a recognition that small-scale agroecology had matured to a point where long-standing knowledge about how plants grow (proper soil pH, mineral balance, irrigation regimes, etc) could be married to an agenda of sustainability. The items of knowledge were not particularly new, but the goals they might serve had expanded significantly. It had become clear that growing things might be a major part of shaping "a clean, prosperous and secure low-carbon future," as RMI's home page currently summarizes what the most important characteristics of American society, economy, and politics would be in a sustainable world. Hunter and Amory had recognized intuitively from the beginning that plants in houses were important among the possibilities they were assembling. They did not extensively foretell the blossoming of eco-agriculture in the succeeding decades as a transformative movement in food production, but that has certainly validated their intuition about good life in buildings with technical understanding that has steadily increased and spread.[72]

Plants as indicators of performance

The banana plants can help us understand another surprising feature of the Snowmass house and its operation: the relative scarcity of measurements. You and I might think that setting out to demonstrate the viability of the soft path would include scattering instruments around the place and generating streams of data. That was the center of Balcomb's project. For a flamboyant project like the Lovins's, with a particular interest in persuading people, such a program of measurement might seem especially desirable. Certainly, having that kind of data would provide more precise evidence for understanding how the building has functioned. But the demonstration Amory and Hunter set in motion and Amory has sustained has not been about living in a laboratory, or about living in a lab-coat mentality, observing themselves and their co-workers and visitors like experimental subjects.

One could say a great deal about measurements, data, lived experience, the values they support, and the tensions between them. Perhaps it's better to just lay down a few brushstrokes. First, the absence of measurements for the Snowmass building is somewhat fortuitous. Amory intended, early on, to have the building monitored. The June 1984 RMI newsletter, the first one after occupancy, says that the University of

Colorado, Lawrence Berkeley Laboratory and the National Association of Homebuilders Research Foundation will help instrument the building. Something must have happened to this plan, however, because there is no later mention of it, and with one exception, there's no run of data on the building's performance in its first 25 years of use.

Reading the charts

The simple existence of the bananas is actually the key information one needs to assess how well the house is meeting its goal of furnace-free operation, but one available run of data is also available. It's a kind that's available to almost every householder—the electric bills. Though so common we take them for granted, these provide fundamental information about houses. This chart shows the monthly electric power use of the Lovins house for six and a half years, between January 1985 and October 1991.[73]

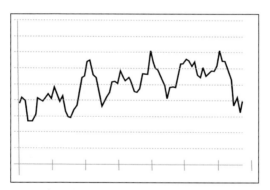

Lovins monthly electric power use, first view

I will devote a little time to this jagged line, to seeing what it can tell us. I hope your first reaction is a puzzled and politely indignant pause. A bare line like this, no matter how jagged or smooth, says nothing directly useful about how well the building has performed. It's based on a series of numbers taken from the electric bills, but presenting those instead of the line wouldn't be any more helpful.

To have the line or the numbers about energy consumption be useful we

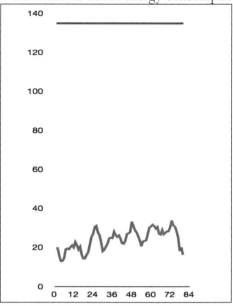

Lovins monthly electric power use with 1987 national
household average

have to ask "Consumption compared to what?" Are these amounts of
energy a lot or a little? The next chart is one possible visual answer.

The jagged line is the same usage data. The higher straight horizontal line
is the national average total energy use in 1987 for houses bigger than
3,000 square feet.[74] It refers to the whole country and households of all
kinds. It includes not only electric energy usage but also natural gas and
oil. It is a suitable reference level for the Lovins/RMI building because
the Lovins data is actually displays the same information—average total
energy use, including any natural gas and oil. It's just that the building
uses no natural gas or oil, so electricity is the whole story.

> It's not quite the whole story, because they did use propane for
> cooking, but we saw earlier that was quite a small amount of
> energy, compared to the electricity used, most of which ran office
> equipment for RMI, not their household gear.

The unit for the vertical line of numbers is kWh per day, the unit we
used before to discuss the energy balance in the building. Eyeball
estimates would put the national average at 135 kWh or so, and Lovins at

15-35 kWh, depending on the month.[75] (The bottom horizontal line of numbers counts months from January 1985 to January 1992.) So this first comparison of the most basic performance parameter for sustainable buildings shows the Snowmass building using only 15-25% of the annual energy of typical buildings of its size at the time. It is important not to let the sizable zigs and zags of the data distract attention from how dramatically low the numbers are, compared with ordinary usage.

> Comparisons like this raise all sorts of detailed questions of the apples-or-oranges kind. I might have compared the Lovins data to averages for Colorado houses, or mountain-located houses, or for home-workplace combinations, or two-person households, or houses built after 1973. A detailed pro and con discussion about the appropriate comparison, of the kind one hopes policymakers have, would be tedious here.

I chose a national average because we'd like the house to provide widely usable lessons, so we'd like to compare the house to the lots of houses. The Lovins house in the 1980s used far less energy in the 1980s than the average American house, four to six times less. The national data for that year (1987) actually indicates that 98% of US houses used more than 100 kWh/day, so even the most efficient houses of the period used far more than the Lovinses' 20-30 kWh.[76]

> I chose to compare it to houses the same size because much smaller houses lose or gain much less heat simply because their walls and roofs are smaller. In 1987, the size of your house was the biggest single factor in your energy use, much bigger than household income, harsh/mild climate, or age of construction. The steady upward creep of US house sizes since the 1950s is problematic in energy terms. Current houses are half again bigger than in 1973, which offsets a significant portion of the other improvements in energy use since then,[77] and the extra square feet may not really make life better.

If you look at the graph again, you'll see that there is a definite rhythm to the highs and lows, and there's a general upward trend. In the last few months, though, something unusual happens.

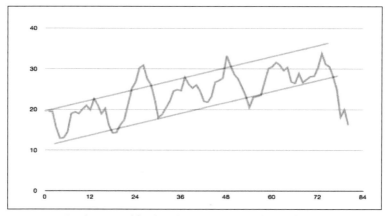

Lovins monthly electric power use with trend lines

These trend lines for the upper and lower levels of use need to be parallel, but their exact locations are pure eye-balling on my part.

> There are formulas for generating trend-lines from data, but they amount to substituting somebody else's judgment for your own, outside of any context for the data and what you want to use it for. When first exploring patterns in data, I think your own judgment should govern, with "objective" techniques called in later, if necessary, as a kind of second opinion.

I see six high-to-low cycles, roughly one a year, up to the downward plunge early in the seventh year (after month 72). A yearly rhythm to energy use is not surprising. Recalling that the data start in January 1985, mid-winter, we can see that the highest usage is in the winter months, and it drops off in the summers. There is one peak well above the upper trend line, about January or February 1987, with perhaps another around January 1989.

Questioning the charts

Patterns like these do not explain themselves, nor are they automatically meaningful. They call out for more information, and if we let them mingle with our wider awareness and information, they can raise interesting questions.

Here is one: if the house is not heated electrically, but by sunlight, why should the electric use be higher in winter than summer? Don't the appliances run all year round, the lights go on every night, and the work activities keep going? There are some minor variations from things like using the lights more in the winter because there's less daylight, but the main difference in this house comes from the use of the air-to-air heat exchangers. They run during the Colorado cold season to capture heat from the outgoing ventilation air, but are not needed in warm weather, when one can just open windows for ventilation.

> I think the winter-to-summer drop in the graph each year is about 5 kWh/day, which is very much in keeping with Lovins' original estimate of what the heat exchangers would use, back on that sheet of scribbled notes in the early design phase.
>
> The upward trend, a quite striking 70% growth in electric use over these years, was primarily a result of RMI's steady growth, from 14 full and part-time staff in early 1985 to 49 in 1991.[78] By then, many were in nearby rented space, but the original building remained a crowded hub, with times when 25 or more staff were based there. The planned occupancy was about 12.

One sign of the nature of RMI's work shows up in the striking drop in power use at the very end of the chart. In those months, the main photocopier was frequently out of order, and the chart shows this reduced the total usage by about one-third. One-third of a business's energy use in photocopying! This testifies both to how little other power the place needed, and to how very paper intensive policy and consulting work can be.

> The two spikes appearing above the trend line also came from temporary events rather than much colder weather; a spate of power saw use in the winter of 1987 and a pump control failure in 1989 which required the electric backup water heater to be on much more than usual.

This exploration of the Lovins power data is typical of what real-world data requires. It never speaks for itself; the numbers are unambiguous, but their meaning is not immediate. There must be interpretive work. Here we've found a suitable basis for comparison, given what we're interested in, and inferred some information about energy use from the rhythm and patterns. Using these additions, we can summarize the six-plus years of energy performance as follows: it was strikingly low for a building of this size; it showed a readily understandable annual rhythm;

there were no lasting disruptions; and energy use grew as the occupancy and activity in the building increased, but remained far below the national average.

Warm enough?

Low energy use doesn't guarantee indoor comfort. In the 1980s the knee-jerk anxiety associated with reducing energy was about freezing in the dark. This was simplistic in the extreme, but it posed a legitimate enough question (even if many of the questioners were not disposed to listen to actual answers). It is fair to ask whether the Lovins house was warm enough. The answer is, yes, definitely warm enough for those who lived and worked there, and for the other living things in residence.

If we had to do without the decisive evidence of the bananas, the available evidence for this would be scattered, uneven, and qualitative, but it still would show it. We need to recognize that comfort is a slippery notion. Here is the official definition of it by the American Society of Heating, Refrigeration, and Air Conditioning Engineers (ASHRAE), a cautious, measurement oriented, self-consciously down-to-earth professional association of engineers:

> Thermal comfort is "that condition of mind which expresses satisfaction with the thermal environment and is assessed by subjective evaluation."[79]

They don't know of any impersonal metric that can tell comfortable from uncomfortable conditions. There is no comfort meter. They know, and we all know, that high and low temperatures have a lot to do with discomfort; so do high and low humidity, winds and breezes, hot or cold surface nearby, and a number of other factors. Unfortunately for the engineers, there is no way of combining all these measures into a single index which guarantees comfort. You have to ask people if they are satisfied or not, or you have to give them ways of adjusting temperatures, air flows, what they are wearing, and so forth until they are satisfied.

> When systematic surveys of thermal satisfaction have been done, typically in white-collar work settings, it's turned out that the average satisfaction for conventionally heated and cooled workplaces and public buildings is only mediocre. A large part of

the problem seems to be that people have no ways of adjusting those environments, so they have to accept conditions that are only tolerable, not positively comfortable.[80]

No one ever surveyed RMI workers about their experience of the building. I have talked with a few, and the striking thing is how little the building figured in their recalled experience. The work was exciting and absorbing. Amory was fascinating and somewhat quirky. There were terrific discussions around the big table next to the kitchen, especially when interesting visitors came through, which was often. There were times when they noticed being cold, but not often. They were actually busy changing the world, and the fulcrum for the lever they were using did not garner much attention.

This is being thermally satisfied in a relatively unconscious way. There is an absence of discomfort. I suspect this comment by Chip Brown, a journalist visiting Amory in 1987, is fairly accurate about the relation between experience and physical conditions in the building:

> A life as elegant as his is bound to acquire an aura of myth, but the truth is that nothing is as exact as a page of numbers. It turns out winters in utopia can be chilly. The energy-efficient appliances extolled in RMI's visitors' guide do not include the two 600-watt space heaters that are occasionally plugged into the grid. The throngs who come on tours do not see the institute staff occasionally donning long johns and fingerless gloves.[81]

One should read this in quite a literal way. "Occasionally" means occasionally; "can be" does not mean "was usually." If the space heaters were on at all regularly, it would show in the electric bills. 1200 watts, on for a full working day, would add 12 kWh to the day's total, about twice what the heat exchangers were adding to the ordinary winter peaks. This could not have happened often, or the difference between winter and summer usage would be much larger than the record shows.

The record doesn't show how much wood went into the two small stoves, but interviews about the 2006-2009 renovation indicate they were on more and more in winter as the years went on and the building's weather stripping and door seals began to leak more.

The one repeated comment from these conversations was about the floor being cold in the early years, even though the air temperature was not. This probably came from the decision not to insulate the underside of the slab. Lovins' thinking was that over time, the building would heat the earth underneath to the average indoor temperature and would then enjoy a great year-round stability from a giant thermal mass effect. This may well have happened eventually, for the comments about cold floors were mostly about the first years, but it didn't happen quickly.

In the end, however, the best testimony about the building's thermal environment is still the eloquence of the banana plants. The original plant produced 27 crops over the dozen years of its life. Its successors have done the same. Banana growth and hardiness vary a certain amount, according to the variety, but they all stop growing at temperatures below about 60° F and above 100° F. Good growth is reported when daytime temperatures are in the high 70s to mid 80s and nights stay above 65. Fruiting is a good sign that these good growing conditions have been continuously present over the 4-6 months between crops. If thermal comfort is expressed satisfaction with thermal conditions, the banana plants have been very comfortable, and if anything, their comfort needs are somewhat greater than ours.

Compact fluorescents

About half the points of interest in the 1984 Visitors' Guide address heat and sunlight—the Heat Mirror windows, the insulated walls, the heat exchangers, and so on, which together make up the passive solar/ superinsulated system of the building. The other half are equipment— energy-efficient photocopier, low-water-use toilets, energy-conserving lighting controls. This list includes a particular lightbulb, "the oddly shaped light-bulb near the south end of the living room ceiling." This was a Philips SL*18, one of the first commercial compact fluorescents.

Philips SL*18 compact fluorescent lightbulb

This bulb is worth a pause for the what it has to tell about how sustainable technology flows onward and how the Lovins project has part floated, part paddled energetically forward in this stream.

The bulb is an archetypal example of the unfolding of a soft-path vision. Looking back over thirty years, one encounters some lessons over and over in the evolution of green building. One such lesson is that a sustainable visionary's role is to point society in a new direction by showing the first steps along a path which cannot be defined very far until those first steps are taken. They're very far from being the last ones, but they are the steps with which the important journey has to begin.

Fluorescent lighting was very familiar in the US in 1984, having proved itself to be a reliable, low-cost source of indoor lighting for World War II production lines. It spread rapidly in industrial and commercial use in the post-war period, but its somewhat harsh light and technical difficulties in making small units restricted its use and desirability in people's homes. The 1973 oil crisis spurred intensive work on energy efficiency by the major lighting companies in the US and Europe, and some key technical moves were found which allowed much smaller bulbs to be made. It looked as if they might be made cheaply in the long run, but the cost would not be low at first, because the major investment needed for mass production facilities would need to be paid off.

> In fact, the major US companies turned aside from compact
> fluorescents in the later 1970s, because they could not see a
> profitable path for tooling up, creating a market, and distributing
> them.

It was European firms who brought this technology to market, and
continued development saw a proliferation of shapes, sizes and
configurations.[82] The SL*18 in the Lovins house came from Philips, the
giant Dutch maker of electrical and electronic gear; its products were
sold in the US using the brandname Norelco, for copyright reasons. It
gained its place in the Lovins house in part because it offered light
equivalent to a 75 watt bulb's, but only needed 18 watts to do it. Just as
important, though, was its physical form; it was small enough to fit in
many existing lamp sockets and fitted with a screw-in base. Finally, it
promised to last five times as long as a standard incandescent bulb, so its
much higher purchase cost would get spread over enough very low cost
operating hours for its total cost of use to come out well below a
standard incandescent's.

This possibility of this double benefit, getting better performance and a
lower cost, flies against the common notion that you get only what you
pay for. For better performance, you should expect to pay more—so
goes conventional wisdom. This notion has plenty of support in
everyday experience, but it's not always the case. Amory's biggest
contribution to the search for sustainability has been his success in
finding and publicizing counter-intuitive double-benefit situations like the
compact fluorescent.

One must admit that pursuing such double benefits often involves
redefining performance or cost or both; these innovative steps expose
you to a different family of risks than the usual ones; often, they turn out
to stretch your mind and values some. Such things are real enough as
burdens, even though they are largely carried in the mind and heart. The
benefits may be double, but they are not weightless. Some complications
like these appeared as the story of compact fluorescents unfolded.

Fluorescent light was not popular in American houses in the 1970s. The
problem was partly about the quality of their light, partly about their size
and shape, and a lot about how householders of the mid-20th century

wanted to live. Fluorescents grew up as long tubes. They provided a low cost, reliable way of illuminating broad areas like factory floors or commercial offices quite uniformly, and they spread rapidly after the war in such settings. By contrast, household electric lighting had grown out of the world of candles and oil lamps, so it naturally developed to provide glowing points or bubbles of light, bulbs instead of tubes. Bulbs in lamp-like fixtures provided plenty of illumination for small, household-size groups, and allowed a familiar differentiation of places in a room. Broadly uniform illumination was not required, or valued; it was associated with factory and office environments.

Adapting the existing technology of fluorescents to make bulbs instead of tubes first called for making narrower tubes, because those could be bent into u-shapes or spirals or the like. Those shapes, more or less the size of bulbs, would be compatible with existing household habits and expectations. They could be made small enough and given the right bases to fit into existing fixtures.

> Unfortunately, there was a major technical problem: fluorescents depend on special coatings on the inside surface of the tubes to emit their light, and the standard coatings for industrial or commercial tubes eroded quickly in the much narrower tubes, much too rapidly for commercial acceptability.

It was fully forty years after the invention of the first commercial fluorescent in 1938 before engineers at Philips found a family of durable enough coatings for narrow tubes. The SL*18 was on the market two years later, in 1980. At that point, it fully met one of Amory's key criteria. He was clear that the first stepping stones along the soft path needed to be solid, not potential, not promises, not "real soon." They needed to be actually available, things one could, in this case, actually screw into a light socket and turn on.

The SL*18 was out of the lab, available to anyone who wanted one. At the same time, it was the first of its kind. One would expect it to be an immature device, and it was. Being on the market didn't mean it didn't have problems. In the words of J. D. Hooker, a historian of lighting technology,

> Although the SL lamp is technologically a great milestone, it is
> easy to see why it was slow to penetrate the market. Most notable
> is its great weight—owing to the conventional magnetic ballast
> inside, the mass of the lamp is more than half a kilogram and this
> was prone to make many table and standard lamps top heavy and
> quite unstable. The larger dimensions meant that it wouldn't fit
> into small shades, and the run-up time of almost five minutes
> also proved unacceptable.[83]

The SL*18 was very much a first stepping stone. Within a very few years,
the "ballast" function, essential for controlling the electric discharge
inside the tube, could be provided electronically, using very light-weight
silicon circuitry. The lamps could now be much lighter and smaller, and
they started up more rapidly when you turned them on.

Even so, the path for compact fluorescents from 1984 to the present has
been rocky, especially in the US. Whereas 40-60% of northern European
households had them by the late 1990s, only 10% of US households did.
The households that did have them didn't have many of them; they
accounted for under 1% of US sales after 15 years or more of
commercial availability. The story is a lesson in sustainability as a search,
and in what visionaries like Lovins do and don't provide.

The basic problem was that compact fluorescents were the answer to a
question no one in the US was asking—not the users, not the
manufacturers, not the sellers. Existing residential lighting was such a
mature and well integrated system that its users could largely take it for
granted. Incandescent bulbs were cheap; their operation was convenient,
their light quality was good, and the systems for manufacturing and
distributing and disposing of them were very well tuned and smooth
running. Replacing them was simple. From a householder's point of view,
they presented no problems.

Much the same went for the retailers and manufacturers. By 1980, the
industry was dominated by three very large firms, General Electric,
Philips, and Osram-Sylvania. The engineering and organization of mass
light-bulb production was well in hand. All the key coordination
questions, like bulb sizes, electric power demands, the physical mating of
bulbs with fittings, or suitably protective packaging, were settled. Retail
was largely through supermarkets, and usually only one brand was

offered in any given chain, thanks to exclusivity agreements with the manufacturers. This meant competition for sales was happening out of consumers' sight, in executive offices, not in advertising campaigns or in the aisles of the stores. Light bulbs were a household consumable like soap or toilet paper, part of the normal, routine, don't-surprise-me background of ordinary life.

Compact fluorescents emerged as technical possibilities from the research arms of the major manufacturers, as part of a normal business process for exploring potential new markets. But their primary appeal was efficiency, which has never been a high priority for American consumers. Performance matters, and purchase cost matters; but cost of operation doesn't matter as much, especially when it's only experienced as a small component of the monthly electric bill, which most people just pay automatically in any case. As far as performance and cost were concerned, "throughout the 1980s, and even into the early '90s, consumers who tried the early models found plenty not to like about the new technology," in the words of a 2006 study commissioned by the US Department of Energy (DOE).[84] The compact fluorescents of that period were bulky, or slow to light, or failed early, or were dim, or hummed, buzzed or flickered, or gave color-shifting illumination—many had several of these problems at once. The very name "fluorescent" reminded people of the somewhat harsh, faintly flickering overhead light fixtures in their workplaces, and word circulating on the grapevine about associated health and discomfort issues. On top of everything else, the first cost was very high, for a light bulb, and that would have been a barrier to acceptance even if the claims of very low long-term cost because of long life had been reliable.

Lifetime was a key issue for this form of lighting; the value proposition had to be that high first cost would be spread over many more hours of use than a conventional bulb could deliver. Knowing this, the manufacturers duly tested their products according to an established industry-wide procedure, and chose a statistically safe claim for expected life. As far as one can tell, this was done openly and honestly; tested this way, compact fluorescents do very reliably last far longer than incandescents. Unfortunately, the procedure had the bulbs on continuously and didn't probe the effects of switching them on and off; household lights are typically turned on and off many times a day, unlike industrial and commercial lights. That doesn't affect the life of incandescent bulbs significantly, but it turned out that it takes a big toll on fluorescents.[85]

The result was that compact fluorescents failed earlier than the advertisements claimed they would. Not all of them failed early, but enough of them did to drastically dampen householder enthusiasm about saving money. Other technical shortcomings of early compact fluorescents have yielded to ongoing engineering improvement, but lifetime has remained a troublesome issue because of the shadow it casts over the whole value proposition.

If Lovins had known all of this he might still have bought the SL*18 for the Snowmass house, and even have highlighted it in the guide. It pointed toward a future that could be pursued, could be reached for, could be brought into being. It fit the standard sockets; its phosphor coatings were durable; its color rendition was good; it used a fraction of the usual power for the amount of light it gave, and it was on the market, produced in quantity by one of the three dominant lighting companies. It also was bulky, weighty, and costly. It was not the ultimate lamp, but it was a milestone in the old sense: it marked real progress and pointed further along a path. It fit with Amory's vision of a future in which familiar forms and levels of comfort will be achieved with low environmental and social cost, thanks to wise balancing of high and low technology.

This path has had its twists and turns, as one should expect. After the "plenty not to like" period of the 1990s compact fluorescents achieved quicker starting, better color rendering, less dimming over time, and other performance improvements, but they were never dramatic enough to erase the early blemishes on its reputation. They were not easy to make, and quality was not uniform between manufacturers, either. The period did see falling prices, widespread action by power companies to encourage their adoption, and slow but continued sales increases. Some governments took all this as justification for taking steps toward banning the old incandescents. That would have increased energy efficiency, but it aroused notable degrees of consumer resentment about "nanny state" intervention. And then a competitor arose, in the late '00s and very strongly after 2010—the light-emitting diode (LED).

LED technology moved very quickly, modestly but genuinely outperforming compact fluorescents in efficiency and the other areas of interest. By early 2016, their costs had plummeted and sales had exploded to the point that General Electric announced it was phasing out production of compact fluorescents in favor of LEDs. The Federal program which awards the "Energy Star" label to top-performing products after rigorous testing raised its efficiency standard in 2017 to a level which excludes compact fluorescents in favor of the current generation of LEDs. The compact fluorescent bulb had come to the end of its pathbreaking role in low energy lighting for American houses.

At the Lovins house, this passing of the leadership baton was marked early, as one would have expected. The major renovation in 2008 replaced the compact fluorescents with LEDs, a new milestone.[86]

The LED takeoff has benefited from the ways compact fluorescents have opened and redirected the lighting industry over the decades since 1980. They allowed energy efficiency in lighting to become an issue; electric utilities, motivated by their own business and regulatory situations, floated extensive incentive and distribution programs which became a completely new channel for providing light bulbs; bulbs also started being sold at home improvement stores, not just supermarkets; performance and appearance became topics of consumer attention and media comment; even the slow pace of US adoption had a good effect, leading to close and constructive examination of the whole chain of production, selling and use. Most significantly, the existence of a viable low energy alternative prompted several national governments to legislate bans on incandescent lighting. For all their shortcomings, compact fluorescents shook things up. The present LED takeoff would have been impossible without them.

Refrigerator

Item 17 in the Visitor's Guide was "passive/hybrid refrigerator." (I am only spending time on these two, not all 27.) For refrigerators, the soft path actually began eight years before, in California, with a breakthrough insight and a chance meeting that the Lovinses had nothing to do with. It has continued unbroken to the present, and is a striking validation of their belief that familiar comfort levels and radical efficiency improvements can go hand in hand.

The story can be told in three pictures. The first two are ads, from Hotpoint in 1973 and KitchenAid in 2015.

Both of these pictures show abundance in the American style. The wide, deep shelves are crammed with food delight; there are pull-out drawers which hold more; there is a freezer as well as the basic cold box. All this could be yours in 1973, courtesy of the Hotpoint corporation. And even more of it could be yours in 2015, because that unit is nearly 25% bigger (25.8 cubic feet compared to 20.8). Moreover, the thickness of the left hand door in the 2015 unit strongly suggests an integral ice cube maker and water dispenser. The path from 1973 to 2015 saw an increase in features as well as in size.

The surprise hidden in these pictures, something astonishing to most conservatives and also to most progressives, is that typical 2015 refrigerators, like this one, use less energy despite their increased size, and cost less in real dollars, than their 1973 ancestors. The reductions are both large—they use 72% less energy and they're 52% cheaper. They resulted from steady downward trends for both energy and real prices over the 40 years, while sizes slowly but steadily increased. The year by year data which confirm this could be laid out in a table or detailed chart,[87] but the meaning is amply conveyed just by the lines themselves: the volume goes up, the price and the energy use go down.

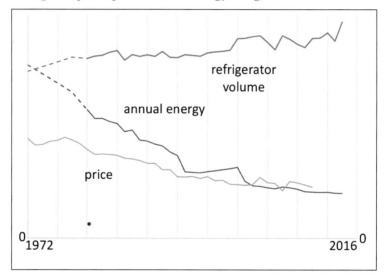

Trends in US refrigerator size, annual energy use and price, 1972-2013. (Redrawn from report by Mauer et al, "Better Appliances"—see endnotes)

These are averages, with the prices adjusted for inflation. As you might expect, the Lovinses didn't install an average fridge; they went to Sun Frost, a small maker of top-efficiency models, and got one whose energy consumption is indicated by the small red dot on the chart. It only used 8% of the industry average. The price was high, but once again the point was to model the future, indeed the readily accessible future. Their refrigerator was commercially available, not just a dream, and nothing in it was intrinsically expensive. If it were brought into mass production, the costs would fall dramatically, in just the way that the costs of the mainstream models shown in the lines on the chart did.

The Lovins' Sun Frost machine did have one feature that challenged an industry assumption about its market. In addition to the normal set of coils for discharging heat from the cold compartment, it had an extra loop that ran out through the kitchen wall to a heat exchanger to be used in cold weather. (Snowmass has plenty of that.) This loop can run without a motor or compressor, provided it is cold enough outdoors, so cooling the fridge at such times is free, in energy terms.[88]

The extra loop's need for an outdoor connection does run counter to the industry's established assumption that its units should be able to be placed anywhere within reach of a power outlet, in a kitchen or elsewhere. In choosing a unit with extraordinary energy performance, the Lovinses were giving up a certain flexibility in their kitchen layout. This was not a profound challenge to American lifestyles, since analogous constraints like bathrooms needing fan exhaust to the exterior, or kitchens requiring direct access to the garage for unloading groceries, are not uncommon. But it does represent a point where lifestyles and the building practices that service them might want to shift somewhat to take advantage of a clever insight into energy performance.

We've seen that the refrigerator industry was making great progress in efficiency during the 1980s in any case, progress which has continued to the present. This was a stream Lovins could float in without having to paddle much. The key insight and the right political moment had occurred in 1976, well before the Snowmass project. A top-notch Berkeley physicist named Art Rosenfeld had been moved by the OPEC oil crisis to take some time away from high-energy particle research to get informed about energy affairs. He was one of several people at the time who realized that increasing energy efficiency could help balance supply and demand in electrical power systems just as well as building new power plants could. Since new plants are expensive and have to be paid for through higher power bills, and since in California, where Rosenfeld was based, there was also great political opposition at that time to nuclear power, it made sense to look into how much efficiency could do, and at what cost.

After some attention to heating and cooling buildings, Rosenfeld and a graduate student, David Goldstein, turned to refrigerators, which were well known to account for about one quarter of all household energy use nationwide at that time. Then they asked the right basic question. They gathered data about the price and energy use of the various models on the market at the time, and found to their surprise:

> There was very poor correlation between purchase price and performance. Some of the lowest priced models showed the same or even cheaper life-cycle costs than models costing $100 to $200 more.[89]

Then came the key insight:

> We quickly realized that if the less efficient half of the model group were deemed unfit for the market, the consumer would not perceive any change in the market range of prices or options.

In other words, public action to ban inefficient units would increase the average efficiency and possibly avoid one or more additional new power plants, without narrowing the scope of consumer choice. No one would have to pay more, or have to forego features. A chance encounter between Rosenfeld and California governor Jerry Brown converted this possibility into a reality. Brown was looking for a way to avoid a controversial nuclear plant; Rosenfeld sketched his data on a napkin (yes, sometimes this is just how it works); and the California Appliance Efficiency Regulations (Title 20) were in place before the end of the year.

Those 1976 regulations were just the beginning of the success story outlined by the three lines (cost, energy use, and size) on the chart above. California tightened its regulations in 1980 and 1987. Federal standards, tighter again, came into play for the whole country in 1990, and were tightened yet further in 1993 and 2001. Performance has steadily improved. Meanwhile, as we have seen, refrigerator prices have kept going down. In this area, familiar comfort levels and radical efficiency improvements have indeed gone hand in hand, as Lovins argued they often could.

At this point, readers may want to pause and take stock. We've looked at just two of the 27 items highlighted in the 1984 Guide. Both developed through stories with twists and turns. One told of basically unbroken improvement; the other focused on a favored technology that is being superseded. Both involved plenty of complications.

There are 25 more items we might explore, and no doubt each has a story, probably intricate or puzzling or surprising in its turn. Is this what living in a green home feels like? Must one always be tracking the latest light bulb? Do you need to know this much about every facet of your home to live sustainably?

If you did it might be a very restless life, always fiddling and tuning; or an anxious one, always wondering if this or that feature is best, or if it is even working; or just a very inward-looking life, always thinking about yourself and your house. It doesn't need to be.

Let's pause and imagine ourselves inside the house in February, helped by the photograph, which was taken just then. The air outside is around 22° F, and has been averaging that since the end of November. There are 10 inches or more of snow on the ground.

Inside, the climate is different. The temperature is in the high 60s, the banana plants are growing well, the overhead fans are spinning gently, and we could be sitting on those chairs in the greenhouse area. Though the building is often busier than it is in this captured moment, it is the busyness of people doing the work it was built to shelter and support. There is rarely much tending of the house and its systems.

The place basically runs itself. All the careful thought that went into choosing the windows, walls, doors, lights, kitchen gear and the rest of the 27 highlighted items (by 1991, there were 46!) has crystallized into this sun-filled stone and wood structure. Daily life and work don't have to review the pro's and con's, the insights and inventions, the measurements and evaluations that went into the initial work.

Much the same goes for any conventional house. It isn't actually simpler, it's just that most of the choices have been made by habit or convention, usually not by the householder but by a builder who knows what has worked pretty well and has generated few complaints. In some important ways, the Lovins house is actually simpler than most—there's no furnace and radiator or hot air system, for example. It is just less familiar. It's true that its owner is unusual—someone who believes that every stone, when turned over, can reveal another step along the soft path, and who has had the energy and persistence to turn over a great many. It's also true that his insights and related soft path efforts by others have spread unevenly into the world of building. Coming chapters will go into that history. For this moment, though, it is enough to luxuriate in what the photograph shows is possible.

I have spent much more time on the wider US context and its evolution than an RMI staffer guiding a tour would have spent in any of these years. Their mission, energized by their enthusiasm, was to get the word out about household efficiency as part of a fully comfortable, up to date, well provisioned American lifestyle. Looking back now it is encouraging to see how that vision dovetailed with what else was afoot in the country. The accounts of the greenhouse, the compact fluorescents, and the refrigerator have shown three distinct ways this happened. Outside initiative, innovation, and dissemination moved these things forward.

PV

We're now, in the 2020s, seeing a wildfire growth in electric generation by solar cells, more officially and precisely called photovoltaics, and known to their friends as PVs. On rooftops, spare fields and stretches of desert, the dark-fronted rectangular panels have become widely familiar. For many, they're now an emblem of sustainability at the household and community level. You have seen that back in 1984 the Snowmass house began its life with electric power from the local utility, Holy Cross Electric, rather than trying to generate some of its own or operate completely off the grid. It took over six years for solar electricity to arrive there. Over the succeeding 35 years, the building has periodically added or reworked its PV setup but it hasn't done anything particularly groundbreaking or innovative. The important PV story during that time has been about dramatic developments in the national picture.

Back in 1983, PV meant "solar cells". They were in the news, but not in people's homes. The space program used them; no one else did. Energy from the sun showed up frequently in technology-for-the-masses magazines like *Popular Science*, not to mention "alternative lifestyle" publications like *Mother Earth News*, but it was being used for heat, not electricity. Collectors were available, but not cells. Solar electricity always sounded just over the horizon; the mainstream news periodically had stories like the following one, from the *New York Times* in July, 1980:

> The Boeing Corporation has developed a highly efficient solar cell capable of converting sunlight into electricity at close to the rate that the Federal Government considers the threshold for commercial application, the Solar Energy Research Institute announced yesterday.

Solar electricity for households was actually still far away. It was still extremely expensive compared to power from coal plants or hydro projects. Industry observers and corporate planners hoped and expected costs to come down steadily as fine-grained engineering and production experience worked their mass-production magic. And so they did; before the Lovins project they'd already dropped over 80% from the mid-70s to the early 80s. Nonetheless, the cost of a kilowatt-hour from solar cells was still far higher in 1983 than the cost of one from the grid. Special situations, like navigation aids or homes remote from power lines, were beginning to pencil out, but it would actually be three decades or so before PV costs started working for ordinary homes.

Even so, one might have expected a benchmark project by energy visionaries to make a centerpiece of PV. Lovins didn't, because he has always focused on how energy is used, not how it is produced. You may recall his maxim that "people do not want electricity or oil, nor such economic abstractions as 'residential services,' but rather comfortable rooms, light, vehicular motion, food, tables, and other real things." The sustainable society will place first priority on finding very efficient ways of providing the "real things." What most needed demonstrating, in the Snowmass house and in RMI's work generally, was that such efficiencies were ready at hand. The energy needs of the soft path would be far lower than those of business as usual, so one could confidently expect to provide them with renewable, low impact sources. Supplying that energy was important, but it was a secondary problem. (In fact, one of the things that made Lovins influential and important later was his ongoing demonstration that the best way to provide new energy was by saving energy through efficiency and using those "negawatts" to meet the new needs.)

Solar electricity is very good in this supporting role. It is quiet, low maintenance, very flexible in scale, quite predictable in performance. It needs no fuel, imported or domestic, mined or drilled or dammed. It does benefit greatly from the efficiency-first philosophy. A PV panel takes up real space and costs real money; the fewer panels one needs, the easier to fit them in and feel right about the expense. The idea is simple, but the difference between conventional and high efficiency situations is drastic. Recall the contrast between Lovins' energy use and the 1987 national average for houses over 3000 sq. ft; those were 20 kWh per day and 135 kWh per day, respectively. Supplying 135 kWh per day with the kind of panels and systems available in the mid 1980s would have taken almost the entire roof area and cost $252,000 for panels alone, equivalent to around $600,000 in today's dollars.[90]

By contrast, the Lovins house, with its much lower energy need, would only have needed panels taking about 500 sq. ft of roof and costing about $37,000 at that time. This was still real money. The Lovinses chose not to spend theirs on it, because it wasn't essential to their vision. But one can just about imagine finding enough trims and tweaks in a project of their size (roughly $500,000 then) to fit in $37,000 for solar cells, while there is no amount of trimming that would accommodate $252,000. It's like the difference between picking up a poodle (40 pounds, heavy but possible) and picking up a pig (250 pounds, out of the question). High efficiency in household energy use makes PV radically more feasible.

Since 1984, the cost of PV has plunged dramatically. High efficiency use patterns are no longer required, though they still help enormously. A large conventional house now would still need to pay something like $24,000 for panels, but that's in today's dollars, in which the overall project cost would be more like $1.2 million. They'd be 2% of the bill. So the cost relation between a PV system and whole house has been transformed. These days, one is picking up a corgi, not even a poodle, much less a pig.

> Lovins may also have been less interested in straining the budget to include PV, because it was already past the visionary stage in 1984. At least three dozen major corporations and research laboratories, including Exxon, General Electric, Texas Instruments, Dow and numerous of their competitors, had substantial development efforts under way.[91] They all had the same clear goal—bringing down the cost of PV to the level of coal-fired or nuclear electricity. They all knew that success would be richly rewarded. (Few of them, perhaps none of them, understood the staying power that would be called for over the three decades until this "grid parity" arrived, but that's another story.) There was no actual need for Amory or any other visionary to wave a banner for PV at that time.

Using today's panels to equip the Lovins house for its mid-1980s use patterns would be more like picking up a month-old kitten. Enough panels to cover its whole electrical load— the 4000 sq. ft house, heat exchangers, circulating fish pond, laptops, high volume copier and all— would cost about $1400.

These numbers are not the whole story, I should add. They are average costs for the panels themselves. They don't reflect differences between manufacturers, or local or seasonal variations in supply, profit margins, or what's called the "balance of system," which is all the mounting brackets and hardware, wiring, inverters and other electronics, as well as the time and overheads of the installer. Back in the 1980s, this all amounted to a very small part of the total system cost, but now that panels are so much cheaper, balance of system can come to half the total cost.

The quoted panel costs are broad averages, not catalog prices, and will probably have changed significantly by the time you read this. They do tell us truly that up-front efficiency opens the door very wide for PV, and that PV now is radically more feasible than it was 35 years ago.

With solar electricity in this supporting role for the Lovins building, it wasn't until 1990, six years after occupancy that PV was finally installed. They used a motley assortment of panels and gear assembled from a variety of donations and discount offers. Amory's reputation and the steady flow of visitors made the house appealing as a demonstration of PV products, and he was not reluctant to seek and accept donations. He describes the result as a "petting zoo," with panels from seven different manufacturers acquired over the next few years.

They were organized into two separate systems, to demonstrate two distinct philosophies about using PV. One system served the household's electrical needs (lighting, refrigerator, and other appliances in the central and west portions of the building) and was "stand-alone," i.e. not connected to the grid.

A bank of lead acid batteries served as storage for nights and cloudy days. Its capacity was 14 kWh, which could supply several days' worth of household use.

The second PV system was "grid-tied." It mainly served the RMI work area at the east end of the building (computers, copier, fax, and so on).

Instead of relying on a battery bank, it was connected to the local utility, Holy Cross, and through them to the regional power network. The grid provided backup for work nights and bad weather.

Of the two system philosophies, the grid-tied arrangement has become by far the most common across the country since the 1980s.

> The owner's up-front investment is a good deal lower, with batteries not weighing into the balance of system expenses, and there's a possibility of selling power back to the grid when household uses are below the PV output. One foregoes, however, the independence of supplying all one's own power, rain or shine. Other pro's and con's are numerous, and are still good food for the debate which has flourished alongside the continuously increasing presence of PV in the electric power systems of many states.

These were some of the central strands in the uneven US evolution of practical sustainability between 1984 and 2006, but a great deal was also happening during that time to the central notions embodied in the Lovins house's design—superinsulation and passive solar.

---

67 RMI Newsletter, 15 December 1984

68 https://www.terrapinbrightgreen.com

69 August 1984; the most recent guide in RMI websites archive is from 2007.

70 The Where To Get It handouts also have very little about plants, animals, or materials and gear for nurturing them.

71 Amory has never been averse to a ripe pun, either.

72 Permaculture has been another important stream of development since the 1990s, for the Lovins house and quite widely in the world. An article by Ferguson and Lovell provides a helpful overview. (Ferguson, R. S., & Lovell, S. T. (2014). "Permaculture for agroecology: design, movement, practice, and worldview. A review." Agronomy for Sustainable Development, 34(2), 251-274.)

73 Redrawn from unpublished chart, "Measured monthly electric intensity of Lovins/RMI building, 1985 "

74 "Household Energy Consumption by Major Fuel," EIA Residential Energy Consumption Survey (RECS), 1987.

75 The Lovins average is 24 kWh per day, but I think it is better to keep all the zigs and zags in view, rather than collapsing the seven years of history into a single number.

76 The 98% figure is a strong claim. The justification is technical: The RECS report for 1987 gives relative standard errors for its numbers. From them and conventional theory of propagation of uncertainty I can estimate the standard deviation of energy per household as 9% of the mean, so my level of 100 kWh/day is almost three standard deviations out, in the very tail of the bell curve.

77 https://www.census.gov/const/C25Ann/sftotalmedavgsqft.pdf

78 RMI December 1984 Newsletter and 1991 Visitors Guide, respectively.

79 Rohles Jr, F. H. (2007). "Temperature & Temperament: A Psychologist Looks at Comfort." ASHRAE Journal, 49(2), 14.

80 Leaman, A. and Bordass, B., 2017. "Productivity in buildings: The killer variables: twenty years on." In *Creating the Productive Workplace* (pp. 301-316). Routledge.

81 Chip Brown, "High Priest of the Low-Flow Shower Heads," *Outside* (September 1987)

82 The Museum of Electric Light Technology displays 22 independently developed variants from the years 1983-2005. http://lamptech.co.uk/index.html

83 http://www.lamptech.co.uk/Spec%20Sheets/D%20FLCi%20Philips%20SL18.htm

84 Sandahl, L. J., Gilbride, T. L., Ledbetter, M. R., Steward, H. E., & Calwell, C. (2006). *Compact fluorescent lighting in America: lessons learned on the way to market* (No. PNNL-15730). Pacific Northwest National Lab.(PNNL), Richland, WA (United States).

85 Spezia, C. J., & Buchanan, J. (2011). "Maximizing the economic benefit of compact fluorescent lamps." Journal of Industrial Technology, 27(2), 1-11.

86 https://www.rmi.org/about/office-locations/amory-private-residence/interior/; One of the renovation task lists shows a start in late 2008, so decisions were made earlier.

87 Mauer, J., deLaski, A., Nadel, S., Fryer, A. and Young, R. (2013). Better appliances: An analysis of performance, features, and price as efficiency has improved. Washington, DC, American Council for an Energy-Efficient Economy and Appliance Standards Awareness Project.

88 Amory says that his favorite number about his Sun Frost refrigerator, with its custom outdoor loop, is that each year it saves its interior volume's worth of coal from being burned at the plant which supplied its electric power

89 Rosenfeld, A. H. (2011, November). "California enhances energy efficiency." In AIP Conference Proceedings (Vol. 1401, No. 1, pp. 7-25). AIP.

90 Panel cost estimates are based on historical data from Philibert, C., et al. (2014). *Technology roadmap: solar photovoltaic energy.* International Energy Agency: Paris, France. Panel costs have continued to drop drastically, though the so-called "balance of system" costs for frames, fencing, connection to the grid, etc are not changing quickly.

91 Roessner, J. D. (1982). "Government-industry relationships in technology commercialization: The case of photovoltaics." Solar Cells, 5(2), 101-134.

8: Superinsulation and Passive Solar in Adolescence (1984-2006)

Meanwhile, in the country at large . . .

. . . there was headline news, full of turbulence, and there was a great deal of business as usual. This was the background or environment in which green building took its next steps, which were partly backward, partly sideways, partly forward.

Headlines

The years between 1984 and the apparently triumphant end of the Iraq war in 1991 produced ample headlines. This was a period of political realignment in America, with Ronald Reagan as the effective leader of a national shift away from activist government; of economic see-saws, including a major tax cut, the breaking of several key unions, the onset of a regime of steadily increasing public and private debt (called by some the "Great Leveraging")[92], and a 1990-91 recession. The digital earthquake began, and the US looked to be the sole global superpower as the Cold War ended, the Soviet Union dissolved, and the Gulf War seemed an unqualified victory. These years also saw the notion of sustainability blossom in a conceptual merger of environmental and development goals, boosted into prominence by the Brundtland Commission's report in 1987, "Our Common Future". Climate change emerged as the world's central environmental challenge, and there was a new surge of green activity and aspirations, changed in intriguing ways. That continues to the present. The next decade or so, from 1992 to the early 2000s, saw generally steady economic growth; a million-fold increase in Internet traffic; the dot-com boom and bust; the impeachment and acquittal of President Clinton; the almost invisible continuation of hostilities in Iraq, the transformative al Qaeda attacks of 9/11 and the consequent US invasions of Afghanistan and Iraq; intensification of American "culture wars" over public morals and national identity; the first female Secretary of State and the first female African-American National Security Advisor. On the climate front, there was the "Earth Summit" in Rio de Janeiro and a year later, an Action Plan by the Clinton/Gore administration. A climate skeptics' movement also launched in 1998, with strategizing sessions at the American Petroleum Institute and the circulation of the so-called Oregon Petition. The seeds of bitter future debates and polarization were sown in these years, not only for the climate question, but for US society as a whole.

Business as Usual

For the home-building industry, however, these twenty years were very much business as usual. A boom in the first years gave way to a partial retreat which ended about 1991 and was followed by steady expansion. The value of private residential construction rose from about $150 billion to $325 billion (in 1996 dollars) over the twenty years.[93] "Conventional" is a good way to describe the industry during this whole period. While the growth in passive solar buildings had been truly impressive in a way, and perhaps 50,000 of them had been built by 1984 for a growth rate of nearly 100% each year from the mere handful in the mid-70s, conventional building was averaging 1.5 million starts a year. It was still in quite a different world. Prospective home buyers might be seeing articles about passive solar or superinsulated houses every month, but could still drive around their area for a year and never see one.

The conventional pattern will be familiar to most readers, in impressions if not in statistics. At the time, three-quarters of US households lived in owner-occupied single-family dwellings built by a highly fragmented industry; 80% of the businesses had fewer than nine employees and the biggest hundred only accounted for 15% or less of all new homes. It was relatively easy to set up as a general contractor; stick-frame construction was a system with modest skills and equipment requirements, able to make fast and reasonably flexible use of widely available mass-produced materials like 2x4s.[94] Financing was provided by the mortgage system, one of the primary social inventions of the post-war period. Before World War II, mortgages were both uncommon and stigmatized, taken by many to be a sign of financial irresponsibility. A merger of New Deal programs and wartime private sector strategizing for postwar prosperity led to government subsidized mass mortgaging that legitimized the practice and proved reliable. Home ownership became within reach of any middle class family that was willing to live in a suburb, and such a life was powerfully attractive. Home-building grew into one of the country's anchor industries.

This system was well entrenched by the 1980s. The turmoils of the 60s and 70s had barely ruffled it, despite the popularity of the satirical song about "little boxes made of ticky tacky" and ample punditry critiquing suburban life. In fact, none of the principal participants, whether lenders, builders, realtors, or buyers had much reason to challenge it. Home-building was not at all ripe for disruption by new systems. Instead, it continued to slowly evolve new but inessential details and features, nicely characterized in a 2013 magazine article surveying the houses listed that spring on Trulia, the online real estate site:

> Ramblers and other homes built in the 1950s emphasize parking, such as side drive, double-wide driveway, and enclosed carport, while homes in the 1960s refer to design features like terrazzo floors and dual paned windows. The 1970s saw homes divided into multiple levels, described as spacious bi-level, split entry, and large split level home – a change from the single-story ranch and rambler homes of the 1950s.
>
> Homes built in the 1980s offer cathedral ceiling skylights, sunken living rooms, and mirrored closets. The 1990s gave us palladium/palladian [sic] windows (a large arched window flanked by smaller rectangular windows), island cooktops, and pot shelves (no, silly, that's a kitchen feature). Next came the decade of water and audio: infinity edge pools, snail showers, and pre-wired surround sound are often mentioned in listings from the 2000s. Finally, phrases emphasizing artisanship and nature popped in the 2010s, like hand-textured walls, hand-scraped hardwood floors, and natural light exposure.[95]

Each decade, in this telling, brought a small number of elaborations and new features to the basic post-war single-family home concept. US consumers have long been excited by auras of newness. The catalog above shows how far from radical this kind of newness has been. In fact, it wards off radical change.

The article goes on to mention that houses built at that point averaged 80% larger than those of the 1940s. Business as usual over the whole post-war period included an unbroken steady increase in the average size of single-family houses. One of the strongest bulwarks of this system was econo-mysticism. Everyone involved in major decisions about houses accepted the narrow concept of the house as an investment. They all assumed that was the proper center of discussion; considerations about comfort, character, and unusual needs or preferences might circle around the questions of how much options would cost and what the house's resale value would be, but they could never matter as much as those. That meant that the guesses about those economic factors that typically held sway at crucial decision points were not about an experienced present, but about an abstract future—projections of resale value, or ways to protect it. It seemed obvious to almost everyone that the anticipated resale value of a house was the obvious standard for deciding what its value for the owners was going to be.

This pattern is so common that it seems natural, but it has troubling consequences. Prudence by all parties buying a house is certainly in order. Bad judgment by a family can have very serious consequences for their lives, and the same is true for lenders or builders making a string of bad judgments. But in practice, this generally meant an excess of caution all round. There was never an outright prohibition on the unusual or innovative, but the pressures against it were considerable, ranging from refusal of mortgages or unfavorable terms to mutterings by realtors or friends about possible resale difficulty.

> Even the Lovinses' national prominence, proven earning power, and strong establishment connections didn't make their path to getting a mortgage smooth. The times did provide them with one favorable factor, the chance to make a person-to-person case with a local banker. This has become less and less available over the past thirty or forty years, as lenders have relied more and more on algorithms and hard data and less and less on their personal judgments about credit worthiness.

Main stream green

The years up to 1984 saw roughly 50,000 passive solar homes built. under the twin impulses of energy crisis and countercultural enthusiasm. The less glamorous, or less heart-touching, superinsulated approach started a few years later but grew somewhat faster, reaching some tens of thousands more quickly. Although it was slow in today's social media terms, this was about as viral a spread as was possible at the time, especially when we are talking about housebuilding and not cat videos.

However, as I mentioned, starting from a few houses meant that this encouraging growth had only risen to the equivalent of 1% or less of the average housing starts in a year. Even under conditions which favored the continued spreading of passive solar and/or superinsulation, it would have taken considerably more time for either to become truly typical.

In fact, conditions were not favorable. The price of oil fell steadily and substantially from 1980 to 1986. The atmosphere of crisis about energy eased greatly. The Reagan administration cut funding for renewables and energy efficiency drastically.

Some individuals did continue pushing the boundaries, notably with alternative materials like straw bales and rammed earth, but potentially mainstream approaches like passive solar and superinsulation still faced the difficulties of being unconventional. They also needed to address some problems of their own which had emerged from the frantic first generation of construction. Superinsulation needed to deal with air quality. Passive solar faced important challenges of predictability and adaptability, and both were part of a general issue about standards. Conventional patterns of home building and financing could continue unchallenged, and largely did. The industry did very well over those two decades; the yearly value of residential construction doubled from its 1980 level.

This growth was accompanied by greening of a certain kind. The energy efficiency of conventional houses began to increase, not in a revolutionary way but slowly and steadily, thanks to incremental improvements in building codes and equipment efficiencies. We saw one strand of this when we looked at refrigerators. The motivation for this was a direct legacy of the 1970s. The 1994 Environmental Showcase Home (ESH), built in Phoenix on the initiative of the regional electric utility, was one example of the ways in which mainstream architecture, construction and utilities were testing the acceptance of green features.

Environmental Showcase Home, Phoenix (1994)

This building descends from the work of Amory Lovins in two significant ways. The Snowmass house/office was one of the projects its designers had in view, but one of his more general insights was also important: reducing a region's need for electric power has the same effect on system capacity as building new power plants, and can well be cheaper and smoother sailing. By the early 1990s, this view made enough sense to the leadership of Arizona Public Service (APS), the electric utility serving the Phoenix region, for them to bring a variety of sustainability concepts into the day-to-day operations of the company, and to launch, in 1992, the design and building of an environmentally responsible home in Phoenix. It was intended to demonstrate the available methods and technologies that could reduce energy, water and materials use.

Their commitment was whole-hearted. The work went on for most of three years. It was well supported by corporate funds and staff; it built constructive alliances with Federal and state environmental agencies, and with Arizona State University; it selected its architect through open competition; and it included extensive research into the environmental designs, materials and equipment of the time. It had a clear goal in mind, which was stated by Mark DeMichele, president of APS, as follows: "to increase awareness and to influence those who impact the construction of entire subdivisions, not just individual homes—the construction industry and its allies." It also had a clear idea about the project's role as a vehicle for moving the region toward that goal; it was to be "a shopping center of environmentally responsible products, architectural concepts, environmental strategies, and a central body of knowledge in one location."

Most strikingly, the work emphasized an elaborate marketing plan: as the project history puts it, "A demonstration is only effective if it has an audience, and the officials first had to identify that audience."[96] They settled on three groups—production builders, custom builders, and home buyers.

> The first group was very well defined. Seventy-eight developers were responsible for 90% of new single-family construction in the area. The second group, the custom builders, were more numerous and had less leverage, but had proved over time to be in close touch with new trends and home buyers' interest in them. And of course the buyers themselves, though diffuse and varied as a group, would eventually have the last word.

This was a thoughtfully designed, carefully executed project, understood by its leaders, associated professionals and staff to be the most natural, straightforward next step in the direction pointed by the Lovins building and the other 24 "environmental demonstration homes" known to the ESH project at its design stage.

Environmental Showcase Home, living room

It did well in immediate terms. There were 30,000 visitors over the next five years, and over a dozen awards for design, environmental leadership, and public spirit. Most awards were from Arizona groups, fitting well with the goal of regional change, and there was national notice from the Electric Power Research Institute and the American Institute of Architects.

The project was not quite a shopping center because the systems on show were not for sale then and there. It was more like a World's Fair exhibit, a House of Tomorrow, in this case a tomorrow that claimed to be well within reach. All the materials and systems were already in the market, although they were often top-end items or the yes-we-can kind of product a maker carries for prestige without expecting to sell many.

Nevertheless, they were not dreams or lab items; they existed as possible elements in a dramatically lower impact way of living in the Phoenix area, and they formed an ensemble of structure and equipment that suggested an expansive mode of life.

> For some major items, like heating, the ESH had two or three different systems installed. A house would only need one, but it felt important to show that more than one option existed.

The project's rhetoric returned repeatedly to the goal of acceptability. This meant avoiding any sense of sacrifice—

> Unlike many experimental resource-efficient homes, the environmental aspects of this home enhance rather than sacrifice the comfort of the inhabitants.[97]

—while equally avoiding any aura of the radical or futuristic—

> Because a showcase home needs to be acceptable to a large number of people, the project team worked toward a more conventional design [than the butterfly roof and sunken garden of Jones Studio's first proposal].

The building actually had no inhabitants. The stream of visitors was not encountering lives actually being lived in it, only spaces the designers and engineers imagined some people might want to inhabit. The talent, hard work, and goodwill that clearly went into this effort aimed, in fact, at something more like Disneyland than the real world, and that was what it achieved.

The clearest indication of its synthetic character comes from "The Environment Comes Home," the informative, well organized, clearly written account of the project published by Arizona State in conjunction with the rest of the publicity program. The book gives a wealth of details about the materials used, with side information and rationales about energy and water systems in the ESH, but it contains no floor plan and no descriptions of the various rooms as rooms. The architect is mentioned briefly as concentrating on the "sculptural elements of the home," which means the relation of rooms to each other and to daylight, but there is little illustration of what this means, and no consideration of which family patterns the house might support well or not so well.

In fact, such an exploration would have worked against the purpose of the project. As a house of tomorrow, the ESH's goal was increasing awareness of physical possibilities and a degree of public education as to why they mattered. Homing in on a specific family life would likely have narrowed the message, and increased the chances of its simply flowing pleasantly by. Or so its proponents believed. No building does everything, and this one did what it set out do.

There doesn't actually seem to be any detailed empirical study of how visitors of any of the three target groups responded to the Environmental Showcase Home. We have no research about how many of them thought it seemed acceptable, or whether any of them were swept away by beauty there. After the immediate exhibition period ended, the site was donated to the Arizona State University Foundation, which made it available for tours and had hopes it would be used as a living laboratory. There is no sign the latter happened. In fact, one of its roles in this period was ironically a part of the utility's campaign to gain community support for expansion of its Palo Verde nuclear plant. The place was eventually sold privately; its last known use was as expansion or meeting space for the church next door.[98] We do know that a great many of the sorts of people the project intended to reach came and visited the building, but it there isn't any clear evidence that those visits led to immediate wider changes. Phoenix didn't become a vital center of home design and construction. It did not lag particularly behind other US cities over the next decades. For example, it is the location of an important

2011 project in retrofitting small office buildings to be "net-zero" i.e. to generate on site each year as much or more energy than is used to run the building,[99] and a university campus expansion recognized in 2012 as a "Top Ten" environmental project by the American Institute of Architects. The documentation for neither project mentions the ESH. The ESH's contribution was only that it unmemorably but usefully helped normalize the notion of green house-building as an acceptable alternative for commercially viable projects in its region.

The dilemma of acceptability

I myself am dubious about the ESH designers' assumption that "a showcase home needs to be acceptable to a large number of people", and more generally about acceptability as a criterion for progress toward sustainability. But my doubts are more ambivalent than you might guess. I think any significant steps toward a sustainable future have to be acceptable enough to establish themselves in the existing world as an increment of progress, but I also think acceptability as a criterion can be domineering and narrowing.

The French author Stendhal once remarked, in passing, "Beauty is nothing other than the promise of happiness.[100]" I first heard this recently, and it instantly made me think of American houses, especially conventional subdivision houses. I'm sorry to say that my immediate thought was somewhat negative: "They aren't beautiful, however affluent they are, and now I see why."

I don't mean that most of our housing is ugly. Certainly not. It is very often pretty, pleasant, comfortable, hospitable, friendly; it has many good qualities that actual ugliness would block. But think how rarely you have been in a conventional subdivision house that took your breath away. Beauty is very subjective, yet there are houses in the world which person after person experiences as intensely and immediately beautiful. Wright's Falling Water or Greene and Greene's Gamble House are famous US examples, and there are less well known and humbler but still truly beautiful houses here and there in every state. But I haven't ever found one in a subdivision.

You can try this thought experiment.[101] Bring to mind some images of a good conventional house. They are there; let them come into your mind. What do you like about these houses, and what is about them that generates those qualities? What provides the sense of comfort or prettiness or whatever other good qualities you have in mind? Now ask yourself what changes in the place would take it toward being breathtakingly beautiful. Not just very pleasant, pretty, friendly or those other things. Breathtakingly beautiful, or definitely moving in that direction. Closer to taking your breath away. What changes would move the place in that direction? This is quite difficult for me and for most people, and I don't think that's because they lack the knack for it, or haven't been trained as architects or artists. I think it can't really be done if your starting point is the 80-90% of US houses built in the usual way.

Shifting your attention from the house to the view may open your experience toward beauty. Many Americans have that breathtaking sensation when looking out into nature. That's not the point of this exercise; it's about the house in itself. So look out for thinking that what the good house needs is a much better view. You should also be on guard against thinking you can solve the problem through sheer scale. That can take your breath away, but not on account of beauty. Simply making a pretty or pleasant or comfortable or friendly place bigger may make it more impressive, but it won't generally make it more beautiful.

If I'm right, conventional subdivision houses, which is to say almost all American houses, are simply not about beauty. They may be about other good things, but not that. This is what came to me out of Stendahl's remark. Maybe these houses are not trying to promise happiness; maybe their designers, builders and buyers are after something different, the promise of acceptability.

This is certainly what the rhetoric of the ESH project centers on, and I at least find it confirmed in realtor, developer, and homebuyer language wherever one encounters it.

You may well ask "What's wrong with that?". This is where my ambivalence comes in. There is something importantly right about acceptability. Mass production, which we count on for low costs, only works when there is a mass market, and that only happens when individual life patterns, which are all unique in their details, don't require unique products. Acceptability, for mass producers, means having created a product that a great many individuals are willing and able to fit into their idiosyncratic lives.

Mass producers understandably but regrettably try to get to this acceptance by a kind of marketing that inveigles buyers into substituting a generic life for their actual one. Buy our item, it shouts, or whispers, or intones, or confides, and you will find yourself in a dream world full of sunshine, high performance cars or spacious dining rooms, and people with perfect teeth. The dream, unfortunately, is the marketer's synthetic dream, not the actual buyer's. It is not composed from elements of anyone's real life, and does none of the work with them that real dreams do.[102]

Mass production has certainly been critical to US material abundance, but the design choices and marketing strategies that have been part of its success have made it a mixed blessing. The system's real flaws and shortcomings coexist with its astonishing achievements in generating possibilities, choices, comforts, excitements, and connections for millions of people. Seekers of sustainability need to keep this in mind.

House building is a fine example of the complications. Acceptability is necessary to enable mass production and reduce costs so houses are affordable for many people, but it's backward looking. Builders and banks are typically only reassured that a market for a certain kind of house exists by knowing that enough sales of houses like that have already been made. Few realtors take pleasure in listing places that look or feel different from what has already been selling well. And house buyers are easily spooked by suggestions that a place may be hard to sell in the future. This all puts a considerable burden of proof on any fundamental improvements, for example in aid of sustainability.

Modest changes in features and arrangements do happen all the time, because US buyers and sellers and their financers like an aura of newness. But whereas the "new" is perennially attractive, the transformative is not. The new has to feel very familiar, or people get nervous. They even get nervous when it is a neighbor's house that might go beyond "new".

Unfortunately, if acceptability is the promise in a house, happiness will be incidental. It may or may not happen, but it has not been the designer's or builder's goal. It has not been the motivation for their care, their imagination, or their effort. Many would actually claim that it could not be a sensible goal, since happiness is so subjective, individual, idiosyncratic.

Maybe so, but I think real progress toward sustainability requires giving thought to happiness. Not the generic happiness of birthday or anniversary cards, but the real happiness of real people in real houses. People will not work to sustain what they do not love. Low impact is not enough, efficiency is not enough. There must be ingredients of happiness in the mix—satisfaction, enjoyment, delight, repose, excitement, whatever they may be.

There is a serious dilemma here which will need both vision and much extended effort to resolve: in this society only generic buildings are affordable, but some real kind of individuality in houses (and workplaces, too) will be essential before they will be sustainable. Spelling out this problem is beyond this book's reach, much less any definiteness about dealing with it. I hope, though, that I have said enough to raise the question as a substantial one.

The two streams of alternative design that had the strongest prospects of reshaping the main stream of American homebuilding in transformative ways, superinsulation and passive solar, each came to 1984 with a considerable stock of completed houses to show. Superinsulation was more or less invisible, and perfectly compatible with concerns about acceptability, and certain versions of passive solar were, too. However, each of them also had some problems to confront, of the kind that show up in any significantly new technology as the number of projects employing it grows.

Some problems of adolescence for passive solar

Passive solar had problems which centered (and still center) on the difficulty of finding the delicate, site-specific balance between underheating and overheating. You have to position the building to get good exposure to the sun, and give it enough window area for daytime sunlight to supply enough heat to cover nighttime and cloudy spells. But rooms must still not get too hot for comfort when in full summer sun. The basic approach is to make walls and floors of massive materials like stone or concrete which can absorb a lot of heat before they get appreciably hot. There has to be enough of this thermal mass, and it has to be exposed enough to any direct sun to absorb its share of heat very readily, so other things like the building's air don't get too hot. The entire bundle of demands—good orientation, adequate and well-placed thermal mass, materials which don't fade, control of glare—creates plenty of difficulty for the designer.

Readers have seen that these issues were very present in designing the Lovins house, and in that case they were very successfully resolved. But each house and site is different, and design aids and experience for passive solar were very limited in the 1980s.

It had a head start as an alternative building philosophy in the 1970s because it could draw on traditional understandings of sun, daily and seasonal cycles, and adobe and other materials. But carrying it into the variety of US climate zones involved twice the challenges faced by superinsulation. A reliable passive solar design needs to be as knowledgeable about heat flows within the structure as a superinsulated one, even more when it comes to heat being stored, but it also needs to be just as sophisticated about the solar variables, which matter much less to superinsulated designs. The sun moves; its shadows move; clouds come and go. Full sunlight is very intense and narrowly directional; reflected and diffused sunlight from clouds, foliage, surroundings in general is meaningful, but much weaker.

Most of these solar factors are amenable to prediction in principle. Balcomb's group at Los Alamos did extensive and reasonably successful measuring, modeling and projecting of these things in the years before and after 1980. They and many others worked hard on converting the results into techniques and routines which could be widely used by designers and builders at large. Sunlight, if absorbed using good passive approaches, could indeed heat houses well without overheating them. But the range of variation and the delicacy of the required heat balance were both so great that each house really needed a site-specific engineering study before its performance could be predicted well.

It's no surprise that many buildings of that period fell short of their designers and owners' hopes. Expertise did grow and spread, and so did the knowledge that passive solar worked simply and reliably to meet a portion of heating needs in many locations around the country, but getting it close to doing the whole heating job was very demanding.

In the US homebuilding industry, "very demanding" generally gets translated quickly by builders into either "not interested" or "it will cost you." The stance is rational enough, given the structure of the industry, but that only makes it more common and less amenable to change. There are many individual exceptions, but they make only a small percentage of the whole. The chances of a random customer finding a non-premium builder with the interest and the skills to make passive solar the main heat source for a new house were small during the 1980s.

The inspiring notion of a fully solar building thus faded for owners, replaced at best by a pedestrian reduction of some percentage in heating bills. For builders, the increased demands and risks of designing one were no longer justified by their increased marketing appeal. The notion stayed alive in green journalism, but the tag "passive solar" went out of widespread use fairly quickly. It was stuck, like "superinsulation" in the US, in a self-reinforcing cycle, with buyers not asking and builders not offering.[103]

From "solar" to "daylight"

Despite the very real difficulties faced by the passive solar design directions of the 1970s and 1980s, the possibility of hearts being touched by sunlight remained strong in sustainable building. The way forward was somewhat unexpected. It explored the possibilities of light itself, rather than the heat that came along with the light from the sun, and it developed in the world of commercial office design.

This progress had to start with head, not heart, of course, given the reigning preference for hard facts in decision-making. At this point in the 1980s, the relevant heads were thinking about energy, not daylight. The Brundtland Commission's 1987 merger of environmental and economic development concerns under the heading of sustainability helped confirm energy efficiency as a critical element. Architects concerned about sustainability were quick to recognize that buildings are the site of just under half the energy used in "advanced" economies, and to accept a responsibility for exploring architectural options for major efficiency improvements consistent with basic comfort and building functions. They induced the American Institute of Architects (AIA) to form a Committee on the Environment in 1989, and convene a major Architecture at the Crossroads conference in 1993, jointly with the International Union of Architects.

A project completed in New York City in 1992 was a true landmark along this path. Audubon House was the renovation of a nearly century-old eight-story commercial building to serve as the national Audubon Society's head office. That was on the upper floors, with leased retail space at ground level and leased office space in between.

Audubon House, New York, 1992 (Croxton Collaborative)

Audubon's mission as an environmental organization no doubt helped it embrace the potential for its new headquarters to take a major step in sustainability. But pioneering projects like this take people who combine the spirit of adventure, an urge to launch into uncharted territory, with the alertness and competence to detect and deal with its dangers. The president of Audubon, Peter A. A. Berle, and the lead architect, Randolph Croxton, proved to be such people. Their project embraced a full range of sustainability issues, including direct heating and cooling, proper ventilation, healthy materials, lighting and recycling. Though all were important, and the project handled them well, the way the project dealt with lighting was truly groundbreaking.[104]

The illustrations almost tell the story by themselves: the design goes to unusual lengths to fill the building with natural light. The original building had generous windows, to which the renovation, literally a "making new", added a large skylight punched through the roof and a major staircase opening carrying daylight down to the next floor. Offices were designed with lower than usual partitions between work stations near the windows, to allow daylight to reach further into each floor.

Sunlight in this building is intended to provide its light, not its heat. Since this was a commercial building taking a bold step, and head not heart (assisted by accounting software) was in charge, the changes were justified by very significant reductions in the bills for lighting. The sun could substitute for artificial light much of the time, especially with sensors and dimmers in place over much of the office to keep artificial light in a backup role. It came on just enough to make up for daylight shortfalls from cloud or shadows.

> There were efficiencies in the electric lighting systems, too— compact fluorescent bulbs, high efficiency conventional fluorescents, and occupancy sensors for switching lights off in unoccupied spaces.

The overall effect was to reduce the building's maximum electric load for lighting by 80% from what New York's code allowed, with savings that paid for the extra cost in two and a half years of operation.

All this took first-class engineering and design time, which is why commercial buildings were the leaders in taking advantage of daylight like this. Office buildings of any size are unique enough for project-specific engineering and design to be a customary part of the work. If some owner decides to push beyond the conventional in some way, the basic budget for the needed professional services is already there. Finding a designer and the budget to pay for one adds a whole new layer of complications to a residential project.

The search for energy efficiency, the prospect of saving money, and the good engineering were all essential to bringing daylight so abundantly into Audubon House. However, looking back from this vantage point, I would say the achieved savings of kilowatt-hours and dollars mattered much less than the dawning, for professionals, owners and workers alike, of the truth that daylight is good for people—good for their their health, their morale, and their productivity as workers.

I call this a dawning, because the sun and the benefits of daylight had been real all along, but had sunk thoroughly out of sight for as much as 50 years, before coming over the horizon again around 1990. In the 1920s and 1930s daylight was common in offices. It was a practical, comfortably familiar form of illumination, supplemented in a matter-of-fact way when needed by incandescent electric light.

Bureau of Printing and Engraving, Washington, D.C., about 1915

But in the post-World War II era, central air conditioning and fluorescent lighting entranced designers and owners with the "space efficiency" and the aura of cleansed modernity they allowed. Office spaces could be enormous, and you didn't need to consider the windows in laying them arranging the space. Workers showed they could tolerate the resulting layouts, which after all were much more comfortable than coal mines or textile factories. Toleration was much more the mood than delight, but few people expected delight would be any part of office employment.

1960s corporate office (a somewhat extreme case)

The white-collar world had indeed shifted in a way that blocked daylight from consciousness and expectation (except as a carefully graded symbol of status, in which the corner office was a pinnacle of ambition). So when it returned, in buildings like Audubon House, the surprise was genuine. It provided a real encounter with unforeseen possibility. The remark of a lead secretary for Audubon was quite typical: "I like the building so much that I give tours." Audubon's senior vice president for finance and operations said, "When you invite friends here, they say, 'Wow, this place looks great!' Sometimes it just stretches their imagination." [105]

The idea that hard-headed engineering and management might, in this case, nurture the feelings and hearts of building inhabitants got joined about this time by the insight that the latter might be good for the former. A 1989 paper in the journal *Occupational Medicine* pointed out that unhealthy buildings might be imposing large hidden costs on businesses and organizations in the form of reduced productivity.[106] The estimates were large enough to put spending on improvements like better light and better air quality in a newly favorable perspective. Staffing can easily account for 90% of their operating costs for white collar organizations, while energy of all kinds is much more like 1% of them. Improving energy efficiency can reduce that 1% even further, but if some improvement, perhaps in daylighting, also raises productivity even a single percentage point, perhaps by reducing sick days or invigorating the last hour or two of regular work, that's the equivalent of saving the whole energy budget.

It would be enough if the benefits of natural light and good air only just balanced the costs, because comments like the following, from the Audubon mailroom supervisor, indicate something very valuable for employees' working lives can happen off the balance sheet:

> We were always sick in the old building, and by three in the afternoon we were dragging and had to get coffee. Here, we don't have to do that. The lighting is better, for one thing.

Even workplaces can touch the heart. This possibility, profound in its implications for what life in a sustainable society might be, had been dramatized in one way in 1983 by the Lovins Snowmass house/office, as we saw earlier. The next years, though disappointing as far as some of the most visible strands of green building went, nevertheless saw a convergence of developments that planted Audubon House as another landmark on the soft path. Energy nerds, the counterculture, equipment makers, bean counters and establishment architects, with all their differences in temperament, insights, and agendas, found they could all reach a good deal of what they were after—impacts reduced, money saved, and working lives improved and inspired.[107] That possibility was not obvious until it happened, though looking back, one can see a certain inevitability at work.

Some problems of adolescence for superinsulation

When people realized how much energy was being lost by cold air seeping in and heated air seeping out through the loose construction of traditional US houses, they took the natural and quite feasible step of sealing them up. This quickly became a standard part of the superinsulation approach. Unfortunately, the air flows that were energy culprits had also been important for removing water vapor and the off-gassing from household materials and chemicals. Unless steps were taken to avoid it, sealing the house was allowing these vapors build up, favoring the growth of molds and rots, and possibly aggravating allergies.

We've already seen what the Lovins house did to avoid these bad effects —that plan had air-to-air heat exchangers from the start, pulling stale air and its moisture and any pollutants out of the house while transferring the heat to the incoming fresh air. Problem basically solved, and not just in a lab sense. Lovins never chose one-of-a-kind or custom technology. He insisted that the equipment he used needed to be in commerce, available for sale, and heat exchangers were. Thus air quality problems in superinsulated houses were potentially avoidable from the moment they arose.

Unfortunately, not every designer was as good or as well-informed as Lovins, and such problems were not always avoided. Enough superinsulated houses had them to create a flurry of concern about health in new construction. This coincided with the appearance in the early 1980s of "sick building syndrome" in offices and similar workplaces. This was a catchall term; certain workplaces began to have quite frequent complaints from occupants about irritated eyes, headaches, asthma-like breathing difficulties, irritated skin, and gastrointestinal discomforts that arose in these buildings and not outside or at home. Symptoms varied from person to person and building to building, and attempts to pin down the causes came up with a great variety of candidates, including organic chemical vapors, very dry air, dust, and perhaps a dozen others. There was nothing conclusive except that some workers were genuinely afflicted, and the symptoms were low-level but enervating. One active leading researcher writing in 2007, and looking back over twenty years of extensive work in the field, could find nothing more definite than this to say:

> Substantial evidence suggests that psychosocial and physical factors in indoor environments, as well as biological and chemical factors, influence the symptoms experienced by office workers, through multiple mechanisms that we still do not understand.[108]

Interestingly for designers of workplaces, occupants with a degree of control over their indoor environment, thanks to such features as local ventilation control, are less prone to sick building symptoms. Unfortunately for managers, research strongly suggests that psychosocial factors like the level of work support available to staff and their degree of control over work demands at work are as potent as any physical influences. On this basis one would expect, for example, that professionals would have fewer sick building complaints than clerical staff, and this is what one finds.[109] Once again, the nature of the life lived in a building is vital, and sick building symptoms may be signs that a workplace's power structure or pace or problem-solving is unhealthy, rather than the physical building itself.

This has played out in some fortunate, some interesting, and some unfortunate ways. Fortunately for building operators, the problem has generally been greatly eased by doing what Leger, Lovins and successful superinsulators did from the start, bringing in much more fresh air. Whatever the physical/chemical/biological factors may be, flushing them away is helpful.

Even though proven solutions were available, the emergence of these indoor air problems meant that "superinsulated" went cold as a feature in US housebuilding. From the later 1980s, the word appeared less and less often in ads and articles. Buyers were no longer inspired to ask about it, and builders were in no hurry to volunteer it as an option.

There's a lesson about change in this history. The difficulties for superinsulation arose from not properly seeing that changing a part means changing a whole. Tightening the construction of a building didn't bring in new toxic materials or exhaust fumes from equipment, increase noise, or change any direct environmental effects of importance. The trouble was that heat wasn't everything that drafts and air leaks had been carrying out of the building; moisture, chemical vapors, spores and the like had been carried away as well. Houses with bad air were houses with only parts of the needed change in place.

Losing sight of the whole is a major hazard in doing technical work. The work often calls for long periods of very focussed attention on the fine details of the mechanisms and materials in question. The watchmaker has to narrow his view to a magnified scene of delicate parts and tiny tools. Watchmakers have mostly learned to come back out into the whole world of the shop and make sure the watch has a watchband as well as keeping good time. Good technical people and teams have learned the same lesson, but the risk of losing track of the whole is always there.

We can formulate the lesson as a stance for change agents to adopt—any status quo is probably doing some good as well as some ill; one should be finding and protecting the good as well as finding and getting rid of the ill. There may be a baby in that bathwater.

Passivhaus

Though it faded in North America, the practice of superinsulating did not disappear from the world. The Leger, Lo-Cal and Canadian successes in constructing houses with no furnaces or radically downsized ones appealed to certain building science researchers in northern Europe, in particular to Wolfgang Feist of Germany and Bo Adamson of Sweden.

Feist was attracted by the idea that body heat and waste heat from cooking, washing, and appliances might supply meaningful amounts of heat to a house. Adamson's knowledge of unheated traditional buildings in China was encouraging. The giant step toward eliminating furnaces entirely came during a visit to the Lovins building around 1985, where he encountered superwindows for the first time. He thereafter directed his research to component-by-component estimates of heat losses and gains in north European conditions, studying window glass, window frames, walls, roofs, doors, door frames, and other construction details in Darmstadt, where he was a research assistant in the late 1980s. These German estimates confirmed the potential of the North American superinsulation formula—heavy insulation, tight construction and air-to-air heat exchangers. Combining the best components of each kind could make an efficient enough building envelope to dispense with a conventional furnace.

Then he and his family put their bodies where his mind was: they decided to build a demonstration house based on his calculations. They found three other families ready for this plunge, and the group was able to secure a long lease on land being developed by the city and get extra funding from the state of Hesse, which was trying to encourage new technology-based enterprises at the time. They had local architects design a four-plex using specific structure, envelope, and equipment details Feist devised. These were the key to the drastic 90% reduction in heating energy that he aimed for and achieved.

The demonstration Passive House building in Darmstadt-Kranichstein, mid-1990s

Feist later wrote, "To those well-versed in physics, it was immediately clear that this [heating] could be done more efficiently; it was only a question of implementation."[110] Implementation means getting the details right, and everyone knows that the devil resides in the details. They often make good intentions actually take you to to hell; Feist's clarity about his goals, and his technical ability meant that his details all provided upward steps instead. His success has been demonstrated consistently since the building's completion in 1991 by the extensive program of measurements he put in place. Each of the four units in the

Darmstadt-Kranichstein house needed only 10% of what the German national code of the time allowed for heating.

The house had no separate heating system, but it did have a heater built into the ventilation system, whose purpose was to keep outside air from being delivered too cold. That is where the remaining 10% got used.

As often happens when one gets into the specifics of a new idea, green or otherwise, readers have to decide for themselves whether this would really allow one to claim that the building has no furnace. In any case, it's impressive that Feist found an eminently workable way of reducing heating need by such an enormous amount. This was perhaps the first demonstration of these possibilities in a building bigger than a single family house, and having the heater didn't much affect the large saving in equipment costs that getting rid a system big enough to heat the whole building provided.

> At the same time, I regret that the cost and performance of available materials ruled out, as Feist saw it, the extra increments of insulation and heat recovery that would have allowed the waste heat from cooking and the like to cover the entire heating load. Zero is a simpler and more powerful index of progress than 10% ever can be, but my regret doesn't nullify my great appreciation for his eliminating the 90%.

Getting to that point did take determination, both personal and professional. In a later interview, Feist said,

> Both our children were still small and were excited about everything happening around them. My wife, Witta, was a dedicated participant right from the start; after all, we completed most of the learning process together. The grandparents were a bit skeptical but had a positive attitude towards this "nonsense" – and supported us as much as they could. Of course we did have to go through the completely normal strains and stresses of a construction process. But the fact that we wanted to build it differently from the usual method didn't make it any easier.
>
> My PhD supervisor had his reservations but had a positive attitude and closely followed the developments. Others – whose names I will not mention here – published theoretical papers explaining that such a concept would never function.

Wolfgang Feist apartment, Passive House building in Darmstadt-Kranichstein

> Our architects Professor Bott, Ridder and Westermeyer were very
> supportive. They went along with almost all our wishes (only
> making fun of the stringently observed principles).[111]

This Kranichstein building was completed and occupied by the four
families in 1991. All the units fully lived up to expectations over the
succeeding years, and have done so down to the present. The structure,
envelope and services are unchanged. There have been no air quality
problems, and the direct heating energy each year has continued to be
down at 10% or so of what codes required in the mid-1990s.

In 1995, four years after the building's completion, came a springboard
moment which transformed Feist's efforts into the base for a relaunch of
superinsulation as a viable factor in the building industry. Amory Lovins
was paying a return visit to the researcher he had met 10 years before in
Snowmass. Feist saw it as a chance to discuss research results, but Lovins'
main comment redirected and drastically expanded the work:

> No, this is not just a scientific experiment. This is the solution.
> You will just have to redesign the details in order to reduce the
> additional costs, and that will be possible, I am convinced.[112]

This was a classic visionary move, opening toward a transformed practice
of building. The path is not fully defined, and neither is the exact nature
of the goal, but the direction is there. Feist seized on it as the direction
he would follow. He and co-workers set to and defined the details of a
path which they could claim, by twenty years later, had been responsible
for a million square meters of what they call Passivhaus building, largely
in northern Europe but also in North America and elsewhere.

The path involved a major strategic move, in which the Kranichstein building only played a supportive role. Instead of focusing on that building, Feist and his associates developed a particular definition of building quality, the Passivhaus Standard, and made that the center of their efforts to promote green building.

There is a very significant difference here from the passive solar story. Passive solar has never so far acquired an organizational center, like the Passivhaus Institut or its US offshoot and competitor, PHIUS, with the specific aim of getting its approach accepted very widely. PHIUS, for example, describes itself as "committed to making high-performance passive building the mainstream market standard." Out of this comes an actively promoted blend of nurturance and advocacy—information transfer, training, certification, and publicity. Passive solar has never had the equivalent.

However, both passive solar and superinsulation led onward. In different ways, both were important as the 1990s tackled the question of what should count as genuinely green building.

---

[92] Taylor, A.M. (2014) "The great leveraging". In *The Social Value of the Financial Sector: Too Big to Fail or Just Too Big?* (pp. 33-65).

[93] *The construction chart book: The US construction industry and its workers.* CPWR--The Center for Construction Research and Training, 2002.

[94] See CPWR Chart Book; Diamond, R.C. (2001) ""An overview of the US building stock" (Chapter 2.1 in Spengler J.D. et al. *Indoor Air Quality Handbook*; McGraw Hill, 2001); Friedman, A., 1995. "The evolution of design characteristics during the post-second world war housing boom: The US experience." *Journal of Design History*, 8(2), pp.131-146.

[95] Found at https://www.forbes.com/sites/trulia/2013/05/02/american-homes-by-decade/#1f60dfa71045

[96] Pijawka, K. David, and Kim Palmer Shetter. *The environment comes home: Arizona public service's environmental showcase home.* Herberger Center for Design Excellence, College of Architecture and Environmental Design, Arizona State University, 1995.

[97] Pijawka et al., *op. cit.*

[98] See https://azarchitecture.com/architecture-guide/aps-environmental-showcase-home/

[99] Ladhad, Akash, and Kristen Parrish. (2013) "Phoenix's First Net-Zero Energy Office Retrofit: a green and lean case study." *J. Green Building* 8, no. 4: 3-16.

[100] Stendahl, *De l'amour.*

[101] This line of thinking owes a great deal to Christopher Alexander's writings about sensing wholeness, though the specific thought exercise is not his.

[102] Jones, Richard Matthew. *The Dream Poet.* University Books, 1979.

[103] Garrett, Vicki, and Tomas M. Koontz. (2008). "Breaking the cycle: Producer and consumer perspectives on the non-adoption of passive solar housing in the US." Energy policy 36(4), 1551-1566.

[104] National Audubon Society and Croxton Collaborative, *Audubon House: building the environmentally responsible, energy-efficient office.* (Wiley, 1994).

[105] *Ibid.*

[106] Woods, James E. "Cost avoidance and productivity in owning and operating buildings." *Occupational Medicine* (Philadelphia, Pa.) 4, no. 4 (1989): 753-770.

[107] RMI case studies were influential in spreading this news. Romm, J. J., & Browning, W. D. (1994). Greening the building and the bottom line. *Rocky Mountain Institute. Snowmass, Colorado.*

[108] Mendell, M. J., and W. J. Fisk. "Is health in office buildings related only to psychosocial factors?." *Occupational and Environmental Medicine* 64, no. 1 (2007): 69-70.

[109] Marmot, A. F., J. Eley, M. Stafford, S. A. Stansfeld, E. Warwick, and M. G. Marmot. "Building health: an epidemiological study of 'sick building syndrome' in the Whitehall II study." Occupational and environmental medicine 63, no. 4 (2006): 283-289.

[110] Interview at https://blog.passivehouse-international.org/first-passive-house-wolfgang-feist/. This is also the source of the interior photograph.

[111] *Ibid.*

[112] Passipedia, "The world's first Passive House, Darmstadt-Kranichstein, Germany". Found at https://passipedia.org/examples/residential_buildings/multi-family_buildings/central_europe/the_world_s_first_passive_house_darmstadt-kranichstein_germany

9: **What Counts as Really Green?**

Audubon House and the Darmstadt-Kranichstein building are landmarks from the early 1990s in the uneven progress of passive solar and superinsulation as approaches to green building. The energies and insights from which they emerged had achieved sound results, but had also shown important limitations. Their successes would be hard to replicate widely in the US; progress called for redirection. Both buildings are impressive physical products, but their primary significance comes from their relation to a turn toward something thoroughly conceptual— general standards of performance.

Products, whether huge and singular like office buildings or tiny and mass produced like corn flakes, are familiar to us inhabitants of this extremely market-oriented society. We know a great deal about how products are made and how to judge their suitability. Most of us are much less familiar with standards, and yet they are a vital part of the infrastructure which enables production, sales, and use to function with the general harmony they exhibit. So a brief excursion into the realm of standards is in order.

The idea of standards was not new in the mid-1990s. The US Pure Food and Drug Act, passed in 1906 to address adulteration and mislabelling, is only one example among many in all countries, of action to temper effects of the explosive growth of industry in the late 19th century. It imposed a legal requirement that foods and drugs in interstate commerce be labelled accurately, and assigned new powers of inspection and enforcement to the Federal Department of Agriculture.

The private sector became important, too. For example, the Good Housekeeping Seal of Approval for household products dates back to 1909. Animated by the wish for advertising claims to be trustworthy, the magazine conceived a facility, the Good Housekeeping Institute, to "test and approve" products in practical household conditions, and awarded its Seal to those that qualified.

The point of the standard, in both these examples, is that a product's users should be able to tell what they are getting. *Good Housekeeping* offered a carrot, the Food and Drug Act brandished a stick, but the criterion was basically the same.

By now, over a hundred years later, standards have evolved and proliferated well beyond their truth-in-packaging origins. Modern industry has blossomed into innumerable specializations and complexities, which creates an enormous need to be able to take many things for granted. Parts produced by different firms need to fit together without special engineering, need to be made of strong enough materials without needing special testing to confirm they're not toxic, and so forth. The degree of complexity is far beyond what can be managed by contracts worked up for each transaction. The situation is captured in the gallows humor of astronaut Michael Collins, on being asked what went through his mind as the rocket engines ignited. "Well, you think about the fact that you are on top of six million parts, all made by the lowest bidder."[113] Specifying all the required details cannot start from a blank slate for each project. Much must be settled in advance, and this is the role of standards and standardization.

> A standard, as we are using the term here, is "a set of technical definitions and guidelines that function as instructions for designers, manufacturers, operators, or users."[114] It can be obeyed, disobeyed, bureaucratized, complained about, valued, or taken for granted like any law, but in itself it has no power of enforcement.

Already in the early 1900s there was need to standardize the sizes of industrial products such as screw threads, letter paper, electric batteries, electric plugs, and lightbulbs. This was tragically dramatized in the Great

Baltimore Fire of 1904, which burned for 30 hours and destroyed some 1500 buildings. It lasted that long and spread that far partly because fire units from nearby cities, rushing to Baltimore to help, found their hoses could not connect to Baltimore's hydrants. A call for standardizing hydrant and hose sizes was a natural part of the national response, and a standard was soon established.

Sadly but typically, firefighting, a public service, has had only modest success with the hose-hydrant standard. By 2004, only 18 of the 48 most populous US cities were using the standard size.[115] The private sector has standardized far more completely on matters with fewer life and death implications. Screw threads, letter paper, and the other items listed above plus thousands of others come in predictable sizes and shapes everywhere in the country. An AA battery from any supplier will fit my AA flashlight. We take this for granted, and that is the point. The variety of standard sizes is enormous, and can be daunting to the do-it-yourselfer visiting a hardware store looking for a replacement nut or bolt. But the item that fits properly is probably there, thanks to standardization.

> In metric countries, the specific sizes and shapes of all these things are different, but they're standardized too. Basic compatibility of this kind is very important, but many standards go further and concern themselves with quality or levels of performance. This started at the beginning; to earn the Good Housekeeping Seal, products had to perform as advertised, and the same was true for food and drugs after the Act of 1906. Standards of this kind remain important, and we now have more assertive standards that define levels of performance validated by third parties. Driver's licenses are in this group: the drivers of taxis, heavy vehicles, or school buses must typically demonstrate additional skill and knowledge beyond what is considered acceptable for ordinary driving to government examiners.

Building codes are a kind of performance standard. They came into being to define minimum acceptable levels of risk to health and safety. Structures need to be minimally sound; ventilation needs to be minimally good; wastewater needs to be kept away from human contact to a certain degree; and so on. Different communities in the US have had quite different views about what counts as the "minimal" requirement needed to provide an acceptable level of risk, but the idea of any code provision is that any worse performance is unacceptable to the community in question.

> Each local building comes out of quite tangled public and private sector negotiations about what's needed and what's practical, with lobbying, vested interests, incomplete information, habits, and community disengagement all at work, producing standards which may have flaws but do represent viable bases for getting on with each community's need for buildings.

One important development in the later 1970s was that building codes began to include energy-related requirements. True to their local nature, US codes have evolved differently in different places, some steadily stiffer, some lagging and less demanding, some almost unchanging. There are still some states that have no building codes at all, leaving decisions about them up to local governments or trusting to the invisible hand of the market to take care of all this.

LEED

By the the mid 1990s large scale commercial green building in the US in was ready for business, but it still didn't have a lot of customers. Buildings like Audubon House were built with materials and equipment already available on the commercial/institutional market, and the needed professional services were equally at hand, available. However, there was only a modest number of buildings like that. Some were done as leadership statements, new headquarters for established non-profits or businesses like Heifer International or the German Commerzbank;

others were we-have-arrived statements for fast-growing new businesses like Genzyme; and there were some new green university or government facilities. About half of the total were general office buildings scattered across the US, Western Europe and Asia. Their owners were motivated by varying proportions of planetary consciousness and the wish to be early participants in the next big thing. Often they occupied some portion of the space, renting out the rest. Design and engineering were often one-off efforts, by firms also interested in acquiring expertise early that might be give them a head start later.

The architectural and construction press paid attention to these projects but there was no quick take-off to a wider commercial or institutional market. By the end of the 1990s there were only thirty or forty buildings at that scale with genuine green ambitions in the country; the number depends on what you count as green. In fact, what one could or ought to count as green was the central issue for the development of the soft path during that decade. We have already talked a good deal about why assumptions and concerns about acceptability mean that change spreads slowly in the world of designers and builders. The dappled character of the situation, its mix of bright spots and shadows, was on show at this time. Audubon House and its cousins demonstrated that markedly greener design and construction was feasible for offices; for this industry, the appeal of the new confronted the perils of the innovative. The temptation to settle for cosmetic improvements and habits of skepticism about trendy puffery each interfered with the adoption of significant improvements. The pressures of day to day work also made the gathering of reliable information about techniques, equipment, and trade-offs a low priority, slowly pursued, for all except the most intrigued professionals. Even they had only their individual judgment about which possibilities to pursue and how to prioritize them.

There was a need for a credible system for assessing how green a building was. Such a system would distinguish puffery from real achievement. It would establish an operational definition of "green" for buildings, and give shape to what had been a confusing variety of means and methods. In addition, a green assessment could become a marketing feature, an aid to establishing buyers' confidence about proposed investments, and a major incentive for professionals to acquire expertise in green design and construction. The result was LEED.

This stands for Leadership in Energy and Environmental Design. Its creation was a group effort, and a purely private initiative at the outset. Several engineers, developers, and researchers convened themselves as the US Green Building Council and started a quite open and widely consultative process with their fellow professionals about what aspects of sustainability mattered most for commercial buildings, how to assess them objectively, and how to combine them into a single score. Each major decision went through a period of general comment and modification before being settled.[116]

The system established a "stretch" standard, a set of voluntary performance targets intended to inspire designers and builders toward much higher than ordinary achievement and then recognize and celebrate it. There are four levels of performance—Certified, Silver, Gold, and Platinum. A project's level is determined by adding up points attached to whichever of over sixty green features, practices, or reduced impacts are present in a design.

> LEED's developers did not try to define what the ultimate green building would be, at all. They aimed instead at getting typical new buildings to be as green as the best 20% or so of what already existed. However, they did announce from the beginning that thresholds for each level might be redefined upward as time went on and (presumably) the best 20% got better and better.

The system was to be outside of government. The US Green Building Council was (and still is) a private organizer, and following the standard was initially purely voluntary.

Projects were to be assessed at the design stage. Later, after the first generation of LEED buildings had been in operation for some years, there was soul-searching when significant numbers of buildings fell short of their projected performance, most strikingly as far as their energy use was concerned. However, as the system was being devised in the mid-1990s the design stage seemed the obvious point of influence. A green building can't come from a purely conventional design; design was the stage at which things were in flux and easy to change, and there was much less risk than in a system in which you couldn't know whether your investment had earned you certification until after you'd constructed and tested a building

After a pilot run in 1998, the first regular version of LEED was launched in 2000. It listed 64 items in six categories spanning the dimensions of sustainability most prominent at the time. In addition to energy, there were water, materials use and recycling, indoor air quality, and others. Most of the 64 items carried a single point and most were independent of the others. To reach the lowest level for recognition, a project needed 26 points. Any 26 would do. There was no single path to LEED certification. It was left to each project's designers and decision-makers to choose which items to go after.

Projects seeking certification submitted a dossier of required evidence for each desired point. Assembling the needed documentation was a burden, as was the fee to pay for the Green Building Council reviewers' time, but LEED's founders had been clear that each point's criteria and the evidence for meeting it needed to be objective. The point was to replace vague claims of greenness with specific, validated protocols and hard data.

Aspects of this approach make LEED particularly suited to the United States. American culture places very high value on individuals being able to choose for themselves among alternatives. This is the country of "28 flavors", not just vanilla, chocolate and strawberry. (As I write this, one national ice cream maker is actually offering 61 flavors[117].) This is a country where the threat of not being able to choose one's doctor has been sufficient to foreclose the political possibility of national health care for decades. LEED makes choice central to its process.

The most basic choice, of course, was whether to participate in LEED at all. It was conceived as a purely voluntary option, and developed entirely as a private sector initiative. When some local governments considered adopting it as a code requirement, later, there was discomfort and resistance from many LEED advocates, who felt the system was ill-suited to function as a general legal minimum. More commonly, governments have adopted LEED as a purchasing policy, by requiring all city projects to be LEED Silver or better, rather than making it a general requirement for local building.

The result of basing certification on a menu of choices was that "LEED-certified" meant a level of green achievement widely acceptable as significant, without guaranteeing a high level in any specific regard. One could have a low or high energy building, very clean or only normally clean air, favorably or ill sited, so long as the combination added up to the right number of points. LEED at that time was like a multiple choice test with demanding questions but plenty of choice and a relatively low passing grade. In fact, of course, most designers were urged to reach the desired number of points by choosing the cheapest options for getting them. Nonetheless, achieving the higher levels, Gold (39 points) or Platinum (51 points), required good coverage in multiple areas.

The system achieved what it set out to do quickly and well. The number of certified projects grew by 60% a year for the first ten years.[118] The rapid increase in the number of building professionals qualified to bring LEED's details into the design and construction process was just as important. The Green Building Council conducted an active training program, and it quickly became the norm for architectural, engineering and construction firms across the US to have "LEED accredited professionals" available for any project.

> This rapid growth should be viewed with the same pair of complementary lenses we used in looking at the growth of passive solar and superinsulated houses in the 1970s and 80s. Growing 60% in a year is a lot, and keeping that rate going for even ten years is truly impressive, especially in the slow-changing world of US commercial building. But this was growth from a tiny base, and the building sector is very large, so even ten years' worth of LEED only changed a small fraction of total building activity.

By 2006, the year the Snowmass building went into its major renovation, LEED was well established as a national standard for green commercial building. As the hose and hydrant history shows, being widely accepted and regarded as a standard does not mean that every organization chooses to adopt it. LEED procedures and scoring have been used for about 20% of total commercial office space in the 30 largest US markets.[119] It has spread remarkably fast, in fact. But this success has been accompanied by a variety of complaints, critiques, resistances, and co-optations. Some are self-interested, like the campaign by certain timber interests trying to get LEED to soften its criterion for sustainably sourced wood. Some are simply discontented with the expense and seemingly bureaucratic nature of the process. Some fault the fact that some points are easier and cheaper to get than others. Some argue that the criteria are not demanding enough given the urgency of climate change and other challenges.

Among those who ultimately held back from the LEED process was Lovins:

> The standards were constantly shifting, there were some knotty definitional questions about new vs. retrofit in a living lab [i.e. the Snowmass building] being continuously retrofitted and retrocommissioned, and in the end it looked like too much of a hassle, so I stopped trying.[120]

The path toward sustainability can't help being just that, a path. An early step, like LEED, can both move things forward and fall short of arrival. A friendly but trenchant critic put it very well in a 2013 article:

> It's not much of a stretch to say that, more than any other single force, LEED has put green buildings on the map and institutionalized building performance measures shown to reduce resource consumption and pollution. A lot of wood, water, and energy has been saved, a lot of pollution has been avoided, and a lot of conditions protective of public health have been adopted because of LEED and because of the hard work of USGBC and their volunteers.
>
> . . .
>
> But, man, there are a lot of warts in this system.[121]

The Passivhaus standard

Wolfgang Feist's Passivhaus standard came from quite different roots—academic study, residential buildings, German conditions—but also found its way forward by defining a stretch standard rather than the perfect building.

Feist and his group wanted to move from the version of I Have Only Myself To Please that his four-plex for his family and their friends embodied to the much more demanding Everyone Should Do This. For houses, and buildings in general, there is a fundamental difficulty in making this move. They're not industrial products the way smartphones, laptops, refrigerators, lawnmowers, and almost all widely used household items are. Building materials are mass-produced, but buildings themselves are not. Marilyn Brown, a distinguished energy policymaker and scholar, has called buildings the largest hand-made objects in the economy.[122] The industry cannot turn out a single product which meets the multiplicity of tastes, needs, site conditions, worker skill levels, and regulations at work in the US economy, or indeed any "advanced" economy. The way forward for Feist and his group, then, could not be simply replicating the Kranichstein house through some ambitious, well-funded campaign of publicity and franchising.

A performance standard is a genuinely different path. The goal would be superinsulated performance, not a specific form of superinsulated house. To the question, What Should Everyone Do? Feist would answer, Put together a comfortable, livable house any way you like, just making sure it meets our standard, by using as little energy as our house. If you pass this test, we will award you the right to use our label—Certified Passive House (Passivhaus in German)—on your place.

Standards shape possibilities

There were four elements to the system they developed: a well-grounded, readily understood standard; a simple way to tell in advance if a house design would meet it; an attractive, well-functioning proof-of-concept building to show that meeting it was possible; and access to low-cost, high-performing building components.

> Feist chose the word "passiv" to highlight the defining feature of these buildings, the absence of a furnace. Heat would be a byproduct of other household energy uses, not something which needed active equipment of its own. Of course, this creates some confusion and irritation in the US, where "passive" points one toward solar heating; solar heat plays no special role in Passivhaus design, though it can be part of how a house meets the standard.

The standard was the heart of this plan. It was not to be a law or regulation. This is typical of the 9,500 or more standards in common use in the industrial world. Some have acquired legal force, but voluntary consensus and observance are far more common.

Though they aren't legal requirements, standards are generally coercive to some degree or other. They typically emerge from meetings and negotiations between businesses' technical staff and professional associations engaged with an issue of compatibility or quality. Agreements that emerge often reach widely enough so meeting the resulting specification becomes a de facto requirement, "the way we do it here," because so much of each industry observes it. So, for example, makers of a new light bulb such as a compact fluorescent have to make it compatible with standard sockets and standard voltages.

Standardization of this kind benefits both makers and users in immediate ways. It also impedes change.

Let us see how this plays out in one detail of US housebuilding. Plywood sheets, used for wall and roof sheathing, partitions and flooring, come in basically just one size, 4' by 8'. There are many different thicknesses and grades of finish, and other sizes are made in small amounts or by special order, but practically speaking, 4' by 8' is the sheet that makers make, suppliers supply, and builders build with.

> Plywood's main competitor, oriented strand board (OSB), comes in exactly the same size sheets.

There is nothing about the basic requirements of any stage that requires these exact dimensions. Builders only need sheets large enough to span wall, roof, and floor areas with few operations, and sheets small enough for one person to carry. But the benefits of mass production are only available through making exactly the same thing over and over. Builders want to be able to use the same sized sheets for their repetitive work. Suppliers like orderly arrangements in warehouses and on trucks, and the fewer adjustments to forklifts and cranes, the better. And the factories have to be set up to produce thousands or millions of sheets the same size, not to keep adjusting everything for custom requests. The particular dimensions don't matter. (In metric countries they are somewhat different, in fact.) But it matters a lot for the product to be uniform.

> With 4' by 8' as the standard, the design of houses is influenced, as well. Designs with affordability in mind will try to use every 4' by 8' sheet intact, rather than incurring the labor costs of cutting any down, and the material costs of unused portions. Making a house a little smaller can actually increase its costs. So there's a subtle pressure to have room lengths and widths in multiples of 4 feet, and ceiling heights 8 feet or less; this kind of thing is never decisive, but the pressure is there.

From all of this, it's probably obvious that once a standard like this is established, it's hard to change. When you consider that plywood sheets are only one of myriad housebuilding components that have settled into standard sizes, shapes, strengths and levels of quality, you can understand the enormous inertia in the housebuilding system. Buildings may be the largest handmade objects in the economy, but the hands have limited options, in practical terms. They can add or subtract island cooktops, choose surround sound or hand-scraped floors, select standard components that are bigger or smaller, and vary the use of them in certain ways, but the basic fabric and services of the house are under great pressure to exemplify the reigning standards at work.

Changing the game significantly, as Feist wanted to, meant finding a way to grow within the status quo. It helped that the Passivhaus kind of standard, a gauge of voluntary high achievement, did not infringe on territory occupied by established compatibility or minimal performance standards. However, as a new arrival from outside the existing constellation of building-related firms and organizations, it had no conventional foundation to provide it with what is often called credibility but is more accurately described as trust. Effective standards embody trust that a thing will perform as expected. Ordinarily that is generated by the stakeholder committee process that defines a standard. One of the big achievements of LEED's founders was to convene a group of green building stakeholders that could command industry respect.

Passivhaus began with no meaningful base in the industry, and indeed ran into just the kind of resistance one might expect. One early Passivhaus staffer captured the breadth and tone of the opposition when interviewed about the early days:

> There were so many voices from everywhere. From the architects: 'The windows are ugly'; from the construction industry: 'This is not traditional. The house will collapse because it is based on insulation. How can you do that? This will not work'; from the manufacturers: 'The components they need are too expensive'; from clients, 'I want to open the windows. I do not want to live in a house where I cannot open the windows'. But you can open the windows.[123]

The mix of fact, rumor, and projected anxiety in these statements is typical; so is the reminder that stakeholders have quite disparate stakes. It's less obvious that stakeholder positions are responses to previously existing options, and the consensus which exists for the current dispensation is usually an equilibrium of opposing pressures. Each stakeholder, having settled for something less than their hopes, defends against getting even less. Proposed changes are not innocent until proven guilty, in standard settings. They are presumed to favor some and cost others, so defense is the stance everyone starts with.

The Passivhaus Institut

Feist and his group wisely chose against trying to change the existing processes. They might, for example, have proposed adding a provision about recognizing high performance to the German energy code. Instead they started their own process, founding a new standard-setting body, the Passivhaus Institut, "Das unabhängige Institut für höchste Energieeffizienz in Gebäuden" ("the independent institute for highest energy efficiency in buildings").

> The major advantage of this move was being able to set the terms of debate. The major disadvantage, the absence of a developed system of communication and working relationships, entailed the creation of new networks and trusted information. That took time, but it was not necessarily slower than trying to persuade the participants in existing processes to work constructively on this new initiative. (The founders of LEED, in the US, made a similar decision to establish a new center of action, the US Green Building Council, rather than working through the existing standards process.)[124]

The Passivhaus Institut was founded in 1996, more than five years after the Kranichstein house was completed. Because Feist had approached it as a research project from the beginning, and had conducted a thorough program of careful measurements, the house had generated five years of data as well as five years of lived experience. The data was solid, and it validated the predictions of very low energy use. The original four families were still in the house, and were enthusiastic about it as a place to live.

The data supported the choice of four basic performance metrics to construct the standard—annual space heating, total energy use, airtightness and thermal comfort.

> Each metric had a specific upper limit: space heating could use no more than 15 kWh per square meter of net living space; total energy for all uses had to be no more than 120 kWh per square meter; there couldn't be more than 0.6 air changes per hour in a defined test; and for comfort, indoor temperatures couldn't be over 25 °C (77 °F) for more than 10% of hours in the year.

These weave together. Total energy needs limiting because one might arrange for low space heating energy in a leaky building by installing very inefficient lamps, stoves or water heaters, whose waste heat would make up the difference. The indoor temperature limit ruled out bad solar design that gets heat in winter at the price of drastic overheating in summer. Everything had to work together, and the trick to creating an elegant standard was finding the minimum number of simple interacting rules to guarantee the functional results they wanted.

> Sharp-eyed readers will have noticed that setting levels on a per-square-meter basis allows larger houses to use more energy than smaller ones, simply because they have more square meters. This resulted from an essentially political decision. They decided that limiting all buildings to a certain amount of total energy would seem unfair enough to owners of larger houses, and would awaken enough of the feeling that energy efficiency is about lower quality of life ("freezing in the dark") that resistance would become unworkable, perhaps especially among owners able to afford the extra costs of Passivhaus construction.

The levels were (and are) demanding. Space heating was to be less than 20% of what average new German residences of the time used. Total energy use was to be under half what was allowed at the time by the toughest energy codes in Europe.

The role of the Darmstadt-Kranichstein house in this was exactly described by Boulding's adage, "What exists is possible." Feist's careful measurements from 1991 to 1996 showed that the standard's demands had actually been met year after after year in the normal use of the building by four different families.

The 1991-96 period had also seen active network building among building professionals and researchers in Germany and even internationally. The Lovins visit in 1995 is just one sign that word was getting out about a way to get very low energy use in housing that felt welcoming and comfortable in familiar ways. A way, moreover, with the potential to revolutionize residential building.

Familiarity had been one of the appeals of superinsulated houses from the beginning, in the Leger house and similar early projects. But welcome, comfort and revolutionary potential had not figured as positive values in the North American work. It had aimed at practicality, and at adequate comfort, but statements from the German Passivhaus promoters like, "What is important is that the occupants of the Passive Houses feel happy in their homes," were never central to the American discussions of superinsulation.

The Passivhaus founders also found a sweet spot in their revolutionary ambitions. Adoption of the standard would promote revolution in a key consequence, energy use, without painful upheaval in anyone's life and work. The ingredients, in form of low-loss windows, careful sealing, and air-to-air heat exchangers, were all basically known, and needed only accessible amounts of refinement and initiative to become low cost and widely enough distributed. Yet the results would be far better than the status quo, if the ingredients were combined in just the right way. The possibility of this kind of revolution added a certain excitement to the Passivhaus project, the sense of being part of history, part of a transformative movement.

Beneath the surface of this plan, there was a tension to be resolved. Enthusiasm for passive houses was to come from personal responses such as comfort or the sense of liberation and personal influence that goes with making major change. Yet Feist and his group knew that the ingredients really did have to be assembled properly, that the Passivhaus label would lose credibility quickly unless it was rigorously applied, and that corrosive bad feeling could easily arise if builders trying for the label found only at the end of their expense and effort that they did not qualify. They were not going to be able to find know whether they'd qualified or not in the design phase, relatively early and cheaply, the way they could with LEED. Avoiding these dangers without dampening individual enthusiasm called for considerable influence over each project's details, applied quite delicately.

The solution was to provide some support in the design phase. Projects seeking to be Passivhaus certified are asked to submit final drawings before construction starts. These are reviewed by a trained certifier and energy use is estimated with Institut software. The designer, builder and owner learn at this time whether the building has good chances of meeting the Passivhaus criteria when in operation. If not, they can submit modified drawings for a new review and estimate. In this way, the Institut (and the applicant) gain assurance that the project is sound before the effort and major expense of construction.

> There needs to be a trained certifier because the estimating software only delivers reliable results if quite a multitude of design details are properly handled. For example, spotting thermal bridges takes a trained eye, and advising the best ways of eliminating them takes human knowledge and judgment. It certainly did in 1996 and pretty certainly does even today.

What about comfort, welcome, and aesthetics generally? The Institut does not review for these qualities. Feist and his group did work hard at the outset to involve architects who produced attractive designs, and succeeded in various locations in Germany, and also in the Vorarlberg region of Austria.[125] The effect was that images of early Passivhaus buildings suited the market in central Europe, unlike what happened in North America where early high performance examples like the Saskatchewan house seemed brutal and unattractive to many people. Aesthetics differ greatly from place to place and person to person. The early German examples look like mere boxes or sheds to many Americans, and American examples may look like self-indulgent McMansions to Germans. Aesthetics do differ. But the core Passivhaus strategies are compatible with a very wide range of forms and styles, so appearance, arrangement of spaces, proportions, lighting design, surface finishes and the other ingredients of comfort and beauty can generally be chosen to suit different communities' and occupants' tastes.

Some of the first certified Passivhaus buildings (1998)

The Institut also strongly encouraged designers to choose components like windows, doors, insulation or ventilation equipment from a certified list which it still maintains. Suppliers could get their gear on the list by submitting data showing measured high performance. The justification for that requirement was that accurate knowledge of how components perform is essential to good estimates of energy use. The incentive for designers to use the list is simple but powerful: off-list components have to be tested, with expense and delays, before the essential Passivhaus energy estimate will be done.

> There is an incentive for suppliers, as well. Inclusion on the list says that an independent body confirms that their equipment performs very well. This helps their marketing, even for projects not aiming to be Passivhaus. And the larger the suppliers' market, the more costs come down, so Passivhaus gets more affordable, more projects get started, more certified equipment gets sold, and an upward spiral sets in.

Once the drawings pass muster and construction starts, there are few formal steps. The builder is required to follow the approved drawings meticulously, clearing any needed changes with the certifier, and the completed building must be tested for air tightness.

> As Passivhaus has spread, the movement has had to become more flexible and accommodating. What started as a simple but very firm energy use criterion, for example, has looked doctrinaire to many in the US, where climates and heating requirements range much more widely than in Germany. A US Passive House Institute (Phius) has now branched off and pursues the same goals with somewhat different procedures. The urge to bring the Passivhaus spirit and its impressive results to other kinds of building than residences has also broadened the movement's approach. (There is naturally a good deal of contention about what is wise or foolish in all this.)

With these four elements in place—demanding criteria for an achievement worth reaching; approval at the design stage; assistance in finding high-quality components; and an attractive, well-functioning proof of concept—the standard was launched in 1996. The illustration shows the first cohort (1998), the wide variety of designs meeting the standard in the earliest certified buildings from the Institut's database.

Now over 25 years old, the strategy has led to steady growth in completed projects, at an annual rate—about 14%—that is enviable over this span of time. It is in active use in North America and Asia, as well as in its original European context. Given the very large scale of housebuilding, which produces 1.5 million new houses a year in the US alone, one sees that the Passivhaus and its US cousin are still far from typical. But it is now legitimate to see this as a movement. It has regained the scale of the superinsulated wave of the early 1980s; it has established two solid organizational home bases (the Institut and Phius); and it has developed techniques for planning projects, training designers and validating results that bode well for further expansion.

Very importantly, the path through Germany has enriched the meaning of the superinsulation approach. The original experiments, Leger and Lo-Cal and their Canadian successors of the 1980s, based their case on practicality and familiarity—the promise of low energy use without changing lifestyle. Wolfgang Feist and his group kept hold of those values, but added believable claims about greater comfort, improved craftsmanship, and wider participation to launch a wave of new green building.

Possible to probable

What does lessons does this history have for us, and how do they relate to the Snowmass house? I think of the first decade of Passivhaus as a study in one way to move housebuilding along the soft path from possible toward probable. Visionaries point to possibilities; powerful visionaries like Lovins provide evidence and concrete examples that are encouraging and inspiring. They go beyond pointing. They move others into action. The advice Lovins gave Feist after visiting in 1995 dramatically enlarged the meaning and potential of his guest's solid but non-visionary research. Feist then set to work to actualize that potential, founding an institute and formulating a standard. Without the action, the vision is ephemeral.

Indeed, during the 1980s superinsulation was nearly lost as a distinctive approach to buildings. Interest in energy efficiency continued, but that was largely pursued as one or another incremental improvement, not as the development of a new philosophy or system of house-building. Feist is the only person I know of who took up that more profound goal in that period.

His action was slow-moving, detail oriented, drawn out. The creation of the Passivhaus standard, with its Institut, research background, and networks of engagement, took years of work. Without that extended effort, the idea of the Kranichstein building as a solution to a pressing global problem would have remained a notion. Conversely, without the expansive idea, the time and effort invested by Feist and his group probably would not have resulted in any significant steps toward sustainability. The visionary and the workaday need each other.

The Passivhaus story continues to the present. This book's concluding chapter describes a very successful use of the ideas in a surprising project, a New York City apartment block for low-income residents.

The early years of Passivhaus in the US, the original source of superinsulation techniques, have been uneven. Having the demanding standard as a target validated by solid European experience has been greeted with whole-hearted enthusiasm by some designers, builders, and buyers, but only with what could be called "two cheers for Passivhaus" by others. The Darmstadt Institut insisted that its European criteria, such as requiring space heating to use less than 15 kWh per square meter per year, be applied intact everywhere across the US. In a country with very diverse climates this generated a good deal of unease and discontent. Differences in house-building practices, attitudes about initiative and authority, and the specific personalities involved increased these tensions, resulting in a schism and the founding of the separate Passive House Institute US (Phius), which has developed a modified set of criteria with standards that vary by location. The original Institut continues a US presence, along with activity in numerous other countries, so there are now two distinct paths in the same general direction for sustainable building performance.

Controversy has probably solidified Phius's identity and direction. As of this writing, it is definitely a going concern, with over 1100 buildings in its database,[126] a standard still pitched at the challenging end of current practice, an active training program, and good connections with makers of relevant equipment and with independent opinion leaders as well as industry insiders.

> LEED has been much less present in homebuilding than in commercial and institutional design and construction, partly because of its breadth of coverage. The Passivhaus standard only addresses energy use, while LEED asks projects to consider several other sustainability-related categories, including materials choice, site characteristics, and water use. Sustainability is a broader challenge than just energy, so LEED is admirable in its attempts at suitable breadth, but this has made for a heavy burden of required documentation. The residential sector has been ill-equipped and unwilling to take it on.

A second observation is about interpreting the energy numbers. The standards we have discussed—LEED, Passivhaus—and others like the UK-based BREEAM all insist on low energy use. But since they have been directed at the design stage of a building, they have had to rely on advance estimates, not actual use. When, in the mid-2000s, operational data covering several years became available, the cat was among the pigeons. Actual energy use is rarely close to the design-phase estimate. This has shown up very straightforwardly in data from 121 LEED-rated commercial buildings[127] and 106-plus German residences.[128] The cynical would immediately guess that the design estimates would be systematically overoptimistic, and the anxious would fear they were right. But the message from these comparisons is more interesting and instructive than that.

In both the LEED and the German samples, the average energy use of all the buildings together is very close to the design phase estimate. The buildings using more than expected, and often much, much more, are basically matched by others using less than expected, often much, much less.[129]

This spread of results turns out to be largely the result of variation in how people use the buildings. Things like when they're occupied, what auxiliary devices from hair dryers to copy machines are used (and how often energy equipment is checked and serviced) can vary a great deal between buildings. There is also some variation in the quality of construction work and installed equipment. The advance estimators can only make guesses about these things; they may be well informed and sensible, but they are guesses nonetheless. The fact that the guesses match average performance is reassuring to the estimators, but the wide spread of individual building results is troublesome for owners and for public confidence in the standards.

This is actually a familiar situation, like the auto industry's practice of providing a miles per gallon figure for each model. That includes a disclaimer: "The EPA ratings are a useful tool for comparing the fuel economies of different vehicles but may not accurately predict the average MPG you will get," or something similar.[130] We can expect that energy estimates for buildings will somehow eventually arrive at a similar cultural position, giving good general indications of the efficiency potential of structure, envelope, and equipment, to be fulfilled to greater or lesser degree by the owners and operators. Standards do help the possible become probable, but they don't provide certainty, especially not about the performance of each individual certified building,

A standard is a tool. No one lives or works in a standard. On the other hand, sustainability is achieved (or not) in actual lives in actual buildings. This is one big reason for having a real-world building at the center of all this book's discussion.

---

[113] This thought has been attributed to several US astronauts. This version is from https://www.daviddarling.info/encyclopedia/C/Collins_Michael.html

[114] *ASME Codes & Standards Writing Guide.* American Society of Mechanical Engineers, 2000.

[115] Seck, Momar D., and David D. Evans, "Major US cities using national standard fire hydrants, one century after the great Baltimore fire." US Department of Commerce, Technology Administration, National Institute of Standards and Technology, 2004.

[116] An excellent short account of context and initiatives in US green building in that era is Cassidy, R. (2003). White paper on sustainability. *Building Design and Construction*, **10**, 132. Available online at https://archive.epa.gov/greenbuilding/web/pdf/bdcwhitepaperr2.pdf

[117] See https://www.baskinrobbins.com/en, accessed 7/26/18)

[118] US Green Building Council, *LEED in Motion 2013*

119 National Green Building Adoption Index 2015. CBRE. Accessed through https://www.cbre.com/-/media/files/corporate%20responsibility/green-building-adoption-index-2015.pdf?la=en

120 Personal communication.

121 Kaid Benfield, January 2013, at citylab.com

122 Brown, M. A. (1996). *Energy-efficient buildings: Does the marketplace work?* (No. CONF-9611133-1). Oak Ridge National Lab.(ORNL), Oak Ridge, TN (United States).

123 Mueller, L. and Berker, T. (2013) "Passive House at the crossroads." *Energy Policy*, 60, pp. 586-593.

124 Gottfried, *op. cit.*

125 Mueller and Berker, *op. cit.*

126 The database for the original Passive House Institute listed 142 US projects in early 2024.

127 Turner, Cathy, and Mark Frankel. "Energy performance of LEED for new construction buildings." New Buildings Institute 4 (2008): 1-42.

128 Passive House Institute, Passive House Standard. https://passiv.de/former_conferences/Passive_House_E/Passivehouse_measured_consumption.html. Accessed December 2016.

129 A footnote for those who may have heard differently: the European Union has had a directive requiring a certain kind of advance energy estimate which does systematically understate what buildings in operation will use. There has been much scrambling to understand the reasons and quite a few changes in procedure have been proposed. The estimates used for the stretch standards of LEED and Passivhaus are made on different, more fundamental bases.

130 For a recent way of putting this, see https://www.epa.gov/greenvehicles/your-mileage-may-vary. Accessed January 2024.

10: **Renovation, 2006-2009**

Sustainability needs sustaining. It's obvious when you think about it, but often one doesn't. The adrenalin of struggling to get something sustainable in place instead of something that's definitely not sustainable can focus your attention on the very short term. But if that struggle leads to success, then a new kind of challenge emerges, the challenge of the long term.

That was certainly true of the building at 1739 Snowmass Creek Road. Over the twenty-two years from 1984 to 2006, its owners and managers generally responded in ways that were conventional, not visionary. They fixed what broke and deferred attention to anything that didn't require it. In a few important ways, they did stay ahead. In lighting, for example, the Lovins/RMI goal of pointing the way forward materialized in an upgrade every seven years or so, to the latest generation of compact fluorescents. They left most other things alone until major changes in the early 2000s brought wear and tear and aging into sharp focus. There were four main areas of work. Besides the improvements to the greenhouse that we've discussed, they set up a radiant floor, converted to LED lighting, and rethought the PV system. There was renovation in the literal sense, "making new again." There was rejuvenation, "making young again." And there was a degree of redirection.

Wear and tear

These twenty-two years saw substantial changes take place for the people and the organization the building housed, changes which converged in a crisis and transition in 2002-2003.

RMI only had three or four employees besides Lovins and his wife in 1984, but the organization quite quickly outgrew the workspace available in the building. Its research on large scale energy and resource strategies continued, in effect defining the soft path for a variety of US and international audiences. It mostly functioned as a think tank, financed by agencies, foundations, or large corporations willing to have Lovins and RMI develop concepts and propose agendas.

It also worked on ideas and services with commercial potential. The encyclopedic in-house knowledge of energy efficiency became embodied in COMPETITEK, a subscription service which generated income for several years, and then was spun off as E SOURCE, a free-standing company, in 1992. The Hypercar project began in the same years. It was another example of the potential of tunneling through the cost barrier— emerging from the insight that carbon-fiber material, then very new and quite expensive, could make a strong, safe vehicle that was radically lighter than conventional cars, permitting a radically smaller power plant, greatly reduced energy consumption, and significant long term savings. Lovins and RMI followed an on-again, off-again, peaks-and-valleys attempt to commercialize this insight, which deserves sometime to be traced in detail for the light it sheds on US ambivalence about innovation, and the complications of trying to transform a huge existing section of the economy. Although the Hypercar never became a commercial success, it was not for want of trying; their vision of the soft path was never anti-commercial or anti-corporate.[131]

Increasingly over these years, in fact, corporations came to RMI to pay it for commercial consulting rather than contributing to sponsor its activities. Consultancy draws on much the same set of skills and knowledge as think-tank work, but it makes decisions and chooses directions to suit the client's agenda, not the consultant's. This is quite lucrative; it supports a larger organization; and it disseminates think-tank thinking into real-world applications. This was all welcome at RMI, the more so because its reputation and presence were such that little or no marketing was necessary to get work of this kind. During this period, Amory and Hunter Lovins collaborated with Paul Hawken, a well-known entrepreneur, in writing *Natural Capitalism*, which made a forceful case to businesses that resource efficiency and environmental restoration were a major new path to profit. The quick success of this book promised well for consulting to continue growing as a major component of RMI's work, and a burst of new work at the end of the 1990s brought that to 40% of its revenue in 2000.

This period, sixteen years of very continuous growth, came to a shocking close with the end of the dot-com bubble in 2000 and the 9/11 attack in September 2001. Consulting revenue plunged. Staff layoffs threatened. And it seems that internal tensions which had been manageable in the good years came to a head: the 2001-2002 Annual Report mentions issues of "staffing, delivery capacity, marketing gaps, and priority-setting."

A personal complication was that the same sixteen years had seen Amory and Hunter's marriage come apart. They separated in 1989 and divorced in 1999. It is no part of this book to trace the whats, whys and wherefores, but it is clear that what was at first a workable separation of personal from professional life, with Amory as inspired researcher and Hunter as forceful manager, plenty of joint authorship and shared visibility in RMI's public affairs, and little shared private life, ended in a total parting of the ways. Hunter Lovins left RMI in the spring of 2002; negotiations over buying out her interest in the building and other terms of separation continued for a year and a half.

For the building, these organizational and personal shifts compounded the accumulated consequences of the quite normal tendency for homeowners to postpone maintenance that is not immediately needed, and not to look too hard for problems. Given the need and wish to present an appealing demonstration of the soft path in action, everything in plain sight was kept looking good. The place may well have been better maintained than at the average house. An appraisal done as part of the 2003 settlement was ready to state that:

> The building has been well maintained during its nearly 20-year life. Its unique design created a need for some remedial work during the first few years of occupancy, including upgrading of the roof cover/insulation system. Most of the building has been re-glazed, with the replacement of fixed glass and, in some cases, window units. Some existing fixed glass units are in need of replacement. Overall, there is minimal evidence of deferred maintenance.

This was an appraiser's once-over, not a detailed investigation. It did not mention various incremental upgrades, like the periodic upgrades of compact fluorescents, nor did it touch on any signs of potential trouble, like the condensation on the upper work area's window edges in cold weather. One can take it as a basic overview of the building's condition as seen by an established real estate professional.

But when fresh eyes and real motivation for renovation arrived, starting in about 2004, an in-house document noted:

> What began as a modest project focused on the greenhouse renovation developed into a state-of-the-art retrofit of the entire building. From the east entrance to the west, hardly a single surface or component has been left unaltered.[132]

The fresh eyes and motivation originated with Judy Hill, a Snowmass resident, the owner of an Aspen art photography business, and a long-standing acquaintance whom Amory began dating early in 2004. The relationship deepened quickly, in practical matters as well as emotionally. Well before the two married in 2007, Judy became in effect the project manager for renovation, and indeed its driving force.

Renovation, rejuvenation, redirection

Her first effort was a thorough inspection—there was 22 years of accumulated wear and tear that called for more than cosmetic treatment. The greenhouse soil had become unproductive, but harbored enough roaches to be "more than a nuisance." Other signs included the cold weather condensation on the work area's windows, a slow year by year increase in the amount of firewood burned in the two wood stoves, and places where the plaster had shrunk and pulled away from the ceiling. The most alarming deterioration was unsuspected until Judy and the intern assisting her began probing the greenhouse window frames. The wood at the bottom of the band of vertical glazing at the foot of the greenhouse was totally rotten, only held together by what Amory called 'termites holding hands'. That called for immediate temporary supporting timbers, pending thorough rebuilding of that portion of the frame.

None of these issues reflected basic flaws in soft path thinking. Some could be traced to the barn-raising phase of construction, and the skill limitations of its enthusiastic volunteers. The greenhouse wood, for example, was simply suffering from builders forgetting to put a copper sheet between it and the concrete supporting it. All this had certainly become more serious during the 1990's, when both Lovinses and the rest of RMI were concentrating on other things than the fabric of their building. Simply restoring the building to its 1984 state, making it young again in that sense, was not the approach they took in 2006. The point of the building had been to show what was possible, and more had become possible after 22 years. Concepts and resources for a more sustainable greenhouse had moved well forward. Technology had made some significant advances, most notably in lighting; market availability of high-performance products had advanced as well. Experience in green building accumulated since Audubon and Kranichstein, and systematized in the LEED ratings and Passivhaus/Passive House standards, had sharpened the definition of good performance. And the occupants' organizational and personal needs had also shifted.

An early project list is explicit about the variety of motivations at work. It suggests five categories: maintenance, demonstration upgrade, RMI-area upgrade, personal upgrade, original uncompleted punch-list. Presumably this was to help allocate costs—defining what Lovins would pay, what RMI would pay as part-lessee, and what would be shared. Sixty-five items are listed; some are quite small, like a motion sensor light at the front door, but most are really whole categories like "floor strip, repair cracks and seal" rather than individual work items. Fifteen of them were tagged as maintenance, nine were personal upgrades, and 46 were demonstration upgrades. (A few got more than one tag, and there were still two "original punch-list" items.)

The demonstration upgrades concerned daylighting, electric lighting, the PV system, a shift to underfloor heating, and an extensive data gathering and display system, as well as a complete renovation of the greenhouse. They bear witness as an ensemble to the swelling of US green building over the previous two decades, in other words to a broadening and deepening of the possible. Where assembling the ingredients for the 1984 house took intensive networking inside and outside established channels and careful sifting of fact from hope and rumor, in 2006-2009 there were relevant products in profusion. Internet search engines would flood one's screen with ads and reviews, and a constellation of activated interest groups were promoting their views of the building industry. Careful sifting was still needed, but now it was distinguishing facts from hype, not facts from hopes.

The implicit message to visitors was to be the same as before, Yours Could Work As Well As This. The place was still not aiming to be either a model to be copied or a statement of individual independence. Neither was it after the carefully smoothed impersonality of the typical demonstration home. It was going to be the home of two real people, leading real lives which balanced public and private spheres in their own particular ways.

The "personal upgrade" items on the early task list reflected the visible surface of personal life—upholstery, furnishings, hot tub, revised storage for clothes, books, and papers. But personal considerations were also behind one major piece of the demonstration moves, the shift to radiant floor heating as the supplement to direct solar. The latter would remain the building's primary source of heat, but Judy objected to wood stoves as the supplement. They were bad for her health and other people's because they leaked small but troublesome amounts of smoke and particulate matter.

The radiant floor

The radiant floor system, in which water is heated outside the living space and then circulated through tubes buried in the floors, was a viable alternative. The original design had considered it, and went as far as placing the needed serpentine tubing everywhere in the floors except the green space, front hall and two bathrooms, to be available as backup if the then very unfamiliar passive solar design failed to live up to expectations. In the event, the passive design worked very well, and modest wood stove supplementing it was all that had been required. The tubing had never been used, but it was still serviceable.

To get a working radiant floor system, they needed a heat source and a suitable set of controls. The obvious heat source was the sun, and solar thermal collectors were the obvious way to harvest its energy. Recall that these simple devices, consisting of a black absorbing surface made hot by the sun and transferring that heat to water pumped through small channels in the surface, were the icons of the solar movement of the 1960s and 1970s. They were "active" solar, on account of needing pumps and controls, in contrast to "passive" approaches like the Lovins greenhouse.

> Active solar had not prospered as a primary heat source for buildings in the solar-oriented era that followed the oil crises of the 1970s. Buildings of the time were not well insulated, at least in today's terms, which made the needed collector array very large and therefore quite expensive. Pumps and controls, though not esoteric, had not been widely enough used in this kind of system to be truly reliable, and solar thermal systems acquired a certain reputation for malfunctioning.

Active solar had actually been employed at the Lovins building from the start, as the heat source for showers, sinks and other domestic hot water. It had proved reliable enough in this role.

> The original collectors, pipes, and large storage tank (1500 gallons) were still in use in 2006; the pump had been replaced once or twice, but no more often than conventional items of household equipment.

To provide the additional heat needed for the radiant floor, the number of thermal collectors was doubled, from four to eight.[133] Since space heating in average Colorado houses calls for about three times the energy use of domestic hot water, a building services engineer might have expected that twelve additional panels would be needed, not just four. But the radiant floors were not to be the sole source of space heat, nor even the primary one. That still came direct from the sun, captured by the generous provision of south-facing glass, and retained by the low-loss shell, superwindows, and heat recovery ventilation.

One might also have expected that more storage would be needed, in proportion to the increased load. US solar hot water systems need storage, because users dislike having their showers, dishwashing and laundry times set by the sun's convenience. The radiant floors would also be most needed after dark, but Lovins had been conservative in 1983 when the hot water system was assembled. Estimates showed that the original 1,500 gallon tank would still be adequate. There would be some shrinkage in the number of days the system could go without direct sun, but not a worrying amount. Once again, the low losses of the shell and ventilation system allowed downsized equipment.

Controls

The last major element in the revised heating scheme was the control system. As you can see from the illustration, it is more than an on/off switch.[134] We don't need to walk through each item and its whats and whys, but the area of controls has been a genuine frontier of sustainable

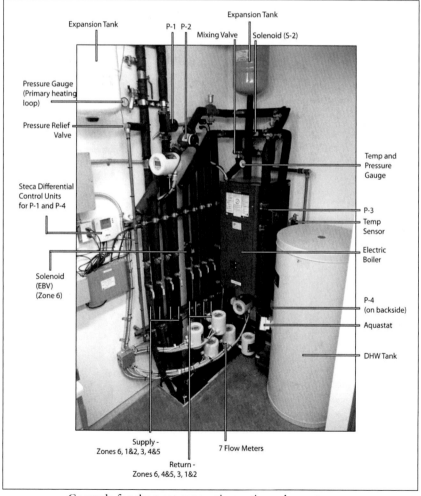

Controls for the post-renovation active solar system
(radiant floor heating and domestic hot water)

thinking over the past ten years. I mean frontier in the fullest sense; it has been an unsettled zone where the right answers are not obvious, and it is not even clear one is asking the right questions.

In fact, the Lovins building was not particularly visionary when it came to controls. It has something to teach, but it doesn't provide a complete lesson plan, and it doesn't point in a decisive direction.

The basic issue seems quite simple, hardly the stuff of careful discussion, much less the inspiration for whole engineering specialties. You want the right amount of heat, neither too much nor too little. Households in the US differ in how warm they want to be, but almost all of them have proved willing to accept a fairly constant indoor temperature as the background condition of their thermal comfort. An unproblematic way providing this had already developed by the 1950s—an oil or gas furnace fed by electric pumps for oil or valves for natural gas, and actuated by a temperature controlled switch, the thermostat.

Active solar systems, like the radiant floors in the Lovins renovation or the hot water system the house enjoyed from the beginning, are conceptually like furnace systems, in the sense of having a specialized, dedicated structure (usually a tank of water), from which heat can be provided when needed. A true passive solar system, like the 1983 Lovins design, also aims for roughly constant temperature, but pursues it quite differently.

Like furnaces, active solar systems need controls. In fact, they need two sets, one for gathering the heat and the other for distributing it. On the gathering side, the basic setup is fairly simple. An antifreeze-water mixture is pumped up to the solar thermal panels on the roof, heated as it passes through them, and returned to heat the storage tank's water as it passes through a finned tube in the bottom of the tank. The control task is just to run the pump whenever fluid at the exit of the panels is warmer than the water at the coolest point, at the bottom of the storage tank, and to turn it off otherwise.

The latter is just as important as the former. Warm water circulating through a collector loses heat, the way any hotter thing loses heat to its cooler environment. When the sun is shining, its inflow much more than makes up for the losses, and warm water comes out warmer. At night or in cloudy weather, there isn't any make-up heat, and the water comes out cooler unless the pump gets turned off.[135]

Distributing the solar heated water calls for a second control setup. This one uses thermostats in the classic way: when the thermostat senses temperature below its setting, it turns on the heat supply. Here the supply is a storage tank full of hot water, not a furnace, but the control setup is basically the same as it has been since the 1950s, with one important departure its important to notice, because it is so characteristic of the present era. There are six heating circuits in this house, six thermostats, six sets of valves and sensors, six different pipe runs.

This was not a Lovins innovation. It was part of a national trend. Once a good average household temperature, maintained by a single thermostat, had been the definition of thermal comfort, but the decades had seen a steady elaboration of housebuilding features and fantasies, with the radical advance of digital technology promising to make it all feasible. Each room at a different temperature? No problem. Different every hour of the year, according to season and likely occupancy? No problem. Some people dream of houses that recognize their different occupants and adjust not only the heat, but also the lights, the furniture, the TV programs, and the snacks on the counter to suit their individual tastes. Thanks to radically cheap and fast computing, embodied not only in computers themselves but also in phones, "smart" appliances, and household control centers, there is no conceptual limit on the elaboration which is technically possible.[136]

In these terms, the remodel of 2006-09 was relatively simple. There were to be six thermostats and sets of valves, but some clever engineering saw to it that a single pump could move all the circulating water, however the needs might vary from zone to zone.

In addition, it seemed desirable to have a backup heat source, in case the solar heated storage proved insufficient, in prolonged cloudy weather or for some other reason. So an electric boiler was installed, to come on only when water supplied by the solar storage tank was less than 105 degrees. This meant one more thermostat loop.

Of course, the original need for hot water for sinks, showers, and laundry was still there. It was to be served from the same storage tank as the floors as a seventh heating circuit, complete with its own thermostat, valves and so forth. It was to have first call on heat in two ways: the radiant floor loops would be closed off temporarily if the hot water system got too cool, and the backup electric boiler would come into play if the solar storage tank was also too cool. The first call required one more control loop.

Gaggle or maze?

One begins to see where the maze of tubes and cylinders in the photo comes from. You may also begin to wonder if there is a simpler way of providing the same services. There is, but it is not obviously preferable. You could have a separate system for each use—separate collectors, storage tank, sensors, valves and pumps. Each system could operate on its own, turning on and off as its narrow circumstances indicated. There would be no maze of interconnections and signaling; instead, there'd be a gaggle of side-by-side units.

This would be simpler. Would it be better? That approach wouldn't have any conflict between uses and would offer much greater ease in diagnosing equipment problems. The most evident disadvantage would be the great proliferation of gear. There would be a lot more machinery to pay for and find room for. Setting up the ensemble would be more straightforward, but it would take more time to do the physical mounting and fastening. There are other tradeoffs.

> Simplicity could also be pursued by reducing the number of zones in the building, but that would mean providing more heat to spaces at times when they are not in use. That's simpler, but it hurts the atmosphere. However, a complex control system that's providing just the needed heat but is malfunctioning can be worse. There is no ready resolution of this dilemma. It has actually sparked lively research into "personal comfort systems," exploring

the potential of buildings providing only a background level of warmth, with local appliances like personal fans and heaters, making things comfortable for each individual.[137]

It's quite important that it might take less time to get the gaggle system up and running smoothly. Troubleshooting the logic of priorities and level settings in the maze system to get it running or repair it could be slow and require specialized training. The instructions for a basic thermostat loop fit in a single sentence ("if temperature at point A is below the set point, turn on the heat"), but it takes five paragraphs totaling over 600 words to cover the variety of conditions and responses in the renovated Lovins hot water system. Temperature needs to be sensed at several points, the domestic hot water needs to be at a different temperature from the radiant floor hot water, and the storage tank's temperature varies according to weather and occupant demands. Keeping track of all this requires more complexity in the controls.

That's in aid of a laudable goal, providing sensitively directed comfort and making the most of the sun's energy while economizing on equipment. There's nothing wrong with complexity in itself. Human bodies, after all, are complex in ways we keep being reminded we barely understand. But it's easy to underestimate or overlook a real cost to setting up complex control systems and getting them running properly.

The weight of the simple, the intricacy of the complex

All these details of the hot water systems show the Lovins project facing a consequential choice which comes up frequently in the search for sustainable economic and social patterns. Is it better to have many simple, independent systems acting side by side or a few systems with complex internal coordination of many actions? An everyday illustration of the same choice is playing out daily in US neighborhoods. Is it better to shop at the stores, or get Amazon to deliver? The first system is a gaggle, with everyone in their individual cars heading to one or more stores and returning home. The other is a maze, with a few delivery drivers following an intricate path that takes them to the houses on the day's list.

In a narrow sense of sustainability, just looking at the fuel used in vehicles and the energy used to make the steel, plastic and other materials they're composed of, the maze approach is much more sustainable. In the much wider sense of sustainability as a mode of life that's not only viable but desirable, the long-run situation is not yet clear. The maze approach is more convenient, but more open to misunderstandings between supplier and consumer, less open to individual initiative, more liable to exploitation of a few (like the drivers) for the benefit of the many, generally quicker to get goods to users, and so on. What is clear in 2023 is that Amazon's maze approach is very successful commercially, despite any burdens of complex coordination.

> Getting the logic right can be tricky even in the simplest thermostat loop when the logic needs to reflect the real world. One notable green classroom/office building in the Pacific Northwest was able to use natural ventilation most of the time, but had a fan to help on days with heavy use and little breeze. The control was the simplest kind of loop: if indoor temperatures got above a certain point, the thermostat would turn on the fan. The idea was to draw in extra air from outside, which in the Northwest is typically cool. Unfortunately, in the occasional heat wave that happens, the indoor air can already be above the thermostat set point in the morning, because it is hot outside. Then the fan would come on, drawing in even hotter outside air, and it would run for the rest of the day, providing really effective further heating of the building, the complete opposite of the intent.

In the building sector these days, complex coordination is on a steady upswing as the preferred approach. Large buildings, like office towers, rely on elaborate systems of ducts, fans, pumps, and chillers to provide thermal comfort. Squeezing down their energy requirements as far as possible without creating comfort problems seems (to industry insiders) to call for the maze approach and complex central control, entailing intricate logic far beyond what went into the Snowmass renovation.[138]

Intricate does not mean esoteric here. The actions being controlled are usually pretty basic ones—on/off for a switch, more/less for a valve or motor. Unfortunately, getting the right switches on or off and the right valve openings and motor speeds when each setting has effects on many others is not straightforward or particularly quick and easy. Even getting all the switches installed the right way up is not guaranteed in a project with thousands of them. Many projects now employ commissioning agents, specialists in checking these maze systems for appropriate behavior. They come in when a project is nearly complete, go over everything, and typically find dozens of adjustments and changes that are needed.

Similar issues certainly arise over the long haul. Complex buildings need good documentation, but all too often don't get it. Repairs and replacements then risk short-circuiting, unsynchronizing or otherwise upsetting the system for want of knowing how its components interact with each other. The Lovins renovation did recognize this problem, in fact, and put together a detailed Operations Manual for the building.

The Lovins setup was far simpler than in a typical office building, but still complicated enough for a typical control system fault to occur. About a year after the renovation was finished, the electric bill began to have giant winter peaks, with monthly totals five or six times the typical levels of the rest of the year. It was some time before this was noticed, but the diagnosis was fortunately quick: the thermostat controlling the water flowing to the solar collectors was failing to notice when the water came down cooler than it went up. So the circulating pump kept running all night every winter night, sending water up to the collectors, which cooled it very effectively when the sun wasn't out. The system cooled the storage tank down every night, to the level where the thermostat governing the backup electric boiler sensed a need and turned the boiler on. Instead of merely providing occasional service, the backup ran daily, doing its main job of ensuring that hot water was available, but also doing a second job —covering the large losses happening every night in the collector system.

There one easy but not particularly helpful lesson here—the fault would have been detected sooner if the Lovinses had looked hard at their monthly bills sooner. Hardly anybody does. However, there's a subtler, quite important lesson about setting up controls. The hot water system was intended to do two things: always provide plenty of hot water, and almost always heat it with solar energy. The unnoticed subtlety was the difference in signals of shortcoming. Falling short of the hot water goal would be obvious very quickly and directly, in cold showers or cold hand-washing. Falling short on solar heat didn't provide any obvious signal. One was there, every month in the electric bill, but nothing was in place to sound an alarm.

There's no technical barrier to having such an alarm. In general, alarms are always possible in digital control systems. One just has to realize one wants one. There is a price to pay in added complexity—one more loop to check—but it's not a large price in itself. Things add up, though. Complexity often arrives like Carl Sandburg's fog, on little cat feet. Like droplets in fog, each loop only impedes perception very slightly, but with enough of them, one can't see at all.

Renovation plans for the Lovins building included a large household data system, with 180 data collection points, a dedicated server and real-time display. The programming could readily have included alarm functions for solar heat and other indices of desired performance. But on top of the difficulty of seeing what alarms the complex heating system might need, the data system had headaches of its own which confirmed another cautionary truth. Technical and industrial equipment is not born mature.

The individual initiative which this society so values is highly generative, but also quite resistant to coordination. So there is always a stage when the hoses don't fit the hydrants, the lamps don't fit the sockets, the data cables don't plug into the server, and when they do the signals they carry are incomprehensible to the receiving circuits. Incompatibilities typically lead to clever workarounds, then rising sentiment for standards, then technically sound but self-interested negotiations, and eventually the birth of a standard. This all takes time and attention.

Eventually everyone revises their product lines, supervisory bodies are organized, and the equipment becomes much easier to set up and use smoothly. A certain maturity has arrived. (We are currently living through this process with electric car chargers, moving from three different incompatible systems of plugs and innumerable systems for paying toward something more standardized and convenient.) The Lovins renovation came before that had happened for building data systems. If we think of the heating system creating a degree of fog, we can think of the data system as having malfunctioning radar. Taken together, and stretching the metaphor, these difficulties made the renovated building sail more slowly than one would expect.

Daylight and its electric cousin

The other major interior upgrades concerned lighting. All but one of the moves that affected daylight were simple, easy to take for granted, and profound. The concrete floor, a maroon colored expanse, was stripped of its sealer and cleaned. Wood surfaces in the greenhouse, kitchen, and elsewhere were brought to much lighter tones through refinishing or replacement. The bare wood of the greenhouse rafters and framing was painted white. The point was to get more natural light into the interior, to the benefit of both plants and people.

For much of the 20th century, until the shift epitomized in the Audubon House, natural light was a resource hidden from US commercial and residential builders. It was hidden in plain sight, to be sure, and valued for some of its effects, but not really recognized in itself. There was much attention to the views windows might give, and sometimes for the fresh air, and poets and painters reveled in sun and shade, atmospherics, dawns and dusks and mid-days, indoors as well as out. People of all kinds certainly responded to the quality of light in the rooms they inhabited or visited—the feeling of bright or dim, sparkling or muted, pure or tinted. Certain theorists, in architecture and elsewhere, also waxed lyrical about such things. But most architects, engineers, and builders didn't pay much attention to them when it came to working on with actual building projects.

Workaday design was largely about providing enough light, with coarse distinctions about quality and source. Fluorescent tubes in a workplace or factory might be somewhat harsh and flickering, as long as they provided enough light to see clearly and read fine print, and did so reliably and cheaply. That was also all that other kinds of electric lighting were expected to do. The postwar era in the US gloried in its control of

Photo Credit: Integrated Design Lab Puget Sound / C. Meek

The Terry Thomas Building, mid-rise office space, Seattle

nature; the sun and sky as sources of light could not match the perceived convenience and flexibility of artificial means, and they fell into disregard in the building sector.

Environmentalism and energy crises began to change this in the 1970s, but for quite a while heating and cooling dominated attention; with sunlight was largely assessed for its ability to replace furnace fuels. This was very important, but it had nothing to do with lighting as a household need.

> In fact, capturing sunlight as heat competes with using it for light, and many solar dwellings of the 1970s were distinctly dim inside.

Eventually, however, the search for energy efficiency in buildings recognized lighting as a major kind of consumption, and efforts to use natural light to replace artificial light and its energy demands emerged. We have seen signs of this at work at Audubon House, in 1992, and commercial design ran ahead of residential in this area.

> Perhaps this was because it took so much artificial light to make deep office and retail spaces workable that the energy bill for lighting bulked much larger than for houses, where almost all

rooms can be day-lit much of the time. Typical estimates for offices and the like in the 1990s showed lighting using 30% more energy than heating and cooling combined, a complete turnaround from household proportions.[139]

Making use of natural light has strong implications for the physical layout of buildings. It calls for higher ceilings, so taller windows can let more daylight in, and shallower rooms, so life and work are not too far from the source of light. This was matter of fact before the twentieth century. Even the most monumental buildings of that time were in the shape of H's, E's, U's or O's, with relatively thin wings facing daylight on both sides.

> This was true of apartment blocks, as well, though not of ordinary houses, which are already narrow enough for daylight to reach well inside most rooms. A rough rule of thumb holds that reading and other ordinary activities can be done by daylight alone as far away as about one and half times the height of the window, even on cloudy winter afternoons. Rooms in most houses satisfy this rule pretty well.

For commercial and governmental buildings, deeper rooms mean more rentable square feet, so green design since the 1990s has given considerable attention to getting daylight deeper into buildings. The methods have turned out to be relatively humble—fewer and lower partitions and lighter paints and finishes. The image of Seattle's Terry Thomas Building shows a dramatic use of this idea. (Two more assertive techniques, light shelves and daylight tubes, have also found some use, but opening up spaces and lightening their colors have been the primary moves.)

Even these humble moves have generated controversy, and here we touch another way in which sustainability is not just a technical matter, but rather something which engages whole lives. Daylight is entangled with workplace habits, patterns, and hierarchies, and with how accountants handle overheads, and with biorhythms and responses of individuals. Opening office spaces for daylight competes with the historic use of windows as status symbols—

> Spotting status used to be simple: you looked for the biggest office with the most windows and best views.[140]

On the other hand, providing more daylight often raises staff spirit, as evidenced by the Audubon House secretary ("I like the building so much that I give tours"), as well as by industry surveys which show absenteeism is markedly lower and reported satisfaction with workplace environment is markedly higher in buildings with lots of daylight.[141] There is also considerable indication from research on hospitals, schools, and workplaces that natural light is good for human health.

At the same time, improved daylight is not the only effect of more open office layouts. They also raise issues that are actively debated in the business press—noise, distraction, and the spread of colds and other diseases. The situation is genuinely tangled. If you recall the discussion of sick building syndrome, real physical symptoms may be caused as much by organizational issues like control over pace and responsibility as by the physical features of workplaces.

Other things being equal, there is no controversy these days that daylight is better in workplaces than artificial, but things are seldom equal.

The Lovins building began with ample daylight in its core, the greenhouse, and what seemed adequate elsewhere. On re-examining the question with the eyes and sensibilities of 2006, however, the office, dining area and kitchen seemed darker than desirable. The hallway between the entry door and the living area, down which you can be drawn now by the promise of light at the far end, looked positively lightless in 2006. The small rooms in the private quarters were still acceptable, but the bulk of the house needed better lighting.

> Light intensity has a very large subjective component; our experience of it is not closely tied to its physical intensity in a space as measured by instruments. Museums, which often want low light in galleries to preserve the artwork, arrange the lobbies and halls on the way to the art itself to be progressively dimmer, so visitors can come from bright outside light to galleries with physical intensity 1000 times less without ever feeling in the dark.
>
> Offices have to manage glare from windows or light fixtures, where quite small differences in the experienced intensity of

adjoining surfaces can be troublesome to the point of unworkability. The subject is very large, multifaceted, and fascinating.[142]

For the Lovins renovation, a key point was that acceptable lighting in 2005 could become unacceptable in 2006, in the same way smudges on eyeglasses can go unnoticed for a long time, but change to constant irritants once they're noticed.

Daylighting in the building was improved by a number of simple yet profound moves toward lighter toned, cleaner surfaces in and around the greenhouse, so the ample daylight there would be reflected and spread into the adjoining spaces more. There was also a profound, less simple move. This addressed the hallway. There are no windows there, and it provides no direct views of any kind to the outside. A skylight was possible but undesirable, because a large extended opening in the roof would have been a major avenue for heat loss and might have leaked over time. Instead, they installed a light pipe. Sunlight coming through a small dome in the roof is channeled down a highly reflective tube to fall on a long translucent panel in the ceiling of the hall. Sunlight is so very much brighter than usual indoor light levels that the small amount captured at the roof can be spread over the large ceiling fixture below and still give plenty of useful illumination.

The artificial side of the lighting was completely reworked. Again, the more advanced sensibilities of 2006 came into play, aided by the rise of LED lamps. The Lovinses worked with Robert Sardinsky, an ex-RMI colleague who had spun himself off as a locally based, nationally active lighting consultant. The goal for this part of the renovation was to "create a luminous environment that is warm and welcoming, versatile for home and work activities, and uses the least amount of energy possible for each application."[143] There's a modest but definite shift in sensibility in the explicit valuing of interpersonal warmth and welcome. The building's first generation had never been opposed to warm welcome, but would have felt it was implicit in the rustic regional aura of the decor, the coffee pot that was always ready, and the flow of conversation. Now the lighting scheme was being directed to do part of this work. Once again, the meaning of sustainability here went beyond the purely technical.

The technical side was also vital, of course. Light-emitting diodes, or LEDs, were an early outcome of the research into semiconductors that generated the transistor, the integrated circuit microchip and the rest of the late 20th-century explosion of solid-state technology. The first LEDs were invented in the mid-1950s, but their use as general purpose lamps was long delayed, because the known materials only generated light at the red end of the spectrum. It was the 1990s before a practical way of getting blue light from an LED was discovered. The science was intricate and arduous enough, and the potential uses of it were wide enough, for the lead researchers to be awarded the 2014 Nobel Prize in Physics.

Once blue LED light was possible, ways were rapidly found to generate the rest of the visual spectrum and mixtures including white; ways to get brighter LEDs also advanced rapidly. During these years, engineering and industrial experience in semiconductor production was accumulating very rapidly, motivated (and financed) by the computer revolution. By the mid 2000s, LED lamps in a variety of configurations were beginning to be available for household and corporate use. They were significantly more efficient than compact fluorescents, and made an even greater step forward in reliability, lifespan, and flexibility. Designing with them was the heart of Sardinsky's business, and the Snowmass renovation was a straightforward application.

The details of the relighting are not particularly important, but one or two features are interesting. The basic light-emitting unit of an LED can be very small, so it is quite easy to make long strings of them to deliver light in lines, as opposed to the bright globes of incandescent lights. The lines could also be any desired length without much difficulty, unlike fluorescents. So the curved walls of the Lovins house are now washed with light in several areas by linear strips which follow the curves. Spotlighting can be incorporated where wanted. The wattage required is very low, more often 3 watts per spotlight than the 75 or more that would have been needed before. The overall result is that you can have many more individual sources of light than before and still end up well ahead on energy, because each source is smaller and much more efficient.

Solar electricity in the renovation

The last area of major work between 2006 and 2009 was on the photovoltaic system. Redirection was the theme here. You may recall that the original building opened without solar electricity of any kind, partly because of its expense, but also because the building was there to demonstrate the possibilities lurking in direct and very efficient use of sunlight. The point at that time was how little industrial energy of any kind was really necessary for comfort and professional effectiveness.

When PV came within reach, it was natural to widen the statement, to show two distinct possible ways of using it. You could remain linked to the grid, and use solar power to reduce your draw. The office ran that way. Or you could sever connections with the grid, as the household side did, and rely on battery storage to make power generated during the sunny days available at other times.

This first period demonstrated the possibility of doing office and household work well in a building that relied almost completely on sunlight. By the time of the remodel, the live questions were different. One way to get at them is to consider changes Lovins made in the PV system and then talk about why.

The physical changes are simple to describe. By 2006, the "petting zoo" of PV panels had grown to a capacity of 3.8 kilowatts (kW), with the household portion backed by a battery bank which could store about 16 kWh of energy. Before the renovation, Lovins estimated that the household portion of the building drew an average of 1/10 of a kilowatt. At that rate, the pre-renovation storage could keep the household going for about 160 hours, which is a little under a week. The renovation nearly tripled the capacity to 9.7 kW and increased the storage to about 60 kWh. The additional capacity went on the roof, in the form of several large flat arrays of several panels each which come close to filling the available roof area. The battery storage remained in the downstairs workroom, stacked up along one wall.

This large expansion was motivated by a significant change in what the photovoltaics were supposed to do. The Lovinses decided that the array should be big enough to handle the whole daytime electrical load of the building, office as well as household. Surprisingly perhaps, they also decided that any extra power produced in daytime would not be stored in the batteries. They would only be used to keep office and household running normally during power outage.

The extra solar power would be delivered to the regional grid for the specific purpose of reducing the need for power from coal or natural gas plants in region. Instead of storing the extra for use at night, the building would draw from the grid then. It happened that non-fossil resources, mainly wind, would generally be adequate in those hours, and could be specified as the sources for the building. They were essentially shipping solar out when the grid was dirty and relatively expensive, and drawing an equivalent amount of cheaper surplus power back in from the grid when it was clean.

Some dramatic developments in US energy between 1983 and 2006 prepared the ground and generated the rationale for this redirection at the Lovins operation. The scientific case for human-caused climate change had become very solid, making electric power production by coal or any fossil fuel a major culprit. In the same years, the price of PV panels dropped by half. Wind turbine technology for electrical generation became far more durable; the cost of wind power fell nearly as much as the cost of PV panels; and wind farms became a normal part of utilities' power portfolios. In addition, these decades had generated radical changes in utility policies and practices that made it possible for many private individuals like the Lovinses to sell to the grid as well as buying from it and to have real choices as buyers about how their electric power was generated.

These days, discussions of human-caused climate change are everywhere, but in 1983, when the Lovins house was designed, it was living under a previous name, global warming, and was only occasionally being noticed by the media, much less the general public. Scientific attention had begun years before and had spread during the 1960s, but it was not until the late 1980s that awareness of the issue became national. Even then, it was only one of a group of environmental issues whose more prominent

Lovins roof-top solar arrays after 2006-2009 renovation. The majority, tilted at 35 or 50 degrees, are solar electric (PV); the eight more steeply tilted collectors (rear center) are solar thermal; the superwindow glass of the greenhouse is toward the right-hand end, set in a raised portion of the building's stone walls.

members included acid rain, ozone depletion, endangered species, toxic spill cleanup, and water quality. It took another ten years or more before climate change acquired its present dominant position as the central environmental issue of our time, around which the numerous other issues need to arrange themselves.

By 2006, those seeking change (not everyone was) approached acting with a certain collective spirit. In the early 1980s people upset with established social practices had often looked for ways to be independent of society, and tried to get themselves out of it. One major appeal of solar energy was its promise of helping with this. But by 2006 the alternatives to fossil-fueled energy were no longer fringe possibilities; they were demonstrating real prospects of becoming genuine replacements. In using their excess solar energy to displace coal and gas, the Lovinses were part of a voting process, in effect. They were signaling their willingness to use their household's economic influence toward changing society's ways, and they saw themselves not as lone voices, but as part of an eventual widespread shared effort to transform the US energy system.

Three developments had made this kind of voting possible. The dramatic drops in the prices of PV and wind electric power had come about through the steady accumulation of small technological improvements in the relevant electrical, mechanical, production, and installation engineering as the green power industry reinvested some of its revenues in further research.

> Solar cells consist of thin sheets of quite pure silicon, judiciously treated with tiny amounts of other elements; electrical contacts are attached, and protective glass (in front, to let light in) and metal encases the whole package. One improvement was to move the active zone of the silicon sheets to the panel's rear side, so the electrical contacts could be made without blocking incoming light. Another was to recognize that silicon that functioned well for this purpose did not require research lab purity, which allowed considerable cost saving at the refining stage. A third was to devise thinner saws for cutting the thin sheets, so less silicon was wasted as silicon sawdust. Each of the multiple stages of making and installing solar cells has seen similar incremental moves.

The third development was the widening of the market. The growth of solar electricity has benefited greatly from the fact that there's no single market for electric power. One gets the impression there is, because one very large market segment dominates the scene. This is "the grid", the large interconnected web of suppliers, distributors, and consumers that handles a very large portion of each region's power. Its prices are usually the lowest available ones, and if meeting those prices had been a requirement for commercially viable solar, it would have stayed a lab curiosity.

Fortunately, the grid is not the whole market. Think about pumping water for cattle in remote parts of their range, far from the nearest transmission line. Think about warning lights for accident-prone country intersections. The cost of solar electric power from a small panel installed right next to the pump or light could be far less than grid power, once the costly miles of feeder line to the remote location were factored in. Remote applications are a different market from grid-connected service.

One very everyday power purchase provides another very striking example—flashlights. If you divide the cost of a flashlight battery by the amount of energy it provides over its lifetime, that electricity turns out to cost several hundred dollars per kWh. Grid power is roughly ten thousand times cheaper, but it's no use for flashlights. They are in a different power market.

Pocket calculators are like flashlights. They need a portable and lightweight source of electric power, and they were actually an important early market for solar cells. The cells work on any kind of visible light, and calculators don't need much energy, so the brightness of full sun is not required. Once again, the cost in cents per kWh of power used by a calculator over its lifetime is egregiously higher than the cost of grid power, but as with flashlights, that's irrelevant to this use of electricity.

The existence of modest distinctive markets like these provided a staircase for growth of the solar cell industry. Experience gained at each step proved effective in lowering costs and enabling the next step outward into wider and wider uses.

> At a certain point, certain European governments and US agencies and state governments began purchase and subsidy programs that further widened the PV market. Such programs have a deserved bad name when used to prop up failing industries, but in this case they have rewarded society by contributing to the ongoing steady decline in market prices for solar.

These three technological and social developments were the major factors in enabling the Lovinses to purchase their expanded PV capacity. But they wanted to relate to the grid as sellers as well as buyers. That has always been technically possible, but it hasn't always been commercially possible. Before the 1970s, utilities would flatly refuse to buy power from other producers. The nearly universal US business model of electric utilities at that time allowed them to own and operate every part of the system, from generating plants through transmission lines and transformers to local poles and wires, right to the user's building.

Things changed radically after 1973. First, progressives lobbied successfully for legislation to require utilities to buy power from small producers. The rationale was that utilities were perpetrators of environmental damage, from acid rain and strip mining to potential nuclear meltdowns, and that as organizations they were deaf to direct appeal. The fruit of this pressure was the Public Utility Regulatory Policies Act of 1978 (universally called PURPA), which required utilities to buy power from any outsider offering a suitable price.

> The legislation did define "suitable", but the definition was unavoidably arcane; there ensued much wrangling about how it would be applied in given situations, the more so as details of implementation were left to the individual states.

PURPA opened a certain kind of market door to non-utility power producers, which at first meant people with a wind turbine or a small hydropower installation, but not solar power, which was still far too expensive. PURPA's real importance, I think, was in smoothing the path for deregulation, a notion dear to libertarians and neo-liberals. Their motives were quite different from the progressives', but they shared a deep distrust of entrenched corporate business. Utilities were thus targets from the right as well as the left. Passing by the quite complex details of Federal, state and private sector maneuvering,[144] it's enough to say that the Federal Energy Policy Act of 1992 took the key step of requiring that non-utility producers of power be given access to transmission lines which could transfer it to a possibly distant customer.

Before that, the transmission and distribution of power was largely owned by utilities and the law left it entirely up to each one to decide whose power to handle. Usually it was only their own. This changed utterly with the new Act. Production and sale of electric power would now be a market that allowed new sellers as well as new buyers.

> The Act of 1992 contained many more ifs, ands and buts than this. A variety of very thorny issues, such as how to pay off the loans that had built older, more expensive plants, had not been settled. Setting up workable ways of doing what the act called for took intense analysis, lobbying, compromises and interpretation stretching over the next 7-8 years or more.

Many of the details were left to the states, which retained considerable authority over electric power inside their boundaries. When the dust had basically settled, in the first years of the new century, things varied a good deal from one of them to another. Colorado adopted a policy very favorable to small producers like the Lovinses. Called "net metering", it equips such households with a bi-directional electric meter, which runs backward whenever the property is producing more power than it is using. The utility essentially guarantees to buy whatever excess power get produced by that household. This access allowed the Lovins house to displace some of the fossil fueled power production in its region.

> One technical feature of electric power is integral to how this displacement works. Until very recently, there was essentially no storage capacity in the power system. At any moment, the amount produced and the amount being used are exactly the same. The physics is such that if I switch off my electric kettle or stove or hair dryer, dropping my use by that much, the interaction of electrons throughout the whole system automatically and almost instantaneously changes the electromagnetic conditions at all the running generators by a tiny amount that just reduces their output to match.

> This means that when sun shines on the Snowmass rooftop array, supplying the building with its own power and thus reducing its call on the rest of the system or perhaps even putting some power onto the grid, the coal and gas plants out there can't help producing less, which means less coal or gas get burned and less CO_2 is emitted. This is the point of the arrangement.

Maintenance vs. sustenance

The shifts in the provision of heat and electric power, the revisions in lighting, and the provision and use of control systems all were part of sustaining sustainability in this building. The intent was to keep the place up to date with what was possible and with changes in the occupants' needs, while keeping a careful eye on the original goals of efficiency, comfort, and environmental citizenship. This is what sustaining sustainability is all about.

I think it matters which words we use to tackle these questions. It matters that 'maintaining' and 'sustaining' differ in their overtones. 'Maintenance' and 'sustenance' differ, as well. To my ear, the former has to do with objects; it suggests keeping something in good condition, while the latter has to do with life, with the basic nourishment of a person. I also feel that sustenance has more flexibility in it; there's more awareness that quite different things at different times may all serve for nourishing or strengthening. Maintenance has an aura about keeping things just as they are, or just as they have been expected to be; there's little suggestion of growth in 'maintenance'. Since this is a time when sustainability needs to be pursued, but we Americans can't yet see the path clearly and still need to feel our way step by step, I think 'sustenance' is the right name for what buildings like the Lovins house and all our other projects need.

This concludes the historical portion of this profile of 1739 Snowmass Creek Road. The next three chapters are aimed at the present and future. Where and how can one go from here?

---

131 Some of the Hypercar ideas, most notably extensive use of carbon fiber materials to greatly reduce weight without losing strength, have been taken up by established car makers, most notably BMW.

132 Aaron Westgate, Lovins Operations Manual (March 2009). This describes how the renovated building and its systems work.

133 Lovins also tilted up the active solar panels from 40º to 70º, which makes the sun hit more directly in winter, when its heat is most needed.

134 Annotated illustration from Lovins Operational Manual

135 Apparently no one has made a business out of fitting solar collectors with superwindows as covers. That would greatly reduce the amount of heat they lose, just as the greenhouse windows in the Lovins building do. Prototypes of such superwindow collectors have been made and tested, but there is no commercially available version in the US. This seems a lesson ready to be learned, but not learned yet. See Giovannetti, Federico, Maik Kirchner, Francis Kliem, and Torben Hoeltje. "Development of an insulated glass solar thermal collector." *Energy Procedia* 48 (2014) 48 (2014): 58-66.

[136] Rich Gold's *The Plenitude: Creativity, Innovation, and Making Stuff* (MIT Press, 2007) is a delightful non-academic discussion of this and related aspects of present-day US society.

[137] For an introduction, see Brager, G., Zhang, H. and Arens, E., 2015. "Evolving opportunities for providing thermal comfort." *Building Research & Information*, *43*(3), pp.274-287.

[138] A contrary view has been forcefully expressed by William Bordass and Adrian Leaman, two British analysts respected for their independent thinking. See Bordass, W. and Leaman, A., 1997. "Future buildings and their services." *Building Research & Information*, *25*(4), pp.190-195.

[139] Lechner, Norbert. *Heating, cooling, lighting: Sustainable design methods for architects.* Wiley, 2014.

[140] From the website of major furniture maker Herman Miller, accessed 4/2020. https://www.hermanmiller.com/stories/why-magazine/there-goes-the-corner-office/

[141] Elzeyadi, Ihab. "Daylighting-bias and biophilia: quantifying the impact of daylighting on occupants health." US Green Building Council. (2011). Accessed April 2020 through https://pdfs.semanticscholar.org/bfa5/2d19c047b0c109ee5db4b11d1c4dc0f3dc74.pdf

[142] A rich discussion of all this is in Heschong, L. (2021). *Visual Delight in Architecture: Daylight, Vision, and View.* Routledge.

[143] Lovins Operational Manual.

[144] Watkiss, Jeffrey D., and Douglas W. Smith. "The Energy Policy Act of 1992 —A watershed for competition in the wholesale power market." *Yale J. on Reg.* 10 (1993): 447.

11: **Sandwich Walls, Superwindows and Fresh Air**

As you read this in the 2020s, the need for a sustainable world is more pressing than ever. The situation calls for each of us to be some part of the solution. The stakes have become higher and higher. Struggles between defenders of the status quo and searchers for a viable future have become intense; the temperature of public dispute has reached fever levels; and the wish for simplistic quick fixes is everywhere. Living through this time will call for attention, spirit of inquiry, hope, and quite possibly courage, and it will call on these from each of us, you as well as me, in one way or another.

In the midst of all this, new buildings keep being built and older buildings keep getting refitted and refurbished. Having their design, construction, and operation be as well grounded as possible matters a great deal. At present, buildings and the activities they contain account for at least 40% of global carbon emissions. Sustainability, "a durable prosperity," depends on us collectively doing better than this. In one way or another you are likely have a part to play. Perhaps it will be as a working professional, perhaps as a client whose home or workplace is being designed and built, or perhaps as one of these people's associates or friends or family. All of us will certainly be employees or dependents or citizens of communities where building takes place. Our involvement may or may not be deep, but we will be in the scene, one way or another. I hope it is clear by now that this is not just the business of experts. You and I need to feel called to promote sustainability, rather than delay, deter, or distract from it.

In the spirit of inquiry, let's consider what can be carried forward into today's work from 1739 Snowmass Creek Road, this one-off, forty year old building and its history. Foremost, I think, is that success comes from buildings that enhance the lives of their occupants, while performing well in technical terms. Next, one can bring to whatever role one plays a willingness to ask important questions and pursue them to satisfactory answers. Surprisingly, a layman's understanding of three or four technical fundamentals puts one in a position to do this. It still takes expertise to get all the many details right, but achieving wholeness, the profound presence of coherence and feeling has to grow from users and occupants, too. They need not step aside while technical experts make the key decisions, because these few fundamentals can be understood in common. Whatever part you play in the building and remodeling going on right around you and in your community, this understanding, the subject of this chapter and the next, should help you participate in the conversations that are badly needed.

❖　❖　❖　❖　❖　❖

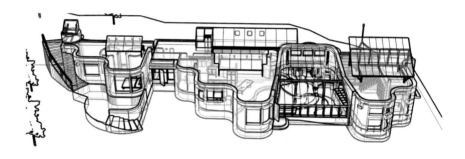

With the renovation of 2006-2009 complete, the Lovins building was well launched on its next phase of life. The vision behind it had born literal fruit and an abundance of the figurative variety—three decades of reliable shelter and comfort for Amory as a person and opinion leader, and for his associates in world-class Rocky Mountain Institute, which by then had offices in Boulder and Washington, D.C. as well as its ongoing presence in the valley.

The search for sustainability had also moved forward over those decades. As we have seen, progress was uneven, largely because of human reluctance or uncertainty. The basic technical underpinnings of green building had not changed since the early 1980s, while society's understanding of their potential, and willingness to pursue it had waxed and waned. The specifics were in flux, as fashions, supply chains, corporate strategies, tax law, and regulations pushed and shoved in their different ways. This continues today, but Nature still behaves the way it did in 1983 when it comes to staying warm in cold climates.

Keeping heat, not importing it

The superinsulation pioneers like Eugene Leger had realized that ordinary living, breathing, and household activities release a good deal of heat into a house. If it can be kept there, it will do a great deal to keep inhabitants comfortably warm. It may even do the whole job. Simultaneously, the passive solar pioneers had realized that the Sun can often provide more than enough heat, but one also needs to keep it in the building for nighttime and cloudy periods. Keeping heat from being lost is a primary goal of sustainable design for cold climates.

> In the US it's easy to forget that our dominant assumptions and expectations about buildings were formed in cold climates, specifically Britain, Germany, and the northern United States. Indeed, most of this country has cold seasons that demand respect. In Hawai'i, though, the outdoors is warm enough almost everywhere to be comfortable all year, so window openings do not need glass to keep in heat. The same goes for all tropical climates. One may wish to enclose buildings completely for cooling purposes, of course, but readers should stay alert to the way cold-climate assumptions creep into US analysis and practice, including in this book.

There are two ways heat gets lost from a building. It can pass directly through the materials of the walls, windows, doors, slab, or basement (collectively called the enclosure) or it can be carried by air (through open windows, open doors, ventilators, chimneys, and leaks). In addressing these two avenues, the Lovins design made one bold, unusual move for each—it used superwindows in the enclosure and put whole-building heat exchange in the air flow. In other respects, the design stayed with approaches quite familiar to architects and builders even then, except that the goal of very low heat loss and very high solar input called for an unusual degree of integration and care in construction.

What I'm calling the Lovins design was at least a three-person effort. Lovins himself generated the concepts and chose their physical implementation, Steven Conger gave them architectural form, and engineer John Ehlers provided all-important energy calculations, crucial to seeing if the chosen materials and form would balance heat gains and losses properly.

Windows and Superwindows

The first important technical fundamental is a basic understanding of how ordinary windows lose heat and what's special enough about the ones at Snowmass to merit calling them superwindows. Getting there involves some general talk about windows, then an apparent detour into solid insulation, a return to ordinary windows, and finally a look at superwindows themselves.

In cold climates, the primary purpose of windows is to let in light while blocking the wind. The latter is often taken for granted, but being impervious to moving air is a primary value of properly sized and mounted glass. Moving air is so effective at transferring heat and shows up in so many ways that the process has a fancy name—convective heat transfer. What is basically going on is not fancy. Air acquires heat in one place, moves to another, and gives it up. (The same can happen in water or any other fluid.) It's not just winds. Breezes, drafts, gales, gusts, zephyrs, puffs and every other variety of moving air can do this; and it happens indoors with drafts, and between indoors and outdoors through chimneys, loose construction, and leaks as well as consciously installed machinery like fans or heat exchangers.

Convection is generally the most effective way of transferring heat, and that makes it the most important one to deal with. The thin fabric of a modern mountaineer's tent, for example, is critical to overnight survival on a windswept snowfield, simply because it blocks the wind.

Windows were already quite highly evolved by 1973, as far as blocking wind was concerned. They were complex assemblies of carefully configured frames and effective seals in addition to glass. The market had a wide range of designs, fixed or openable in several ways, and available in a great variety of styles.

In terms of heat loss, however, the typical windows of 1973 were little better than those of 1773, and were usually worse in practice, because they were much bigger. They blocked the worst kind of heat transfer, convection, but lost heat readily by two other kinds of transfer, conduction and radiation. The more window a house had, the worse for heat loss, and it was usually a lot in 1973.

Some historical data about tall US buildings over the 20th century indicates the problem. The Woolworth and Equitable Buildings, two classic New York skyscrapers from before World War I, gave 21% and 25% of their facade areas to glass. Lever House, a famous NY building from the 1950-70 period, went to 53%, and Lake Shore Drive Apartments in Chicago, an equally iconic project, reached 72%. Unfortunately, the glass in these mid century buildings lost just as much heat per square foot as the glass 200 years earlier had, and there were many more square feet of it.

As long as energy was cheap and abundant, houses could make up for losses like this by turning up the furnace, but the energy crisis ended any complacency of that sort. Among the multiple responses it touched off was an intense, creative, and lasting effort to radically improve the energy performance of windows. The Lovins "superwindows" were mileposts in this work. It involved understanding and specifically addressing the ways that conduction and radiation are at work in windows. The basics are not hard to lay out.

Some things you already know about heat

You and I and everyone know a great deal from ordinary life about heating (when heat's flowing in) and cooling (when it's flowing out). Hot tea cools down (and makes the air around it a bit hotter, though we don't notice that.). The tea water got hot by contact with the even hotter metal of a kettle or electric heating element. This everyday fact—when left to itself, heat flows from hotter to cooler places—is now recognized as one of the most fundamental truths about the universe we live in.

It shows itself at every scale and in every place, from the grandest galaxy to the humblest tea cup, without exception or qualification. Suitably sharpened by careful definitions, it goes by the name of Second Law of Thermodynamics, and sets a fundamental boundary between things that can actually happen in Nature and things one can imagine but will never happen. The fundamental limit on energy conversion mentioned earlier (in the section on cooking in Chapter 5) is a surprising but thoroughly tested and confirmed consequence of this familiar fact.

Another piece of common knowledge is that kettles or heating elements only stay hot if energy is steadily supplied from outside, via gas flame or electric power. They would actually get cooler, as heat flows from them into the water, but we're making up for that loss with the heat flowing into them from the gas or electricity. Keeping things cold also takes outside energy. Otherwise, hotter things around them get cooler as heat flows out of them, and the cooler things into which the heat flows get warmer.

This is another of the most fundamental things we know about the universe. One major achievement of 19th-century physical science was demonstrating that heat and other forms of energy can be converted one into another, but there is never an increase or a decrease in the total amount of energy in the world. This is called the First Law of Thermodynamics. It took persistent and extensive experimentation to trace and measure the various forms energy may take, but the conclusion has been inescapable. Whenever energy has seemed to be appearing out of nowhere, or disappearing, close investigation has always found the sources or the sinks, and the amounts have always confirmed this law.

How fast does this cooling down or heating up happen? That depends on the difference in temperature between the hot and cold places. A house kept at 78 degrees loses heat faster than one kept at 68. A sign of this happening is that the furnace comes on more often.

You may not notice it because much effort on recent American housing has gone to making heating and cooling work silently and invisibly. I personally think this is a mistake, because it makes us unaware. There's no need for heating or cooling to be noisy, but a little hum would help householders know when things are working properly, and be a clue about how much heat they're using.

Temperature difference governs all heat flow, other things being equal, but insulation and windows don't need to be equal between one building and the next. Make good choices about them, and the temperature difference you want to maintain between the inside and the outside will have less impact on the climate (and your budget). Back during the energy crisis of the 1970s, reducing the temperature difference by turning down the thermostat seemed like the only option for saving energy, and it was the only way to get immediate changes in household use. Now, in the 2020s, most Americans don't face short term cutoffs in their heating or gasoline, and there are choices available that reduce climate impacts without reducing comfort.

Doing this with windows comes down to dealing with two ways heat can flow—conduction and radiation. Conduction is about direct contact. A hot water bottle is a classic case: hot water in contact with the rubber container heats it up; the rubber surface in contact with my clothes heats them up; they in turn warm up my skin. Radiation, by contrast, acts across space: the heat from a blazing fire comes directly through space to me from the glowing flames and coals, with no material contact involved.

We look at conduction first. It is fundamentally a mechanical process, atom knocking atom. The atoms of hot objects are highly agitated, and they transmit this agitation by contact to anything they are in contact with. Conduction is a bucket brigade process, with each set of atoms agitating the next. In solids and liquids, atoms are in close contact with each other, while in gases they are far apart. The illustration[145] comes from a careful computer simulation in which the differences of atomic life in gases, liquids and solids show clearly. It depicts a drop of water, the heap of tiny green spheres, on a flat solid surface, the very regular array of gray spheres. The space above and to the right of the drop is taken up with water vapor, a gas. Each molecule moves randomly, according to collisions with other molecules. The inescapable tendency is to move from dense regions with more collisions to less dense ones with fewer. That is what evaporation is all about.

Everyday gases like air have their atoms or molecules even more sparsely spread; they're mostly empty space. This means the bucket brigade is much less effective in gases. Thermal agitation at a hot surface still

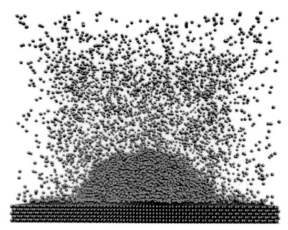

One moment in a computer simulation of evaporation of liquid (green spheres) from droplet on solid surface (black spheres).

creates agitation which spreads through the gas, but much more weakly. This is just what one wants, if slowing heat loss is the goal.

Different substances conduct heat at different rates. Other things being equal, copper conducts almost 500 times as much heat per second as brick or glass, aluminum almost 300 times, and steel about 70 times.[146] Wood does better than glass, allowing only one quarter the flow.

> Actually wood itself varies greatly. Moisture content and direction of heat flow relative to the grain make noticeable differences, and the species matters even more. Oak and redwood differ by a factor of two, for example. So the ratio of ¼ is the middle of a range.

Still air is what keeps you warm

Air is the unassuming, unsung champion among common materials for providing insulation. It is cheap, stable, available everywhere, and other things being equal, conductive heat flow through air is 33 times slower than through glass. Its virtues were put to use quite early in the form of storm windows, the extra layer of framed glazing which was installed and removed seasonally over the windows of some houses as early as the 18th century. Such extra layers obviously made houses warmer, but understanding of what was happening only accumulated slowly.

It's now clear that the trick is avoiding convection. When free to move, air very readily circles in loops; a familiar example is the winter situation where room air is being cooled by a window, flowing along the floor as a draft, rising slowly as it picks up heat in the room, and then flowing back toward the window at ceiling level to complete the circuit by flowing down along the window and giving up its heat to the outdoors. This kind of convection is a very effective way of transferring heat, to the dismay of that room's occupants.

The function of the double layer of glass in a window outfitted for winter storms, or in the permanently double-glazed units that were first patented in the 1840s and became commercial in the 1930s, is to create a layer of air in the window opening that isn't moving. This still air does essentially all the slowing of heat loss, and serves as the "blanket" proudly claimed by this advertisement.[147]

In fact, on investigation, it turns out that still air is also the operative ingredient in real blankets, and indeed in most commercial insulating materials. Not just wool, but fiberglass, cellulose, rock wool, cork and

other materials used for insulation get their effect from the very many small cells or pockets of air they contain. The fur of seals and otters works the same way: under a dense water-resistant layer is a layer of very fine, loosely packed hairs which holds onto air even while the animal is swimming. The structure of fibers, strands, foam or whatever just has the role of keeping the air in place and not moving; the structural material itself doesn't insulate any better than other solid materials like glass or brick would. However, when it takes any of these open forms with very small, loosely packed fibers or thin cell walls, the solid portions are too narrow to conduct much heat, and any significant heat flow takes place through the trapped air, which conducts quite poorly.

Air, in fact, is responsible for the very modest but real insulation against conduction provided by traditional single-pane windows. Although their glass blocks moving air, it does almost nothing in itself to reduce the amount of heat flowing by conduction from a warm interior to a cold outdoors. However, a quite thin, quite still layer of air forms along both the inside and outside glass surfaces of the glass, and that does provide some insulation.[148]

How effective are these air films? Insulation is never all or nothing. The question is always how much it reduces heat flow, and a key part of the answer is never to zero. So one wants a metric for comparing the effectiveness of insulation. The US has a standard one, called R-value. The R stands for "resistance," and the larger the R-value, the better the insulating. Conveniently, the R-value for a traditional single-pane window is about R-1. If one can create a full inch's worth of still air, that insulates at R-5.5. By contrast, an inch of concrete or stone is rated at something like R-0.08. These two numbers, 5.5 and 0.08, show how very great the difference is between solid materials and air or materials like insulating foam which are largely composed of air.[149] The ratio, 5.5 divided by 0.08, tells one that heat flows almost 70 times faster through solids than air.

Unfortunately, a single inch of air is too mobile, too readily induced into convection, to actually insulate at R-5.5. The way to get that to happen, we have already seen, is to trap air in the tiny spaces of a fiber mat or a foam. The narrow space between panes has the same effect.

Various kinds of foam insulation are advertised with R-values more than 5.5 per inch. The ads are true, in a way, but somewhat misleading. The bubbles in these foams are not made with air, but with other gases that are less conductive. In the short run, this makes them perform better, but over time, the filler gas diffuses out and air diffuses in, so after some years it is air, not the other gas, doing the insulating. This takes years, so the wall in question may be replaced before air has largely replaced the other gas. But if you're building for the long term, you should design using the R-value for air.

Walls and roof—things get complicated

Aside from igloos, one never sees a house made entirely of insulation. Walls and roofs need to do more than insulate by keeping the wind out and heat in. They're responsible for holding the roof up against the pull of gravity and for holding it in place against the varying pulls and pushes of the wind. Walls need to deal with water, both rain from outside and moisture generated inside by the occupants cooking, bathing and just breathing. They need to provide surfaces suitable for decoration, especially inside, and they need to deal in some way with the chance of fire. This complex of functions has meant that present-day walls consist of several layers—wallboard, structure, insulation, sheathing, surface treatment, and so on.

Heat flows through each layer on its way from hotter to cooler. Each layer has an R-value, large or small but never zero. You can also think of the whole assembly as having its own R-value, the overall effect of the thermal properties of its components and it turns out that the R-value of the whole is simply the sum of the R-values of each layer. There's this much for the inner wallboard, that much for the insulation, the sheathing, and so forth, all just added together in turn from inside to outside.

Something similar happens with windows. Even the simple single-glazed window is multi-layered when it comes to heat flow, because the air films that always form on the inner and outer surfaces play the decisive role in governing heat flow there. So there are really three layers—the glass and the inside and outside air films. The R-1 value of an ordinary window comes from the combined effect of the latter. The glass itself does nearly no insulating, but without it, the air films would not form.

What about the opaque portions of a wall? In the US, most houses have the "stick frame" system of evenly spaced studs, vertical members to provide a skeleton which is covered by external sheathing and internal panelling to create a continuous surface. This gets complicated in heat flow terms, because the studs conduct differently from the spaces between them. The same goes for corners of all kinds, including the frames of dormer windows and the major joints where roof meets wall.

US "stick frame" construction.

The spaces can have insulation of different kinds. Panelling and sheathing on the inside and outside of the wall also have R-values which depend on exactly what they are made of; there are even air films on both inside and outside surfaces. Estimating the overall R-value of this kind of wall is expert work if one wants any precision, but a decent value for an ordinary insulated wall these days is R-18.

This R-value is about what one would get for 3 inches of still, stabilized air. The ordinary wall in question will be a little over twice as thick. All the structure that's needed to get the wall doing its multiple jobs comes with an energy price. A particular price worth noting comes from the skeleton of studs, because each stud is a weak point for heat flow, connecting inside and outside with a solid path that makes a thermal bridge.

The walls of the Lovins house largely escape thermal bridging. They have two layers of steel-reinforced concrete, which do the structural work. There's a four-inch gap between them filled with polyurethane foam. It was rated at R-33 at the time of construction.

> It will not be performing at that level now, because the slow diffusion mentioned above and the 40 year span of time will have taken some toll, though it's hard to say how much without boring into the wall and measuring. (The particular foam also couldn't be installed now, because the filler gas used in 1983 has been implicated in depleting the atmosphere's ozone layer and removed from production. But at the time, it was the only foam available.)[150]

The masonry layers and the surface air films do their bit, and the original wall came to R-35.

The Lovins roof, aside from the sloping glass of the greenhouse, was insulated with polyurethane foam averaging seven inches in thickness. This was held up by a deck of oak planks, and several waterproofing layers were in place to keep rain and melting snow from leaking into the house or wetting the insulation.

> There are important technical details in making such a roof, such as sloping the insulation to direct water to drains, but they don't affect the basic thermal behavior of the roof, provided they keep the insulation dry.

What decides what

There is nothing "super" in themselves about the materials and methods in these walls and this roof. All were widely used and readily available in 1983. But something important and special went into their deployment in the Lovins house. It is worth a line to itself.

Insulation decided structure in the Lovins house, not
the other way around.

In the longstanding tradition of American house construction, the primary choice has always been the framing system, which has usually been stud walls and rafter roofs, with timber dimensions adequate to bear the weight of the structure. Insulation has been a secondary choice, sometimes omitted entirely, and otherwise limited to what would fit in the chosen framing. The stud and rafter systems did happen to provide some space for it, but offered no ways of accommodating greater amounts, and imposed thermal bridges every 12-18 inches as well. Within these quite rigid limits, the actual amounts of insulation were decided by habit or a cost-balancing exercise in which the cost of insulation was set against expected fuel savings.

The Lovins design reversed the priority. The building shell had to be insulated enough to hold each day's solar heating through the succeeding night, indeed to hold heat well enough to manage a number of cloudy or stormy days in a row. That came first. It meant the structure had to allow enough room for that required insulation in roof and walls, and had to do it with minimal thermal bridging. It did also need to hold up the building's weight, but it had to do that in a way which allowed meeting the energy goal. There was no thermostat in this house to turn up.

In effect, long before LEED and Passivhaus, Lovins had set up a performance standard for himself.

Heat flows down, too

There is another way houses lose heat by conduction. Heat also flows downward, into the ground. The basics are familiar by now: in cold weather, the inside of the house is warmer than the ground underneath it, so heat will flow from house to ground; the flow is through solids, usually a concrete slab or basement floor, so it is by conduction, at a rate governed by the low R-value of the concrete and by the temperature difference between house interior and the ground beneath. The ground isn't as cold as the outside air, so typically in 1983 a slab or basement floor would be cool, but tolerable. One could always turn up the thermostat.

Lovins had quite a different attitude about saving energy, but he did choose not to insulate the floor slab in his house. He thought that heat would flow to start with, but would accumulate underneath the building, because it would not flow away around the edges quite as fast as it flowed in from the house. This would establish a somewhat warm volume below, which would slow heat loss from the house markedly, down to a level where the house's solar input could manage it. He encouraged this with an insulating skirt around the foundation, extending four-inch thick slabs of foam board to six feet below the ground to reduce heat flow by lengthening the path it would have to follow.[151]

This notion was definitely in circulation at the time. Advocates for superinsulation recognized it as a likely long-term feature of houses in cold climates. Expert analysts flatly disagreed with each other about this, and the computational tools available could not give decisive answers. It cannot be said it worked well for the Lovinses. The ground underneath may have warmed enough over time to slow downward heat loss usefully, but the floors felt cold for years, until the radiant heating system was installed during the renovation. If he were doing it over now, Lovins would insulate his slab, and this has independently become the standard in general housebuilding around the country; in fact, it's often required by local building codes.

Radiation—in other words, light and heat

So far, we have been talking about conduction alone. For walls and roof, conduction is the main story. Windows are another matter. They deal in radiation, too. Superwindows are super because they do this in a sophisticated way.

In physics, radiation just means light. Light is pervasive in the universe., visibly and invisibly. All light has the same basic and relatively simple nature; it's a traveling electric and magnetic disturbance of space. Some light stimulates the eye, while other light, such as what's called infra-red radiation, does not. but Some of its interactions with matter—with walls, glass, painted surfaces, water, the molecules in the air that create clouds and rainbows—produce visual effects that are extraordinarily rich, varied and complicated. However, the invisible ingredients of matter, atoms and electrons, also react in a great variety of ways to different varieties of light. Superwindows turn this to advantage.

The variety of interactions has generated multiple names—visible light, infra-red light, ultra-violet light, radio waves, microwaves, X-rays, gamma rays, and others—but they all refer to the same basic phenomenon.

This electromagnetic disturbance is basically an oscillation, a periodic growing and shrinking of its electric and magnetic components. The only essential difference between one kind of light and another is the rate of oscillation, the number of cycles completed in a second. The technical term is "frequency", which is somewhat familiar from radio broadcasting ("This is WABC from Bigburg, coming to you at a frequency of 1020," or the equivalent). AM radio uses frequencies between 550 thousand and 1.7 million cycles per second. The frequencies of visible light are far, far higher, between 400 and 800 trillion cycles per second. Each frequency in that range triggers a sensation of pure color in our eyes, running from red at the lowest end through orange, yellow, and green, to blue and violet at the high frequency end.

Frequencies out of this range don't trigger our optical sensations. Ultra-violet light, X-rays, and gamma rays all have higher frequencies than visible light, while infra-red light, microwaves, and radio waves all have lower frequencies.

All light, of all frequencies, carries energy. Whenever light is given off, by a light bulb, the sun, an X-ray machine, or a radio transmitter, and no matter how it's generated, it carries energy with it. When that light is absorbed, by skin or black paint or the eye or desert sand, its energy is absorbed and makes changes.

The discovery that light interacts with matter in discrete units, which came to be called photons, was a great milestone in the 20th century physics. Each photon carries a definite amount of energy, and the higher the frequency of the light, the higher this amount of energy; it's directly proportional to the frequency. Thus the upper end of the visible, at 750 trillion cycles, has photons almost twice as energetic as light at the lower end, 430 trillion cycles.

It turns out that visible light carries enough energy to rearrange atoms and molecules without knocking them apart. The visual system counts on this. When light is absorbed by specialized molecules in the retina, it shifts them to a form which triggers neural impulses, after which other retinal molecules shift them back, ready to absorb again.

Since all light, visible and invisible, carries heat, it can heat things up, including buildings. However, all material objects also give off heat all the time in the form of light, mostly at frequencies we can't see, and that is part of cooling them down. It's no surprise to anyone who has relaxed in a south-facing window seat, or has shielded their face while rearranging the logs in a blazing fire to be told that light carries heat. Nor is a person coming back to a parked car on a sunny day surprised that the interior is baking hot. The microwave oven that makes a steaming bowl of ramen uses light too, in a frequency range which water and other molecules in food are very ready to absorb.

However, the second fact, that objects give off heat all the time in the form of light, is not at all obvious. I'm not talking about the visible light by which we see things. Usually, that's generated somewhere else, by the sun or a lightbulb, and is partly reflected to us off the objects. What I'm talking about is best illustrated by the glow we see in hot iron coming out of a furnace. Everything is giving off that sort of basic glow all the time, strongly or weakly. The intensity of the glow and its visibility vary greatly, from dramatic and dangerous (flame, molten metal or the surface of the Sun) to soothing and invisible (the warmth of a wood stove). Even things that are apparently inert, like a rock on a hillside or a night-time cloud, glow. Everything gives off light, visibly or invisibly, according to how hot it is. Everything glows, literally everything.

> How intensely an object glows varies strongly with its temperature, specifically by the fourth power of the temperature measured from absolute zero. The white-hot color of the Sun corresponds to a temperature of about 5500° C.

For things at everyday temperatures, the glow is weak and invisible. We sense it as relative heat or cold: a pane of single glazing on a winter night chills me more than an insulated wall nearby partly because the latter glows at me more strongly.

The glow spreads over the wide range of infra-red frequencies, from 430 trillion cycles, just slower than the eye can register, down to about 300 billion cycles. (That's 300 billion at the lower end, not trillion; in other words that kind of light oscillates more than a thousand times more

slowly than the other.) Cameras sensitive to infra-red are available, and can generate images like the one here of a London outdoor cafe. The camera's software translates invisible infra-red into visible light by pairing each infra-red frequency with a visible frequency, and displays the latter.

Warmer areas appear as red, yellow (even warmer) or white (even warmer than that), and cooler ones as greens to blues or purples. The walls are cooler than the windows, which in turn are cooler than the people.

It's no surprise that the windows show up warmer than the walls or roof. We know windows are usually poor insulators, so more heat gets through the glass to the outer surface than gets through the wall. It's not obvious in this image, but the glow of the windows is not showing us the interior. Window glass blocks infra-red light. An infra-red camera looking from outside at the clear glass of a window only sees the outer surface, not any details of warm and cool areas inside, just as it can only see the surfaces of the rest of the exterior.

This means that a hot place inside, like a fireplace, doesn't send any of that heat straight out through the glass. Infra-red radiation that reaches the window does not pass through. It's absorbed there, and the heat it carries goes into the glass. What you see from outside is just the glass's own glow, corresponding to whatever temperature it has. So even ordinary single-pane windows are a partial barrier to heat loss by radiation, though they aren't much of a barrier to losses by conduction.

Opaque walls and roofs also glow with infra-red light, but usually much more weakly. From this point of view, then, a window is a relatively warm and brightly glowing surface in a weakly glowing wall. And the brighter the glow, the faster the heat loss.

Heat gets lost through the glow itself, as infra-red light carries heat away, and also through the conduction between the relatively warm glass surface and the cooler outside air reduced a bit by the stationary air films next to each side of the glass.

Double-glazing was an early idea to reduce the conduction loss, and it definitely works, roughly doubling the R-value of a single pane, if you make the air gap about half an inch wide. However, if you look at the numbers for the R-value of air there's something of a puzzle. The measured R-value for an inch for still air would lead you to expect a much higher R-value for that air than R-1. Heat losses through radiation are to blame.

The two panes of glass which face each other across the air gap both glow, as everything does. They glow with infra-red light, which carries heat, and the inside pane glows somewhat more intensely, because it is warmer. So more radiative heat heads outward than comes back inward from the outer pane. On balance, radiant heat flows outward in addition to the reduced conduction that's still happening through the gas as molecule hits molecule.

When you add up the amounts, you find that radiation is transferring over twice as much heat across the gap as conduction.[152] One could take this as bad news, because the same radiation would happen even if one made the gap wider. But it turns out to open the door to good news. You only have to find ways to reduce the radiation given off by the glass, and it turns out this is possible, and possible in commercial production at affordable costs. We have come to the "super" in superwindows.

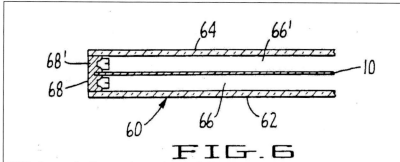

FIG. 6

"Window unit 60 contains a sheet of film 10 stretched under tension between glass or plastic panes 62 and 64, 66 and 66' are air voids and 68 and 68' are spacer plugs for holding the film in proper position and properly under tension."

The numbers here are just labels to connect the drawing with the description.

Superwindows (at last)

The basic structure of the superwindows that went into the Lovins house is laid out in US Patent 4,799,745: Heat Reflecting Composite Films and Glazing Products Containing the Same, issued in July 1989.

The sheet of film labelled 10 is the heart of the matter. Referred to commercially as "Heat Mirror©" or "low-e film," it reflects infra-red light but lets visible light through. This reflecting doesn't entirely block infra-red heat flow, but it reduces it very drastically, to two or three percent of its original amount. The Lovins windows achieved R-5.3, over five times better than the traditional single pane.[153] This was essential for making the large central greenhouse area a major net gainer of heat rather than a very large loser.

It's easy to describe how to make such a film and not hard to demonstrate it in a suitably equipped laboratory. You coat a transparent surface, like glass or plastic film, with very thin alternating layers of silver and some electrical non-conductor. If the silver is thin enough, only 40-60 atoms across, and the thicknesses of the non-conductor are just right, the coating reflects infra-red light very strongly while transmitting visible light very well. This selective behavior enables sunlight to get into the Lovins greenhouse without letting heat radiation out.

The patent application gives measurements for this: transmission is best (86%) for light at 700 trillion cycles (violet), still good (74%) at 545 trillion (green), down to 24% at 350 trillion (just into infra-red), and essentially zero in the range (20-60 trillion cycles) of the much lower infra-red frequencies for light emitted by objects at room temperature. Zero transmission for this infra-red means that it can't escape a house through this kind of window.

The image shows the difference this treatment makes. The left side has a person (actually Stephen Selkowitz, a long-time leader of this kind of research) holding a piece of ordinary window glass. You recognize the lively colors of his body and clothing as signs that this is an infra-red image. He glows much brighter than the other surfaces in that room. In the glass one sees a faint reflected image. Ordinary glass does reflect about 10% of this range of infra-red.

In the right-hand image, Selkowitz is holding glass with a low-e coating. Now the reflection is very strong; almost all the infra-red reaching the coated glass is being sent back into the space it came from. In a house, this would be heat kept inside instead of being absorbed by the window glass and passed along to the outdoors.

Reflected infra-red radiation from ordinary window glass (left) and glass with low-e coating (right)
(Courtesy Stephen Selkowitz, Lawrence Berkeley Laboratory)

If you're wondering why the ordinary glass is not glowing as warmly as in the previous images of windows seen from outside, it's because infra-red cameras often adjust the color range to fit the range of temperatures they find in a scene. These are software-chosen colors, not real ones. In these images the coolest temperature is 19° C (66° F), so it shows dark blue. In an image taken from the colder outdoors, things at this temperature would be close to the warmest and would show red or even white.

The 1983 windows in the Lovins house had a heat mirror film stretched across the air gap between two panes of glass, like the three layer assembly in the patent diagram. (The film was heat shrinkable, on top of its other virtues, so wrinkle-free stretching could be achieved at the factory by putting the whole assembly into an industrial oven for a short period after it was put together.) Since infra-red radiation accounts for roughly two-thirds of the heat flow between the inner and outer panes of ordinary double glazing, and heat mirror film in the lab transmits essentially none of the infra-red emitted by things at household temperatures, we might expect that only one-third as much heat would get through these superwindows. The Lovins windows did not do quite as well as this. But they did achieve R-5.3, compared to roughly R-2 for a double-glazed window with just air in the gap. This is an improvement that genuinely makes a difference. Some of this improvement in R-value also comes from filling the air gaps in these windows with argon gas rather than air. As with the foams mentioned above, slow diffusion over the years will see the argon replaced by air, so the long-term R-value will be somewhat less.

Since 1983, top of the line window performance has steadily improved. R-values as high as 20 have been offered, and R-10, which is twice as good as the original Snowmass windows, is available in volume. This has largely come from multiplying the number of glass panes and heat mirror films. There has even been some work on vacuum windows, which completely eliminate conduction by having no gas of any kind in the empty space between panes. This requires a glass structure which can hold back the full pressure of the atmosphere, since there is no balancing pressure from a filler gas. Workable windows of this kind exist, but so far only for special situations.

Keeping heat in while air goes out

We now turn to the other main way heat gets lost from buildings, and what the Lovins house did about it. Houses need fresh air and they need to get rid of used air. We need oxygen replenished, and we want to get rid of the humidity and odors from kitchens, bathrooms, and our bodies. In cold seasons, this has usually meant getting rid of warm air and replacing it with cold air, or at least with air from the cold outdoors. Traditionally, you just said goodbye to the outgoing air and just stoked the fire or furnace enough to heat the new air, minute after minute.

The amounts of energy involved are significant. In a well insulated house, getting outside air up to room temperature can take one-third to one-half of all the heat needed for winter comfort.

This continuing energy drain, day and night, could be addressed simply by reducing the amount of fresh air; warm air that stays inside doesn't need to be replaced by cold air from outside. This was everyone's first thought when the energy crises of the 1970s arrived. Much thought and effort went into constructing new homes more tightly, and finding and plugging the leaks in existing ones.

Open fireplaces and their chimneys were fairly obvious channels for escaping warm air Investigation revealed many other pathways, from loosely fitted doors and sash windows to the numerous holes for wiring and plumbing in walls and floors which had token covers but no kind of seal.

> The blower door was a simple but effective test for general air-tightness developed at this time. It relies on a large fan mounted in a panel which fits snugly in a normal doorway. The fan blows air into the house, and you measure the pressure difference between inside and outside. In a drafty house, the blown-in air escapes relatively easily, and the inside pressure does not go up much. In a tight house the reverse is true.

A great deal about controlling air flow in and out of houses was learned in those years. However, it also became clear that simply making a house tight led to a number of new problems, including mold growth, rot from condensation in the walls, and persistent odors.

Rather than accept a limit on possible savings, home energy activists in the 1970s began to explore an old idea from outside the building sector. Why not get the outgoing stale air to give up its warmth to the incoming fresh but cold air by putting both streams of air through the right kind of device—a heat exchanger? There were already devices like this, in industrial boilers, car radiators, and chemical refineries—ways of getting one fluid to heat another without mixing them. Here are three examples of existing heat exchangers. A version for buildings would have to be different in many details, but it would not have to start from scratch. The pioneers borrowed or adapted from existing devices.

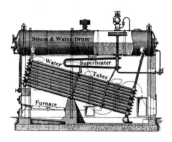  

Three heat exchangers: (left to right) old boiler; car radiator; refrigerator coils

The first image is an old boiler, which has fire and hot gas in the white space marked "furnace" and has many small tubes carrying water through it to be heated. The next is a front view closeup of a car radiator, where water heated by the engine flows crossways in the small tubes and air flows front to back, receiving heat as it passes between the tubes and past the zig-zag fins between them.

> Not everyone is used to thinking of air as a fluid. Water, yes; oil, yes; but air doesn't seem the same. Indeed, it is a gas, not a liquid. But fluids are just substances that flow. Gases and liquids are both fluids; they have no fixed shape; they give way to external intrusions and arrange to go around obstacles.

The last image shows the coil at the back of an ordinary refrigerator. The system absorbs heat from the food compartment with a refrigerating fluid, and runs that through the thin serpentine black tube; the rows of attached thin ribs help transfer that heat to the air in the room.

In all these examples, and in heat exchange generally, the two fluids are kept separate. Heat leaves one and enters the other, but the fluids don't mix themselves. The same goes for heat exchangers in buildings: odors and everything else that makes air stale gets carried away with it, but warmth from that outgoing stale air is transferred to incoming fresh air.

The examples all have many small elements—tubes, fins, ribs—for a fundamental reason. Heat is to flow from one fluid to the other, and must do it across the separating surface, so the more shared separating surface there is, the more heat can flow at a time. Put another way, one wants as much as possible of the hot fluid to be as close as possible to as much of the cold fluid as possible. So one naturally makes as many small tubes or thin layers as one can; they have more surface area than a larger tube carrying the same amount of fluid would.

> The limitations to this solution are not fundamental, only practical. Creating many small features can be unworkably fussy and expensive, or one can have clever ideas that do the several needed things, i.e. keep the flows separate, make it easy to divide each flow into small streams, have thin and conductive walls between the flows, have durable construction, and minimize labor and assembly time.

The illustration shows two ways of doing it.

You can see that the "cross-flow" arrangement in the left-hand image keeps the flows separate in an elegant way, and it looks as if the folded

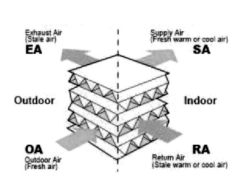

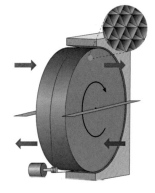

Household air-to-air heat exchanger, cross-flow configuration

Rotary heat exchanger:

structure might be very strong, like corrugated cardboard. It is not the most efficient possible setup, however. That honor goes to the "counter-flow" configuration, not illustrated here. In counterflow exchangers the hot fluid comes in right beside where the cold fluid goes out. This sets up a situation where no matter how much the cold fluid warms up, it finds warmer fluid just across the barrier, so it can go on absorbing heat right to the end of its pass through the exchanger. Such a set-up can get as close as you like to 100% efficient: just make it long enough.

Keeping the two fluids separate at the inlets and outlets of a counter-flow exchanger typically requires a fussy design and much more time spent in fabrication, which can be acceptable in industry, but rarely works for the mass-produced equipment used in households.

A different, quite elegant approach is rotary. As the right-hand image shows, a disk made of many small passages is placed across the flows, half in one, half in the other. The passages allow flows to go straight through, and seals around the edges keep the flows from mixing. The disk is made to rotate, and passages that have been warmed by outgoing air now have cool incoming air flowing through them, and vice versa. The cool air gets warmed by the walls of those passages and carries that heat with it into the house. The opposite happens at the other side of the wheel, where the now cooled passages come back into the warm outgoing flow, gaining heat from them. Their heat gets put into the incoming air when the wheel rotates to that side.

The net effect of all this is that heat carried by ventilation air stays in the house even though the air leaves. Exchangers like this, which are also called heat recovery or energy recovery ventilators, do not capture all the available heat, but efficiencies can be greater than 80%.

> The efficiency of a heat exchanger is somewhat slippery to define; it's even harder to establish meaningful averages. There are two streams of air, each carrying two kinds of thermal energy, the energy of sensible warmth and the energy carried by evaporated water (what's called latent heat). The devices also use energy to run the ventilation fans and turn the rotating disk, and some of that

leaks into the incoming air. Unsurprisingly, marketers, building operators, and researchers tend to make different choices about what to measure and report. Nevertheless, it's fair to say that the best available products extract more than 90% of the possible outgoing thermal energy.

Tight buildings do face the question of power outages. Fan driven ventilation needs power. The issue can be resolved, however, in two different ways. One can have on-site battery storage to provide the quite small amounts of power needed by this kind of fan. Or one can have windows that seal well when shut, but can be opened wide when direct fresh air is wanted. Both options are feasible with today's equipment.

As we know, the Lovinses had aimed at lowest energy use from the beginning, and they had no fear of the unfamiliar; an air-to-air heat exchanger was in Lovins' notes about his ideas from very early on. In fact, they ended with the six we described on the tour, to make sure all parts of the building got enough fresh air.

Residential heat exchangers really only make sense in buildings which are well sealed. Tight buildings caused problems in the early going, and heat exchangers were brought in to deal with those problems, but tightness is also needed when one goal is to capture outgoing heat. Heated air leaking past ill-fitting windows, wiring and plumbing penetrations and the like evades capture, so your exchangers may not be conserving very much of the interior heat in a building like that.

Superwindows and heat exchangers were the two most dramatic ingredients in the Lovins merger of passive solar and superinsulated building. A third ingredient, a much more massive, tighter and better insulated shell than usual, was also vital to the building's prospects, both by controlling air leaks and by tempering swings in temperature, but it held less drama and less mystery. The shell mainly involved doing more than usual with the same materials, and doing it more carefully than usual. Construction professionals know that this is not necessarily easy, but for our purposes we can pass it by, and move to the question of how these ingredients fit together in the final design.

---

145 Source lost; if rediscovered will amend future printings.

146 http://hyperphysics.phy-astr.gsu.edu/hbase/Tables/thrcn.html

147 Image found at https://www.pinterest.co.uk/quinsippimercan/vintage-railroad-ads/

148 These thin films of air arise from the fact that atoms of all kinds are weakly attracted to other atoms of all kinds. The formal name for this is van der Waals attraction, and the basic, somewhat oversimplified slogan is, "Everything sticks (weakly) to everything else." The attraction is much weaker than proper chemical bonds of the kind that hold molecules together or set up the crystal structures found in solids. It is somewhat weaker than the average energy of thermally agitated atoms or molecules at everyday temperatures. Nevertheless, there is a tendency for air molecules of all the usual kinds—nitrogen, oxygen, water vapor, argon, carbon dioxide, and so forth—to stick temporarily to any glass surface. They are jostled around constantly and frequently bounced loose and replaced, but the main effect of this coming and going is to make the population of molecules near the surface take on the average speed of the surface, namely zero. There is no tendency for molecules near the surface to progress significantly in any direction along it. In other words, there is no convection in the zone close to the surface.

The effect reaches out quite a distance in molecular terms, to something like a million or more times the width of a single molecule. But because molecules are so very small, this amounts at the human scale only to 1-5 millimeters for the air films on window glass. The actual width varies with conditions. In heavy winds, for example, the films are much thinner than in light airs. But they are always present.

149 There is a simple interpretation of the US R-value. It is the temperature difference (in degrees Fahrenheit) that gives rise to a certain standard heat flow from one side to the other of one square foot of the material. Temperature difference is the driving force of heat flow. Heat not only flows from hotter to colder, but basically does so in proportion to the temperature difference. So if an inch thickness of still air needs a thermal driving force of 5.5 degrees to create the reference amount of heat flow through each square foot, then an inch thickness of concrete would only require a difference of 0.08 degree to have the same heat flow.

---

[150] Designers and builders would also be more conscious now, forty years later, of embodied carbon, the carbon dioxide emitted in making construction materials and assembling them. Concrete is a major emitter, for example. Were Lovins building today, he would be looking hard for ways to reduce the large amount of concrete that went into the 1983 design. Now that people are looking, they are finding some potential for making cement with far less heat or with different chemical reactions—see Fennell, Paul, et al. "Cement and steel—nine steps to net zero." *Nature* 603.7902 (2022): 574-577.

[151] Two recent closely studied examples are the Las Vegas zero-energy house comparative project run by the University of Nevada, (Hurt, R. et al. (2006). University of Nevada Zero Energy House Project. *ACEEE Summer Study on Energy Efficiency in Buildings*) and the Equinox House project at University of Illinois (Newell, T. & Newell, B. (2011). "Ground heat transfer." *Ashrae Journal, 53*(2), 62.)

[152] Manz, H. (2008)."On minimizing heat transport in architectural glazing." *Renewable Energy, 33*(1), 119-128.

[153] The 5.3 amount refers to the so-called "center of glass." The window unit as a whole also loses heat through its edge structures of spacers and sealants, so the average R-value for the whole unit is somewhat less than the center-of-glass value.

12: **How to Tell If It's Enough**

So much for the most important components of this building. What any inhabitant most wants to know is what happens when they're assembled into a complete building. That means any designer wants ways of seeing in advance what the whole will amount to; this is one major role of architectural drawing at the design stage. Where will the stairs go? If here, circulation will be one way. If there, another way. No matter where they go, the stairs will do their immediate job of letting you get from one level to the next and back again. But some locations are much better for the whole life and function of the building than others, and the drawing is a powerful way of helping you think about that.

The same goes for energy-related features. Walls of a certain construction, windows with multiple layers, ventilation of a certain kind, this roof, that floor—what do they amount to as a whole? The lead energy designer, Amory Lovins in this case, hoped they wouldn't need a furnace in the Rocky Mountain winter; he needed to know if the ensemble would keep the place warm. The main tool available in 1983, and still for most projects, is the kind of energy budget we have already glimpsed in his scratchy notes on energy uses. One lists the energy needs and energy sources, estimates a numerical amount for each, and tallies them up.

Unfortunately, this budget approach is far less powerful than architectural drawing for revealing difficulties or opportunities. Drawings show relative sizes and relative positions in two or even three dimensions quickly and clearly; they readily embody numerical information without stifling the viewer's intuition; they can be rough or very precise or anywhere in between, and drawing technique signals quite naturally what level of precision is intended. Little of this is available in budget documents. They contain vital information, but it's typically in a single dimension, and has little capacity for showing relationships between different entries. Even with liberal use of color and text annotation, the result is much weaker than what drawing achieves easily. Budgets also strongly tempt you to think only of the final tally—is it positive or negative? Is it larger than last year? And so on... It's as if the whole meaning and import of the complex entity that generates the budget can be boiled down to a single number. No one imagines doing that with a drawing.

Nevertheless, budgets are the usual means (so far) for grasping a project's energy features as a whole. And they do useful work, within their limitations. For the Lovins house in its design phase, the energy budget's tally of inflows and outflows did give an answer to the key question—furnace or no furnace?

Back in the chapter on designing, creating an energy budget for a whole building looked fairly simple. Amory listed the electrical appliances he expected to use, looked at their labels to find the wattages, made some reasonable guesses about how many hours a day they would be on, and added up the results. Unfortunately, the structure of a whole house doesn't come in a standard package with a wattage printed on a label, and a solar house doesn't even have a reliable heat source.

Nevertheless, there is a one-line answer: you list all the inflows of energy, solar and electrical and body heat and the others; you list all the outflows, heat through the walls and in the ventilating air and so forth, and you make a grand tally.

Like most short answers to big questions, this is tidy but insufficient. In the actual making of a design, that answer has to be unfolded, and the key to doing that is to notice that a vital question and an important closely linked issue have been missing from the explanations so far. The vital question is, "How big?" One way or another, this has to be asked and answered about every component of every building. Without answering it, no house can be built at all. You have to decide how tall the walls will be, how pitched the roof, how wide the door, how high each step on the stairs, and so on, component by component.

For energy arrangements at 1739 Snowmass Creek Road, you can probably begin the list yourself. How many square feet of greenhouse glass? What's the thickness of the roof insulation? How large are the tubes to supply the heat exchanger? These are good starters on what the builders needed to know. Some of the questions were about physical dimensions, heights or diameters or lengths. Others were about capacities, such as cubic feet per minute or kilowatt-hours per day. Without the answers to this string of questions about sizes, the ingredients of a building are merely possible. Regardless of how effective the heat exchanger technology or how high the R-values of its superwindows may be on paper, the building can't be built.

The closely linked issue is about integration. The many components of a house should end up as an effective whole, in which the parts support and enhance each other. Thinking about the sizes of everything is actually a primary way of getting integration and effectiveness onto the table. The different jobs components do (insulating, carrying air, letting in light, and so on) are all connected, so the right size for this depends on the size of that, and vice versa.

> The technical data and reasoning needed for making decisions about "how big?" for real projects are complicated and can be left to the professionals involved. Unfortunately, the people with the expertise needed for these decisions are almost always not the people who will experience their consequences.

The general thinking that organizes this work can't very well just be left to the professionals. To make good buildings, there has to be some understanding from each side of what the other side is up to. The basic ideas used by the experts are actually not hard to understand, even though carrying them out is complicated and fussy. I am convinced that successfully exploring and approaching sustainable building requires finding a middle space where experts and owners/inhabitants can discuss the issues and options in mutually intelligible ways. The roles are quite distinct, but both are essential. Sustainable buildings have to work in technical terms, and they also have to work experientially for the people who use them.

> You yourself may even need or want to get energy estimates done sometime, and it's helpful to have some idea what the estimator is up to. (I also think estimators should be expected to explain what they do, and it helps in that to meet them part way.)

How big? (typical 1983 answers)

In conventional building, many of these sizing questions get answered by doing what everyone does. How thick should a wall be? Most 1983 builders would have said, "The thickness of a 2x4." At that time, each stud in a wood-framed wall were almost always a "2x4", 1½ inches wide by 3 ⅝ inches deep.[154]

> A piece of this lumber starts roughly cut to 2 inch by 4 inch dimensions, which is where the name comes from. By the time it has dried further and been planed for smooth surfaces, it has lost about half an inch in each dimension, or about 1/3 of its volume.

Every conventional American builder in 1983 knew that the studs should be 2x4s placed 16 inches apart. This made a frame 3 ⅝ inches deep. The frame was covered with sheet materials like plywood and sheet rock to make the inner and outer wall surfaces, but the basic thickness of the wall was set by the 2x4s. There were variations in how they were placed and reinforced and connected to deal with windows, doors, and corners, but everything was done with them. How big they should be was never a live question for conventional builders at the time; the answer was a given.

> The same goes for most other sizing questions in conventional building. A house is a real embodiment of "the ten thousand things," the Buddhist phrase for the complexity and entanglement of the world. No builder can work out each component from scratch.

Of course, simply doing what everyone does can't be the whole story. To become taken for granted in that way, a solution has to satisfy some real-world requirements. There are actually several layers of requirement for framing lumber, and they are disparate. Availability, reliability, reputation, structural strength—all of these need to be at least adequate before everybody uses something without thinking about it. Logistical matters are the builder's most immediate concerns. In the 1960s and 1970s, 2x4s were produced in enormous quantities, were available everywhere in a variety of standard lengths, and were subject to an established system which graded them for strength. A builder with a preference for 2x5s would have had a hard time finding them, and might also have faced regulations which called for an engineer to certify their suitability, rather than being able to use them without question.

Reputations also matter to builders. 2x4s were widely held to make satisfactory walls, if used in customary ways, and relying on them was not going to make other people in the industry or your customers think you were odd or untrustworthy. Staying with the crowd generally makes one seem reliable.

Logistics and reputation are about whether the job has a good chance of getting done, but they aren't about the job itself. That has physical requirements, which were unrelated to energy performance before the 1970s. 2x4s became a standard because they were manageable by a single worker, robust enough for the handling they received on building sites, rigid enough to support their share of downward load, nail-able, and low enough in cost.

"Enough" is the watchword here, inescapably. When this many criteria are in play, few can be met with Platonic perfection.

In thinking about the energy performance of a house, we can narrow the view. We can bypass the structural and construction-site questions and just think about the properties of a 2x4 that relate directly to energy use. In the context of the Snowmass house, just two of those mattered. The 3⅝ inch depth of the cavity between studs governed the thickness of insulation which could be installed without disturbing standard ways of sheathing the structure, and the R-value of spruce-pine-fir, the typical softwoods of housebuilding, governed the amount of heat that would bypass the insulation and flow out through the structural wood.

Does a wall framed with 2x4s meet a house's energy requirements well enough? Before the 1970s, it did; but after the OPEC embargo and ensuing events, it seemed not good enough to many. Putting more insulation in the cavity quickly became normal for new construction, and that vastly reduced heat loss and heating bills. In colder regions, framing with the next larger size, "2x6s", which were actually 1½ inches wide by 5⅝ inches deep, was an easy way of taking performance up another notch with very little change in what builders needed to do.

Econo-mysticism was ready with a prescription for how much insulating to do: stop when the last increment of insulation costs the same as the energy it saves one from buying. Like other prescriptions originating in this world-view, this elevated an important insight (insulation isn't free) into a sweeping doctrine (least cost is all that matters). It was easy and tidy, and it was used with tunnel vision. This approach just looked at insulation and fuel, not surrounding factors like the furnace size, the length of the heating season, and so forth.

However, Lovins was not simply aiming to maximize the cost benefit of his insulation, and do better than the average conventional builder on his construction budget. Not having a furnace is a qualitatively different goal; it imposes a quite different discipline on the design. How was he going to know that his building would be warm enough?

There's a critical difference between the challenge of designing to end up with better insulation than usual and the challenge of having it be enough better to meet a high-stakes performance target like having no furnace. It's the difference between walking along a path and jumping over a stream. Across a stream, a shorter than expected jump lands you in the water, where a path just asks your next step to be a bit longer or shorter. A somewhat under-insulated conventional house just asks you to turn up the furnace. This is like walking. A house with no furnace has no such escape hatch; you face a jump over cold, cold water. The energy balance in freezing weather had better live up to your design expectations.

The Lovins building had stone and concrete walls, not wooden ones, but that posed no special problems for energy design. The thermal properties of stone and concrete were just as well known as wood. The superwindows were quite predictable, too.

The troublesome factors were the two environmental ones, cold air and sunshine; the trouble was their variability. Lovins couldn't know for sure when solar heat would be available, or what outside temperatures would be drawing it away again through the windows, walls, floors and roof. The design needed to address these uncertainties, and the building would have only a temporary cushion, the heat stored in the massive walls and floor, if the design fell short.

The main design challenge about the building's functioning was to set up an adequate balance between these two fickle flows—solar heat taken in and building heat leaking out.

It was in this critical arena that John Ehlers made his contributions. At that time, computer methods for projecting energy gains and losses were just emerging, but the Lovins project would stand or fall on the quality of the estimates made. Making them called for very good engineering judgment about how to approximate the complexities of the building's form, the Sun's movements in the sky and local weather into manageable formulas and how best to build in safety factors for the unavoidable uncertainties. Ehlers was the primary agent for this work, and as the building's history shows so clearly, he did an excellent job.

Enough sunlight?

The heat supplied to the Lovinses by the sun is far greater than from any other source, and very safely more than needed. You have seen earlier that a rough estimate, using information Lovins might have had at the time, has the sun supplying 150 kWh per day in January, the least favorable month.[155]

> This kind of data was available in abundance already in the mid-1980s, and continues to be collected to this day. Several hundred long-standing weather stations which record temperature, precipitation, pressure, wind speed, solar intensity and the like every hour are spread across the country. 150 kWh per day was more than 30% larger than his estimated heating need for January, so his estimates of average supply and of average needs and uses could all be off by a great deal without setting up an incapacitating shortfall of supply.

Now recall that having enough average solar heat is good but not the whole story. Though the Sun's brightness is very constant, Earth's weather is not. A workable solar heating scheme has to take account of variability.

To get a line on this, one can use the hour-by-hour solar data collected by US weather stations to construct a chart like the one below for the Aspen area. I will talk it through shortly, but here in brief is the main thing it shows: enough sunlight to maintain the building's temperature is available on most days of every month, and the longest spell of insufficient sunlight in a typical year is about one week. That only happens about twice in a typical year.

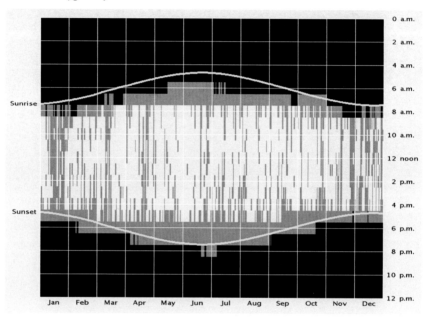

Solar energy available in Aspen, hour by hour

Here is where that summary comes from. We'll work slowly in from larger features to small details. The chart as a whole represents every hour of every day in the year. Each day's hours run vertically; the successive days are laid out horizontally. Black indicates night hours or such early or late daytime that essentially no solar energy is available. The curved yellow lines indicate the official times of sunrise (above) and sunset (below). Notice that they're wider apart in June (midway along) than in January or December (left and right edges), as they should be, since daytime is longer in June.

Yellow or gray indicate sunlight above or below the amount where six hours would supply the house's whole-day need for solar heat. Six hours with that much sun would heat the house for a full twenty-four. You probably don't want to try to decide which of these lines is yellow for six hours, but you can see that there are about nine hours of daylight between the top line and the bottom one on the shortest days, so you don't need a solid yellow line to have six hours with enough sun. Yellow periods will typically supply some excess, more than the threshold amount, and there are many yellow patches. This is encouraging.

> There are already implications for the design in this information. The walls and floor need to be extensive enough to absorb and hold most of the solar heat arriving during the eight or so daylight hours, so they can feed it back into the living space for the other sixteen.

Now for the next level of detail.

Each hour is a thin vertical rectangle of color whose vertical position indicates its place in the day, from very early at the top to very late at the bottom. Each day is a thin vertical strip.

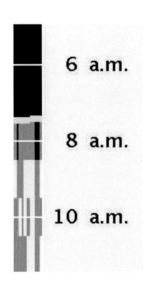

This is probably clearest along the right hand edge of the chart, for example in the portion marked 6 a.m. to 10 a.m. About nine days are here, side by side. The hours run downward from the top. The sunrise line hits the edge about ¾ of the way between 6 a.m. and 8 a.m. That would be about 7.30 a.m. Reading down from there along the very right-hand edge, one sees a gray, then a yellow, then another gray rectangle, all very thin. Read this sequence as follows: threshold sun from 7.30 to 8.30, then above-threshold sun from 8.30 to 9.30, then below-threshold again from 9.30 to 10.30. After that, we have a yellow band which on the full chart runs down to 3.30 p.m, five hours later.

Thus, the whole day in question had six above-threshold hours, so enough or more than enough solar input came in that day to keep the house from cooling off.

And which day is this? The months of the year are laid out in order from left to right, as indicated by the labels at the bottom. Within each month the days are laid out in the same left-to-right order. Though they are unmarked, one can gauge the width of a single day by looking for the thinnest rectangles, of which the day we have been looking at is one, December 31, the last day of the year. Its solar story is that low light, starting at official sunrise, intensified in the next hour, but dropped away again, probably from temporary cloud cover, before getting above our threshold around 11:00 and staying that way until 3:30. Sunset came about 4.30.

With a bit of fussing, one could read each day's story this way, but that's not the chart's purpose. You should scan the whole year visually, looking for vertical bands of gray. A band spanning a whole day from top to bottom indicates a whole day with low solar inflow. If the band is wider than one day's width, it represents several low-sun days in a row. If there are too many days like that, or if they come one after another too often, furnace-free solar heating is in trouble.

The 1980s had the same concepts available, but not the same richness of hourly data or fast computing for handling it. John Ehlers used the coarser methods of the time to good effect, and Lovins made careful study of information from a "zero-energy" demonstration house built in the late 1970s at the Technical University of Denmark. Though not performing quite up to its name, it had generated data which confirmed Lovins' approach to the Snowmass project.

If you look at the same chart for Seattle (the right-hand chart below) you can see that its solar potential is more limited. (It's too small to read details, but the general features are all we need here.) Seattle is said to be cloudy, and the chart bears this out. At the left side, which represents January, and the right, starting as early as October, the hours are frequently gray from top to bottom. This means weeks of day-long cloud cover. The Lovins house might be a chilly place in Seattle,[156] but the

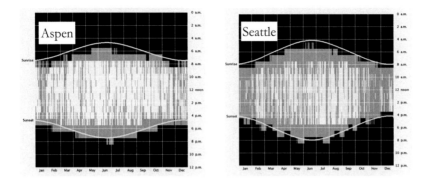

Hour by hour solar energy available in Aspen (left) and Seattle (right)

story in Aspen is quite different. That chart shows increased gray in January and late November through December, but the bands are not wide, and most do not run the whole day. Even in the cloudiest times, the data indicates that the house should actually only cool off about twice a year.

The thought of the house cooling off at all may be distressing. However, the house actually only cools off very slowly, because its insulation is very thick. Lovins estimated at one point that the house would only cool by 0.8 degrees per day. The massive walls, interior arch and slab floor are also reservoirs of heat that gets released slowly and partly replaces the heat lost through the windows and other exterior surfaces. The cooling off during a single week of bad weather remains quite manageable.

Making it manageable is the designer's job. Once again, the operative question is, "How big?" How big does the mass of the house have to be to hold the heat needed? And, very importantly, how much surface area is needed? Stored heat can only get in through an exposed surface. If there are too few exposed square inches, not enough heat can get in. It's like bottles and bottlenecks. The bottle has to be big enough, and the neck has to be wide enough to let the bottle fill in the time allowed. If you had a warm wall ten feet long, but only the end of it was in your building, the heat in it wouldn't do you much good.

This focus on a single year's data may seem troubling. Surely each year is different from others... How can one pronounce that some definite amount of sunlight will happen during such and such a specific hour? Actually the claim here is somewhat different. This hour-by-hour data set is a so-called Typical Meteorological Year (TMY), an ingenious weather data table aimed at embodying not only the customary averages for temperature, rainfall, sunlight, wind, and so forth, but also the hour to hour and day to day correlations which make up the weather patterns typical for the location in question. It is assembled from carefully selected segments of real weather data.[157]

The specific days and hours are not meaningful here, but the distribution of sun and cloud, hot and cold, wet and dry through the successive days and weeks is what usually unfolds in the given location. Any specific real year is likely to have a few unusual highs, lows, or variations which would mislead the engineer who took them as conditions to design for. So the claim is that this data set shows a year's worth of typical conditions, and perhaps does so better than any real year's data.

Slow enough heat loss?

If we know how much solar heat would be available, it's equally important to know whether we can keep enough of it for long enough. How can one tell how fast heat will get lost? That depends on how quickly conduction and radiation will move heat out, and getting numerical estimates for the rates of those processes in a given building is somewhat fussy, though much less than doing a Federal income tax return. For our purposes, there's no need to work with the formulas. To think about what matters and why, it's enough to know two qualitative things about them.

(a) Heat flows from hot to cold, and the bigger the temperature difference between them, the faster the heat flow, in direct proportion. If there is a certain heat flow for a 10 degree difference, the flow for twice the difference (20 degrees) will be twice as much, for three times the difference (30 degrees) three times as much, for half the difference (5 degrees) half as much, for 1.17 times the difference (11.7 degrees) 1.17 times as much, and so on.

(b) The whole effect of the building's physical features on heat flow, walls, roof, windows, and floor, can be boiled into a single number, the amount of heat leaving the building for each degree of temperature difference between inside and outside.

> The official name for this quantity is the "building load coefficient".

To derive this single number, there are various approaches, approximations, and shortcuts. If I wrote out the formulas, they would look horrifying. But the same would be true of the income tax Form 1040 and its swarm of Schedules A, B, C, their cousins and their sub-forms. The work is actually straightforward, mostly adding and subtracting.

> The difficulty is tedium, just as in financial accounting. In fact, energy estimating is a form of accounting, working with kilowatt-hours instead of dollars but otherwise very similar in mentality and technique. Like finance, it is no longer a Dickensian matter requiring great quantities of paper and ink, thanks to computers and software like spreadsheets. Tedium is still present, in the need for checking every detail of the formulas used, but there's much less of it.

In any case, what the formulas generate is an estimate at best. It's like the mileage figure for a car. It tells important things, like whether or not a furnace is required for comfort, but it will not be very precise. Actual mileage of cars is never what the official number says, but it is usually close enough to make meaningful choices between models. The same goes for heat loss.

> When the stakes are real, a good way to generate a decision from an imprecise estimate is to build in a safety margin, and that is just what happens with these solar heating and heat loss estimates.

To estimate the building's load coefficient, one considers each square inch or square centimeter of the outer surface of the building. Some square inches have insulation in them, others are doors or superwindows or concrete floor or whatever. Often they have multiple layers. Heat flows through all of them, slower for some, faster for others. The thermal properties of all the common materials are well known and publicly available—as their R-values! The way to get an overall R-value for a layered assembly is also well known, so each area of the surface will be assigned its particular heat flow, and the total for the building is the simple sum of all areas.

> There is a whole engineering subfield devoted to ironing out wrinkles and dealing with complications. (What about thermal mass? Does it matter if sun shines on the outside wall? what about curved surfaces? What if there is wind blowing? What if not all rooms are heated all the time?). Computers and good software have generated an ability and a willingness to tackle increasingly complicated details. This is important work, and it tunes up the estimates usefully.

The story is not quite over. As you know from the previous chapter, fresh air is another way heat gets lost from houses. The amount may be large or small, depending on how tight the construction is, and how effective any heat exchangers are, but some loss is unavoidable. Surprisingly, this does not make estimating heat loss much worse. The effect of ventilation can just be added to the other heat loss number.

This much can be done before thinking about the actual climate at a building's location. But to meet the no-furnace challenge, you have to estimate the actual, numerical amount of heat loss, so as to set it alongside the solar inflow. That takes real data about outside temperatures. The number one gets by adding up the R-values for all of the surface areas only gives you an R-value for the whole building, and that only tells you the heat loss for each degree that the outside is colder than the inside. You still need to know what the outside temperatures will be.

For any real location, temperatures change all the time, but the estimator faces no great difficulty these days. The illustration indicates the distribution of temperatures in Aspen over a typical year. As you might guess, it comes from the same database (Typical Meteorological Year) as the solar energy data discussed above, and is laid out the same way. Once again, this approach is an approximate yet well-grounded way to account for extended warm or cool spells and other variability that affects heating needs but would be smoothed out of account if you only used daily averages.

> Weather stations that record outdoor temperatures every hour are even more widespread than solar energy stations, and have been in

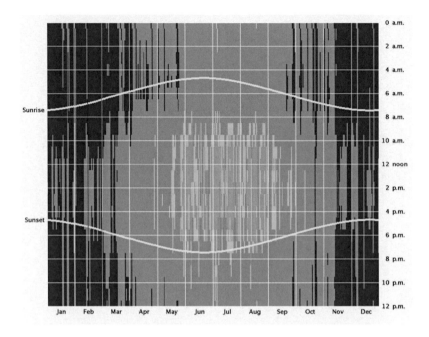

Hour by hour temperatures for Aspen (Typical Meteorological Year)

place for many years. You can readily get a whole year of real local data wherever you are in the country.

As before, each thin top to bottom strip represents one day, with light blue for temperatures between 68° and 75° Fahrenheit, orange hotter than that, lavender colder down to freezing, and dark blue below freezing (a full 30% of the year). Some general features you might expect show up here. There is much more freezing weather in winter, on the left and right sides, than there is in the central portion for the summer; mid-days and afternoons are typically warmer than mornings; there are many more warm days after the midpoint of the year than before.

> Finding these basic patterns in the chart can help one have confidence that other, unexpected patterns are also real.

One quite important but often forgotten pattern that shows here is that hot weather is not continuous in the summer months. There is a fairly steady alternation of hotter and cooler spells, roughly a week in length. One might guess that the solar chart would show alternating spells of cloudy and clear skies that line up with this pattern. Using these estimated outdoor temperatures, our expected temperature for the inside of the house, and our R-values, we can estimate how much lost heat we'll need to be replacing during the coldest stretches of the year.

Getting gains and losses to balance

We can see now that the diligent designer has handles on the big-enough question; there is a way of telling if the many parts of the building which affect heating and cooling will be the right sizes to take in and hold enough solar heat when it's cold, and to keep out or get rid of excess when it's hot.

For many US locations, getting enough solar input in winter is less of a problem than getting too much in summer. As recounted earlier, this was the downfall of a surge in passive solar interest in the US right after World War II, remained a thorny issue in the 1980s and 1990s, and led to heating taking a back seat to daylighting as the primary way to use sunlight directly.

Amory Lovins was well aware of the danger. Any building that takes in all the available sun in the winter and holds it tightly is bound to have trouble in the summer, when much more sun arrives, unless something changes about how much gets in or how tightly it is held.

One can put it this way: passive solar houses need to have seasons. They need to be different in winter and summer. In conventional houses, being different in different seasons is so thoroughly built into people's habits that the need never presents itself as an insight. You just open windows when it's hot and close them when it's cold, and you turn the heating system on for the winter and off for the summer. There was a time when there were significant season-change routines, especially in cold climates. Storm windows went on in the fall, came off in the spring. In some areas, families shifted their activities out of the colder side of the house in the winter, and back in the spring. In others, screened sleeping porches were common summer amenities from which people retreated in winter.

Somehow the postwar passive solar boom lost sight of this.

I suspect this was a comeuppance to the major glass companies. In the years immediately after World War II, they were major promoters of the solar house idea, seeing it as a huge potential market. A housing boom was underway, and if a good portion of it involved large sheets of south-facing glass, what a nice prospect for the industry. Unfortunately, their way of using large sheets had them fixed in place, like picture windows; that meant any seasonal changes would have to come from other features, like shades or vents or fans. The glass companies were probably not interested in making owners or builders realize that their new glass would call for fussing with these additional items, and many people may simply have forgotten summer in their enthusiasm for this new way of dealing with winter.

The important point here is that the Lovins building needed to be seasonal, and so it was. The top of the greenhouse has a line of good-sized vents, to be opened when necessary to release excessively heated air. A line of windows along the lower edge of the greenhouse enclosure could also be opened, encouraging circulation to flush hot air out the top.

Automatic or manual?

These vents were manually controlled. The three large upper ones had a cord and pulley arrangement for pulling them open from the floor below. An earlier photo shows that end of the set-up. They closed by gravity, relying on the weight of the vent to rotate it down snugly into its frame when the pulled cord was unfastened and released. Automatic control, with thermostats and motor-driven opening and closing, was possible at the time, but it would have been much more expensive and prone to breakage, without much advantage in effectiveness.

US householders, it is true, have often responded enthusiastically to the promise of houses that run themselves. Not having to do the work of basic functions has been one of the recurring appeals of affluent living. The washing machine, the refrigerator, automatic transmissions in cars, and the prospect of self-driving vehicles are prominent examples among many in US life. Alongside this has run a quieter but very persistent stream of satisfaction in doing things for oneself, without servants (human or mechanical). This dual tendency manifested itself as one of the sharper divides between conventional and alternative culture in the 1960s. Environmentalism called, among other things, for a much increased awareness of the natural world and human impacts on it. Alternative living seemed to many people, both conventional and alternative minded, to imply reduced use of machines and reduced involvement in the industrial world that was chewing up nature to manufacture them and the energy they needed to run.

To the conventionally minded, the sense of comfort and convenience suburban life offered was worth the impacts, which seemed manageable. Alternatives, including efforts at solar heating, seemed like returns to less appealing ways of living. Across the divide, in the counter-culture, there was a variable blend of forward and backward thinking. Amory would stoutly maintain that his thinking looked resolutely forward, but he was actually delighted to find future uses for good ideas of the past. In his eyes, the cord and pulley vent openers were quite like the halyards of small sailboats, lightweight simple devices for responding to the environment, and not at all like laundry lines in old tenements, creaking and perhaps rusty accommodations to cramped living conditions.

Because of choices like these, human occupants were essential parts of the Lovins house system. It wouldn't function acceptably without a degree of human perception and active effort. The amount of attention and effort the house required were certainly not truly taxing, compared say, to cutting and splitting enough wood to feed stoves all winter. It's also true that ordinary houses, with their furnaces and thermostats, do call for some effort, but their primary mode is automatic. People only need to make adjustments for special circumstances like visits from cold-sensitive older people, while adjusting the vents in a passive solar house is a routine task, even though the effort is small.

On the other hand, the rest of the operation of the house was thoroughly automatic, even in 1984 The heat exchangers ran on their own all winter; the insulation silently insulated; the superwindows needed no attention to let in sun when there was some, and to hold in heat all the time. I am sure it is already clear that Lovins' approach was eclectic. The design was guided by the end goals of using energy efficiently, relying on renewable sources, and having a comfortable and satisfying living and working space, but not by a preemptive purity in how any of these would be pursued.

The debate or dialogue between automatic and manual continues to this day, and is probably with us forever. We've seen that the 2006-2009 renovation brought in more elaborate systems and controls, for several reasons particular to the building's inhabitants, and we've also seen that the benefits came with some shadows.

In society at large, the decades since 1984 have brought wavelets of excitement about household automation, which now include possibilities for control at a distance and quick responding voice control inside the home. With this has come possibilities of surveillance and manipulation by the providers of these automatic services. Any progress toward sustainability through these expansions of our capacities for controlling our buildings will be accompanied by this debate.

---

[154] Smith, L. W., & Wood, L. W. (1964). "History of yard lumber size standards." *USDA Forest Service, Forest Product Laboratory.*

[155] This is a rough estimate, based on January data from the Department of Energy for nearby Aspen. A horizontal surface averages 2.1 kWh per m^2-day. Glass tilted up receives more, about 3.4, but the two glass surfaces and the heat-mirror film together reflect back a little under half of what arrives, so the final amount received is about 1.8 kWh per m^2-day. The greenhouse and two small roof windows have 65 m^2; south-facing vertical windows are about 18 m^2 more. Very roughly, this makes 150 kWh/day from the Sun.

[156] The chart is a little unfair to Seattle. It uses the same threshold as for Aspen, but the climate is not as severe in Seattle, so actually somewhat less solar input is needed to maintain steady indoor temperatures. Seattle is still cloudy for extended periods in the winter, so an appropriate furnace-free design would probably have more insulation and less glass. But less sun is needed, so the threshold for steady temperature would be lower. Seattle is somewhat yellower, so to speak, than it appears in this chart.

[157] Wilcox, Stephen, and William Marion. *Users manual for TMY3 data sets.* Golden, CO: National Renewable Energy Laboratory, 2008.

1983

2011

13: Looking Back and Ahead

It is time to draw this extended reflection to a close. The path to sustainability does not end here, though. This chapter is a pause along the way, a chance to look back, see where we are, and look ahead.

I have pursued five themes. There is the physical functioning of the building, the way it shelters the Lovins household and office. There's the relation of those functions and materials—heating and cooling, daylighting and artificial light, stone and glass and wood—to the lives lived in the place, psychologically, even spiritually, as well as physically. There's the wider world and what it was doing about buildings. There's sustainability, evolving over several decades. And there is the role of the visionary. There has been plenty of background and explanation for each of these themes, and many pointers and clues for future progress have presented themselves. Glimpses, I called them on page 1, glimpses of tools, practices, insights, and partnerships from which a world can be made that is not only sustainable but desirable. Now is the time to organize them and highlight the most important.

From the Introduction, you already know I am a longtime college teacher, but this is not a class, and there is no grade. When it comes to sustainability, we are all learners, not teachers. I have thought hard about the topics that have come up, and you can tell I have opinions about them. But sustainability is not at a point where one person's knowledge and opinions can settle anything.

One person can point out possibilities. An exceptional person like Amory Lovins can take hold of the jumble of ideas, techniques, and experiences in society at a given moment and assemble them into a coherent and inspiring account of how we might move toward a better world. Describing his vision of this kind, the soft path, a path toward "the enduring prosperity of all living things," has been Lovins' most important contribution to world energy affairs. The Snowmass house has deserved our extended attention because it is so firmly and obviously committed to the soft path. It is not trying to hedge its bets. It is not a baby step. It is a major stride.

I have called the place a benchmark because it has served as a reference point. It could be called a trailhead because it indicated the beginning of a way forward into untamed territory. In fact, one can see the building as a stride along that path, a big one, but by no means the last. This is what we should hope for from visionaries like Lovins—a big first stride in a newly defined direction with inspiring prospects. Then it's the responsibility of other people who recognize the prospects and understand the direction to work out the next steps and keep going. I see three general lessons to keep in mind.

More than hardware

The new direction, as I see it, involves more than a change of hardware. If you go on a tour of the Lovins house, as we did vicariously in Chapter 7, your immediate attention goes largely to architectural features, equipment, and services. However, the striking feel of the place—the light, the growing things, the connection with the environment outside, the sound of running water rather than mechanical sounds—is always in the background. As you know from the chapter on reflections, as well as my comments in other places, I think the house owes its persuasiveness as much to this general character as to its technical features. It has the "surprising and complex" relation of parts and the depth of feeling that make it whole, in the profound sense that Christopher Alexander teaches us to strive for.

Of course, the fittings and services do matter a great deal. The place would be uninhabitable if the passive solar and superinsulation design had gone awry. They have not. This large, well appointed, multifunctional structure grows banana crops in the Snowmass winter, welcomes dinner parties, has sheltered and supported a business winter and summer, all with sunlight, a good heat-holding structure and only occasional and quite minimal assistance from wood and propane. What exists is possible. Other buildings in the area could readily do the same, if their owners and designers wanted to, and if they brought appropriate critical understanding to the task. Design teams do need accurate detailed knowledge, not just a vision, and owners need to know enough to quiz the designers constructively.

But the tacit message of the place, "Yours Could Be This Good", is about more than staying warm. It is about the importance of materials—the stone and the wood, the extensive glass. It is about the curving forms, the play of light during each day, the acoustic environment, the immediate green of the plants. It is about a circulation pattern and set of spaces closely adapted to the life the owners aimed at. That life, with its large public component and its interweaving of workspace and household, has been quite unusual, even idiosyncratic. The lesson is not that the building should be cloned. The lesson is that owners and designers should be thinking about the intangible dimensions that we encountered in Chapter 6—about how a place can contain one's concerns, how it may be taken as one's own in satisfying ways, how it can connect with what one knows and believes and thinks.

This is not an easy or straightforward lesson for our country today. Neither the building industry nor their customers are particularly organized to pursue it, and they are even less inclined to because the customers' side is so often an uneasy alliance of buyers, speculative builders, bankers and realtors. Nevertheless, it is there to be absorbed and learned from, at 1739 Snowmass Creek Road.

The vision did what some visions can

There was plenty of uneasiness in the quite different, one-of-a-kind alliance that built 1739. That alliance is not a model for future buildings of this general kind, any more than the building itself should be cloned. Almost everywhere in the country now, forty years later, there are builders and architects who have the skills and experience to make a structure that holds heat and uses the sun as effectively in its area as this one has done in Snowmass. The possibility was already demonstrated in Eugene Leger's 1979 superinsulated house in the chilly, overcast outskirts of Boston. The succeeding years have seen materials and equipment become widely available, and the know-how to use them has become widely dispersed as well. There remain, as one should expect, important variations in the knowledge, skill, and care of builders. "Caveat emptor" is still good advice for homebuyers. But a great deal has changed since 1983, and the capacity for very low energy buildings of style and sound construction is present almost everywhere in the US.

One particular lesson from the 1983 saga is important, however. You may recall the collision of vision with reality when the unskilled and inexperienced foreman and crew found their progress too slow for the onset of winter. At that point, the project teetered between collapse and continuation, and what made the difference was the quality of the vision. In this case, it makes sense to say that reality gave way to vision.

To put it more carefully, reality turned out to harbor alternatives compatible with the vision, and the vision turned out to be adaptable to short term changes without giving way on what it promised for the long term. It kept a good grip on the baby as it let the bathwater go. This is one of the most important of the various possibilities Amory and Hunter Lovins revealed at the Snowmass site: when vision and reality conflict, the right vision can get reality to reveal new ways forward.

Such a vision needs to be both inspiring and well grounded, and this one was. It was inspiration that kept work going, kept problem solving alive, and kept generating new interest and resources when the old ones had dried up. It was the good grounding of the design that allowed each increment of work to be a genuine step toward completion. True, there were some reversals, like the cold fall day when the concrete pour would not set and had to be cleared away and redone. But the completed building was true in detail to the promise held out by the first full rendering of the design in 1983.

Sustainability acquires a history

When the notion of sustainability emerged in the late 1980s, it reshaped reality in something like the way the notion of a soft path had reshaped energy policy. Articulated on a far broader scale than the soft path vision, and neither so inspiring nor so well grounded, it got plenty of kneading, pounding, and reshaping from reality in its turn. Some of this is illuminated by what has changed and not changed about the Lovins building over its 41 years of existence.

We've seen that the building's basic structure and function worked very much as planned from the start, but the structure aged and function slowly declined over the next twenty years until the renovation of 2006-2009 tightened things up again. Doors loosened and window frames weakened. This kind of wear and tear accumulates quickly or slowly according to how careful the maintenance is, but it always does accumulate. The Snowmass building's history doesn't have new lessons to teach about maintenance. That was adequately done in most ways, though it allowed certain problems like moisture wicking up into the greenhouse window frames to go unnoticed. It generally unfolded acceptably but not instructively. The lesson lies in the readiness for changes.

I dwell on changes here, because sustenance, the activity of sustaining life, needs to be about adapting to circumstances, and circumstances inside and beyond the building did change notably between 1984 and 2006. Examining the changes in a visionary structure can shed light on the fruitfulness of the originating visions.

Within the structure, these two decades saw the rise and fall of compact fluorescent lights, the rise and continuous flourishing of banana plants, the decline of a first approach to soil and water in the greenhouse and the installation of a new one. The heating system started using solar driven radiant floors, and the building shifted from modest consumption of electric power, highlighted by efficient appliances and equipment, to the deliberate production of power beyond the building's own needs to displace fossil generation on the grid. What lessons are here?

The clearest is that practical actions aimed at increasing sustainability must keep adapting as the search for it reveals both obstacles and opportunities. It would be nice to find enduring solutions right away, but sustainability is too transformative a goal for that, except occasionally. First-generation moves, like compact fluorescents, must often give way over time to better ones. The greenhouse renovation is a prime example. Its first incarnation proved its point: the ample local sun, well held by an efficient structure, would deal with Rocky Mountain winter. The major reworking of 2006-2009 could take this for granted and bring to it what the wider world had done by way of assembling possibilities since 1984, uniting longstanding knowledge about plants with an urgent new goal, agricultural sustainability. The result, out in that wider world, was the new field of agroecology. The greenhouse area could simply tap into this new synthesis, and did.

The change in Lovins' philosophy about on-site energy production was a different kind of adaptation, more about outward engagement. He had originally come to the soft path approach out of deep concern with the social and political implications of ever more centralized power production, the dominant tendency of the 1970s. Activists of that era often went for cutting all ties with the national system, having as little as possible to do with the grid as a matter of principle. Lovins worked instead, from the beginning, toward transforming that system by direct engagement—policy critique, formulation of alternatives, and major demonstration projects. By 2009, thanks to the work of other theorists and activists focused on economic issues, the national system for providing electric power had entered a period of quietly intense turbulence that continues today. The creation of markets in which old utilities and new independent producers bid against each other in short-term and long-term offerings had been instrumental in opening the door for renewable sources such as solar electricity. Awareness of the threats of climate change had spread widely enough to make reducing CO_2 emissions a significant motivator of actions by individuals and some governments, so choices about household electricity had a new dimension.

Putting his personal chips in 2006 on displacing coal power with extra rooftop solar on his house was a personal action right in line with the policy choices he'd always advocated, an important moment of adapting newly available means without losing sight of the ends.

Looking forward

Neither the search for sustainability nor the Lovins building are ending now. The building is fifteen years into its renovated second generation, and it is safe to say that another fifteen years will see more changes in its use, even if its shell and services stay the same. Amory turned 75 in 2022, and so far shows little sign of slowing down or shifting gears; Judy is 78 and continues her work as a master photographic printmaker and advisor. Aging is unpredictable but hard to avoid. The building offers some advantages for aging in place, and some disadvantages. There's no way to speculate on whether or how it might continue to suit their lives. It may be easier to talk about thirty or more years from now, when these individuals will have left the scene, at least if we respect the comment attributed to Yogi Berra, "Prediction is hard, especially about the future." Without making predictions, we can consider some connections between this very specific building and general tendencies in American culture.

First must come the truth that our culture gives no automatic respect to older buildings. The catalogue of notable buildings that have been demolished or condemned is extensive, from New York's Pennsylvania Station to San Francisco's several Cliff House incarnations, from Houston's Astrodome to the original Chicago Stock Exchange, and everywhere in between. Many others have survived, of course—including Taos Pueblo, Monticello, Fallingwater, and Hearst Castle. Those histories are full of near losses and fortunate escapes, though, and one must admit that the statistics of survival are gloomy. Recently they have become even gloomier in places like the Aspen area, where expensive houses are frequently demolished right after being purchased to allow even more expensive houses to go up.

The Lovins building may seem quite vulnerable because of the shadow side of one of its strengths. Its persuasiveness as a real-life embodiment of sustainable ideas gains greatly from its having been designed for actual lives lived by actual people. It has none of the synthetic aura that demonstration buildings like the Environmental Showcase Home in Phoenix can't escape. However, actual people wanting a house in the future would have different lives, and might well balk at features such as the two small bedrooms and the very large library/office area. Certainly the professional appraisals of the property in 2003 and 2007 were dubious about these points in relation to typical buyers.

On the other hand, any Internet search for images of "unusual US houses" shows dozens of truly outlandish shapes and sizes, all apparently in use. What exists is possible, as I keep saying, and what these houses prove is that non-typical buyers exist. So it is possible one may appear when needed. It's also possible that the place could continue as a combination home and research institute, which its current special use zoning permits. Nonetheless, this kind of continuation is quite rare, depending as it does on the existence of a suitable organization that's the right size, solvent enough, and ready at the right time.

This building faces long odds against surviving in its present form, then. However, its place in the stream of work on green building is well established. It has been a lively part of that stream for forty years, providing memorable images like Amory with his heavy bunches of bananas, direct encounters for tens of thousands of tour visitors, and inspiration to others in green building, like those in the Passivhaus movement. That work has steadily broadened and deepened, and now touches every kind of building in all parts of the country. In true American fashion it rushes forward in some places and merely idles or creeps in others. To give two glimpses of how far it has reached, I'll describe two more buildings. They are on opposite sides of the country and speak to quite different goals.

Zero Cottage

The first is called Zero Cottage. It's located on a difficult, narrow lot in the Mission District of the city of San Francisco, and is the home of David Baker and his life partner, Yosh Asato. Baker is an architect whose practice centers on affordable and multi-family housing in fully urban locations in the Bay Area. His firm, David Baker Architects, has about 30 design professionals and consistently wins awards for infill, mixed use, neighborhood, and affordable projects.[158]

The building is located on the rear portion of a narrow lot in the middle of a block, flanked all along its south side by a long, high concrete wall. There is another narrow three-story building at the front of the site, with two small apartments above a storefront.

Baker undertook the project in 2010 as a personal and professional challenge and experiment: was it possible to both meet the Passivhaus standard and achieve "net-zero" operation in a residence on this site, in a way he would choose to inhabit?[159] (It would be his home, after all.) He used the occasion for some experimenting with reclaimed materials as well: the outermost wall surface is a rain screen of sheet metal rectangles held in with Baker-designed clips that make them individually replaceable.

"Net-zero" means the building will produce at least as much energy as it uses over the course of a year. (We encountered this goal, though not the term, when looking at the PV aspect of the Lovins building renovation.) This goal has become a key symbolic benchmark for current green building. Zero has a clarity and a grounding in actual performance that have been very welcome, especially as evidence has accumulated that design-stage estimates are often considerably below (or above) actual usage.

The eventual design has two floors of living space above a workshop or gallery space at ground level. This amounts to 712 square feet of indoor living space, and it has a vegetated roof garden with a small solar hot water heater. The shell has the technical features you would now expect —thick insulation, superwindows (triple-pane in this case), very tight construction and heat exchangers for ventilation. Construction to the desired tightness was quite tricky in the rear of the site, where adjoining buildings made access and the positioning of air barriers difficult, but the structure passed the Phius tightness test.

Electric power is produced on site with a 3-kilowatt array held up and off to one side of the roof by a custom metal frame. This elaborate mounting was the response to insistence from the fire code inspectors

Zero Cottage, San Francisco; David Baker, architect
(images by Matthew Millman)

that the roof allow access for firemen; the array needed to produce enough power over 12 months for net-zero would have taken too much of the actual roof to leave room for them. The images make it obvious that this is no mass market design. The interior layout is equally individual, tuned to the lives of the actual people who live here. On examining the details, however, one finds a structure that is straightforward and efficient to build, and quite adaptable to different choices about overall size, space allocation, windows and so forth.

One unavoidable feature of the design is its small size. The site would have accepted somewhat more than the 712 square feet, but not very much. Suburban expanse was impossible for this project, but that's the situation of most city dwellers. Zero Cottage is of interest because it speaks to the possibilities for imagination, eco-soundness, and individual lives to coexist in high density settings.

Ten years of operation show the building has cleared the annual net-zero threshold continuously since October 2013, the end of the first full year of occupancy. Indeed, it produced more than the commercial energy it consumed almost every month, winter as well as summer. (It did this in 41 out of the 48 months in the first four years). This is a step beyond net-zero, and not unusual for recent buildings that take net-zero as their design goal. Prudent design for solar energy naturally builds in a certain amount of extra capacity to deal with the year-to-year variability in sun conditions. Some might be content with a system that averaged out to net-zero over several years, accepting some below-zero years in the run if they were balanced by enough years above zero, but pride in that achievement would feel strained to most interested householders. Much greater satisfaction comes from knowing one's building can be counted on to do its job every year. Zero is not really a target, it is a threshold. Above feels quite different from below, so aiming for a positive balance every year becomes the norm.

Green building advocates and enthusiasts have recognized that this kind of satisfaction should be reflected in language, and have started touting "net-plus" as the way to describe a building that is really making it. David Baker has kept the name Zero Cottage, but his descriptions of the place are quick to mention net-plus as its performance. I like this usage myself, because I think it helps in one more small way to acknowledge that each building is connected to a larger whole, and that these buildings are connected in a way that contributes to it. The extra power production that justifies "plus" goes out to be used at large, balancing the help that comes from out there when sunlight is scarce or absent.

Net-plus is not a viable goal for high-rise residences, nor even mid-rise ones above perhaps six or seven stories. Only so much sunlight falls on the roof, and the more floors it must supply, the less is available per floor. One Seattle office project, the Bullitt Building, has done it for six floors, but getting enough PV power for all of them required extending the array out over the city sidewalk, which needed a special exception to the Seattle code. Lower buildings need no such special measures, even in cloudy locations like the Pacific Northwest. Zero Cottage, with two floors of habitation and one of workshop/gallery in San Francisco, had no difficulty.

120 Grove Street

The second glimpse of present-day continuation on this path toward sustainability is a four-story multifamily building at 120 Grove Street, Brooklyn, NY. It's owned and managed as affordable housing by Riseboro Community Partners, a multi-pronged local non-profit, and is a testimony to the potential for drastic improvements in existing buildings. Originally put up in 1932, it was taken through major retrofitting in 2016-2020, bringing it to the Passivhaus standard of performance.

The moving force behind this project was New York architect Chris Benedict, who had been working since the mid 1990s on low energy designing for mid-rise apartment blocks at the scale of 120 Grove St, some retrofits, some new construction. 120 Grove Street is actually part of a group of 12 buildings in Brooklyn she has been working on with Riseboro, and New York City has many, many more buildings of this general kind.

Benedict has collaborated from early on with an engineer, Henry Gifford; they share a no-nonsense approach to both new-build and retrofit projects. Committed to reducing energy use, impatient with fads, patient and thorough with details, and focused on fundamentals, they have an impressive track record completing low energy projects in this unglamorous but abundant building type.

Their approach relies on the fundamentals of superinsulation—a building shell with as few gaps as possible in the insulation, tight construction to eliminate air leakage, and carefully managed ventilation, including heat exchangers. However, their work stands out in two ways. First, they compartmentalize. As fully as possible, they make each apartment a separate unit for heating, cooling, and fresh air. Each gets its own heaters, thermostat, air ducts and fans, and each is well sealed on all sides. This means heating or cooling is only being generated for units that feel the need. This avoids the far too common situation (at least in New York City) in which a large central boiler overheats most units, and they then regain comfort by flinging open their windows. Compartmentalizing also has good side benefits: noise, smells, and pests are much reduced, and the lived experience of tenants is much enhanced.

120 Grove St, Brooklyn. (Left) Before retrofit. (Right) After retrofit.

The second stand-out feature of their work has been a commitment to costing no more than conventional projects of this kind. This needed to be established to the satisfaction of financers and owners before construction could ever start. All parties to a building project are reflexively suspicious of the unconventional; builders typically ask for more money as a kind of insurance or reward for taking on risk, while owners and financers assume that will happen, putting such proposals out of consideration.

Benedict and Gifford's tactic was to go to the relevant party—builder, owner or financer—with a set of drawings and detailed bid sheet for a conventional way of doing the project, get some agreement that this was basically reasonable, and then produce a bid sheet and drawings for their unconventional proposal that came to the same cost. It took some talking, but the worked out details and the equal final costs were enough to get their first projects okayed, and after they came in on target, later similar projects had an easier time.

The cost balancing requires some good insights and a lot of careful legwork in buildings to be retrofitted. A sample insight: a six-story building with a large boiler in the basement for building-wide heating would have required a solidly built 70 foot chimney for the exhaust. Going to individual air-source heat pumps cost plenty for the multiple units but saved plenty on the chimney. This was a case of tunneling through the cost barrier. Not all their projects had this particular trade-off available, but Benedict and Gifford have been very good at spotting this kind of possibility, and their costs have routinely come out even.

Attention to details, on site, was the other key ingredient. The comparative cost schedules needed each item worked out and ready to be explained and defended. It turned out that building code minimums for fire-stopping, waterproofing and acoustics would take care of a good deal of air tightening, if the minimums were actually met over the whole building, so Benedict was frequently up on the scaffolding, looking over builders' shoulders. This was not always popular, but she got good results. Later, spray-on sealants came on the market, which made air-tightening much more straightforward. It still required unremitting care, though, and Benedict continued to look over shoulders often.

It was a help to avoid talk of grand goals in working with the builders. Benedict says she tries to make everything feel as normal as possible in carrying out these projects, as if it all came from Home Depot. Her close supervision was an exception to this, of course, but that, too, was workaday, rather than being a matter of planetary significance. She just seemed like an unusually picky architect being stringent.

Eventually, as awareness of climate change slowly permeated the country, grander reasons for taking this kind of trouble became part of their work. A significant change happened around 2005, when the Passive House effort made its real US appearance. Working largely independently, Benedict/Gifford and the Passivhaus/Passive House project had come to very similar strategies for achieving low energy buildings. Benedict says:

> When people started to tell me that the Germans were making these buildings that didn't need heating systems and that the insulation and the air barrier was what was functioning to keep them warm, I kind of got that because I knew from my own buildings that if I stepped it up, I could get to that.[160]

And indeed, it was not long before Benedict and Gifford finished their first Passive House project, a new build successfully certified in 2014. Generally, the German roots of Passivhaus and the careful construction of the Passivhaus standard lent reassuring weight to the performance claims that Benedict and Gifford were already essentially making.

As a retrofit, 120 Grove Street raised a particular challenge. It was not the usual one for retrofits, the difficulty of working with the existing structure; Benedict devised a clever scheme for applying her basic technical solutions there. However, the building's 24 units were occupied by sitting tenants; Riseboro was legally and morally bound to look after them during the major work proposed, which was nothing less than complete reworking of the building's heating and ventilation. After extensive consultation with all parties, Benedict proposed to have tenants remain in their units throughout the work, except for a week or so of final steps, when they would be housed in a vacant unit or in a hotel.

How was this possible? Her key insight was that they could put all the new systems—the air sealing, insulation, heating/cooling and ventilation—on the outside surface of the existing building. The new "tight building" sealant against air and water leaks, a liquid, could be painted on to provide an unbroken barrier. A continuous layer of insulation would then be fastened on over the whole exterior of the building, and new windows fitted to it. New heating, cooling and ventilation systems would be mounted on the roof and distribution to individual apartments would sit underneath the insulation layer, supported by the existing exterior of the building.

All this could be done without displacing the occupants of any apartment. There would be scaffolding outside, there would be noise and some degree of mess, but the apartments would remain livable.

Then there would be the brief final stage, taking a few days for each apartment, when workers would bring the heating pipes and small ventilation ducts through the wall, install the indoor units, remove the old windows, and clean everything up.

Technically, this is superinsulation grown out of adolescence, and provided for existing buildings through a clever and sophisticated process. As always, very good insulation and windows make it possible to have very low capacity gear for heating, cooling and ventilating, so the building's energy use drops to 25% or less of its previous level.[161] Experientially, lives improve, as well. Tenants can adjust their heating and cooling individually; the apartments are much quieter; and the unbroken barrier to air leakage also keeps pests at bay. In case of power outages, the renovated building loses heat far more slowly than originally. Benedict and Gifford provided all this without elevated cost, for users without privilege.

Remember the bananas!

Zero Cottage and 120 Grove Street are just two noteworthy indicators of where the insights that shaped the Lovins building are now at work. Neither will get thousands of visitors; both are doing their part in what continues to be the American pattern of uneven but genuine progress toward a sustainable world. In 1983, net-zero was an ambition only for the few who hoped for complete, isolated self-sufficiency. Now, in 2024, it has become technically far easier and can be considered by the many people who aspire to live sustainably in the highly connected, socially complex settings of urban centers. In 1983, generic low-rent four-story apartment buildings in unfashionable city neighborhoods were a big part of the country's energy problem. Now there are materials and tested techniques at hand to make them part of the solution.

Each of these buildings also present some of today's unresolved questions. The 1930s cornice and decorative brickwork of the original 120 Grove Street building are now buried under several inches of block foam. The blocks have been thoughtfully shaped to suggest Art Deco cornice and decorations, so some of the feeling of the original survives, but hardly all of it. How much should history remain present in these material forms? We do not know.

Zero Cottage was clearly built as a special project, to reflect the preferences and rhythms of its particular inhabitants, one of whom also happened to be an architect and a developer. For most people, the mass production of materials and the routinization of construction enable energy-efficient, low impact building at affordable cost, but as we now do things the results are generic, not individual. How can these things square with the thought that we won't sustain what we don't love, and the knowledge that love grows from particulars, not generalities? We do not know.

We do know that the soft path has a wider base than ever. A 2022 tally by the Energy and Environmental Building Alliance (EEBA), an industry association, found 63,000 zero-energy residences in the US. This included all comers, only some of which were certified by Passive House, LEED or their cousins. Nevertheless, the numbers in the EEBA's surveys have grown markedly over the past decade, and can certainly be taken as a strong indicator of widely shared intentions. In relation to annual new-home sales in the US in the hundreds of thousands, these numbers are still small. The 1980s waves of passive solar and superinsulated houses ran up to levels like this but never spread to become conventional practice. Unlike the earlier waves, however, this one has strong encouragement from state policy in California, Massachusetts and New York, and growing support in certain Western states, including Texas. There is a well-developed network of industry newsletters and publicity, spreading information and encouragement. This run-up is slower than earlier ones, and has already lasted much longer, for twenty years more or less. I would bet on its long continuation, but the story is far from over.

What is clear, above and beyond any fine distinctions and cautions, is that buildings, in which we Americans spend 85% of our time, matter a great deal for sustainability. It is also clear that the building stock is not sustainable yet, that much is known about how to make it so, but that getting there is not guaranteed. This is not merely information, either. As I pointed out, you the reader are likely, one way or another, to be part of how this plays out, directly or indirectly, close-up or at a distance.

If you find yourself thinking about how to make a building more sustainable, or choose to get involved somehow in the public or private work of deciding what the buildings in our communities will be like, I hope that the ideas, practices and history unfolded in this book will make it easier for you. Keep the Lovins building in mind. It remains a significant milestone. It stands for technical insight, determined execution, and the courage of one's convictions. It stands equally for being clear about what life one wants to be lived in a building, and for faithfulness in making that life possible. This dual witness may be easiest to keep in mind if you remember Amory's bananas. They testify to the particular personal wholeness achieved in this particular building. The right technical moves got married to the right experiential intuitions. Do your part to find their equivalent in the buildings you become involved with. They can only end up whole if the right people engage in the right conversations, working out a coherent relationship for all the ingredients and finding the depth of feeling that animates them and moves their users. Remember the bananas!

---

158 The firm is David Baker Architects; its informative website is at www.dbarchitect.com/

159 This account is largely from two interviews with David Baker in 2015 and 2016.

160 From 2014 interview of Chris Benedict by Andrew Gardner as part of the Bard Graduate Center Craft, Art and Design Oral History Project. This is an excellent account of the origins and development of Benedict's work. Available through https://bgccraftartdesign.org/items (consulted 12 November 2023)

161 There's a comparison of Passive House energy usage with existing New York buildings at https://www.swinter.com/party-walls/the-numbers-are-in-nyc-passive-house-performance-data/. 120 Grove Street is about 10% better than the Passive House threshold level.

Selected Bibliography

Alexander, C. et al. *A Pattern Language: Towns, Buildings, Construction.* Oxford University Press, 1977

Balcomb, S. (1984). "Living in a passive solar home". Energy and Buildings, 7(4), 309-314.

Bayard, Pierre. *How to Talk About Books You Haven't Read.* Bloomsbury Publishing USA, 2007.

Bloomer, Kent C., Charles Willard Moore, Robert J. Yudell, and Buzz Yudell. *Body, Memory, and Architecture.* Yale University Press, 1977.

Denzer, Anthony. *The Solar House: Pioneering Sustainable Design.* Rizzoli, 2013.

Gold, Rich. *The Plenitude: Creativity, Innovation, and Making Stuff.* MIT Press, 2007

Laird, Frank N. *Solar Energy, Technology Policy, and Institutional Values.* Cambridge University Press, 2001.

Lechner, Norbert. *Heating, Cooling, Lighting: Sustainable Design Methods for Architects.* Wiley, 2014.

Lovins, Amory B., "Energy Strategy: the Road Not Taken?". *Foreign Affairs* **55**, p. 66 (1976)

Macy, Joanna. *Despair and Personal Power in the Nuclear Age.* New Society Publishers, 1983.

Mott-Smith, Morton. *The Concept of Energy Simply Explained.* Dover Publications, 1934

National Audubon Society and Croxton Collaborative, *Audubon House: Building the Environmentally Responsible, Energy-Efficient Office.* Wiley, 1994.

Passivhaus Institut, Passipedia—The Passive House Resource (online at https://passipedia.org/; updated periodically)

Perlin, John. *Let It Shine: the 6,000-year Story of Solar Energy.* New World Library, 2022.

Image Credits

Front and Back Covers and pages 17, 31, 37, 164, 225	Judy Hill Lovins
Page 33	Mr.mu517j under https://creativecommons.org/licenses/by-sa/3.0 via Wikimedia Commons
Pages 40, 41, 52-62	Sara Balcomb *Energy and Buildings* paper, see endnote 22
Pages 179, 180	Arizona Board of Regents
Page 189 (all)	Croxton Collaborative Architects
Page 199	International Passive House Association
Pages 211, 218	Passivhaus Institut
Page 266	Jaksmata under http://creativecommons.org/licenses/by-sa/3.0/ via Wikimedia Commons
Page 272	David Skinner under https://creativecommons.org/licenses/by/2.0 via Wikimedia Commons
Page 279	Tomia under https://creativecommons.org/licenses/by/2.5 via Wikimedia Commons
Pages 292-294, 298	Climate Consultant 6.0, developed by UCLA Energy Design Tools Group; © Regents of University of California 2014
Page 312	David Baker Architects under https://creativecommons.org/licenses/by-nc-nd/4.0/
Page 315 (right)	© 2024 Google

Note: Some images are credited in their captions. Images without captions or credits noted above are by the author, are supplied by Amory Lovins, or are in the public domain. Any credit errors will be corrected in later printings